# MARTYRDOM AND LITERATURE
# IN EARLY MODERN ENGLAND

*Martyrdom and Literature in Early Modern England* is the first literary study to compare how Protestant and Catholic martyrs were represented during the Reformation, the most intense period of religious persecution in English history. Through its focus on martyrs, it argues that Catholic and Protestant texts are produced by dialogue, even competition, with texts across the religious divide, rather than simply as part of a stable and discrete doctrinal system. The first part of the book clearly traces the development of competing discourses of martyrdom; the second part considers the deployment of these discourses through a range of Protestant and Catholic literary texts in the sixteenth and seventeenth centuries. Monta pays extended attention to many texts popular in their own day but now considered unliterary or insignificant. This study is an important contribution to scholarship on early modern literature and religious history.

SUSANNAH BRIETZ MONTA is Assistant Professor of English at Louisiana State University. She is co-editor of *Teaching Early Modern Prose*, which is under development for the Modern Language Association of America's "Options for Teaching" series, and has published widely on topics including Shakespeare, Spenser, and early modern drama.

# MARTYRDOM AND LITERATURE IN EARLY MODERN ENGLAND

SUSANNAH BRIETZ MONTA
*Louisiana State University*

CAMBRIDGE
UNIVERSITY PRESS

CAMBRIDGE UNIVERSITY PRESS
Cambridge, New York, Melbourne, Madrid, Cape Town, Singapore, São Paulo

Cambridge University Press
The Edinburgh Building, Cambridge CB2 2RU, UK

Published in the United States of America by Cambridge University Press, New York
www.cambridge.org
Information on this title: www.cambridge.org/9780521844987

First published 2005

Printed in the United Kingdom at the University Press, Cambridge

*A catalogue record for this book is available from the British Library*

*Library of Congress Cataloguing in Publication data*

Monta, Susannah Brietz.
Martyrdom and literature in early modern England / Susannah Brietz Monta.
p.   cm.
Includes bibliographical references and index.
ISBN 0 521 84498 3
1. English literature – Early modern, 1500–1700 – History and criticism.   2. Martyrdom in
literature.   3. Christianity and literature – England – History – 16th century.   4. Christianity
and literature – England – History – 17th century.   5. Christian martyrs – England – History – 16th
century.   6. Christian martyrs – England – History – 17th
century.   7. England – Church history – 16th century.   8. England – Church history – 17th
century.   9. Christian martyrs in literature.   10. Martyrdom – Christianity.   I. Title.
PR428.M364M66 2005
820.9′38272′09031–dc22    2004054630
ISBN-13 978-0-521-844987 hardback
ISBN-10 0-521-844983 hardback

# Contents

# Acknowledgments

I am happy to acknowledge Louisiana State University's English Department, filled with generous and learned scholars. Anna Nardo and Robin Roberts read the entire manuscript, for which I am deeply grateful. Angeletta Gourdine and Robin Roberts commented upon multiple drafts of my work (and took me to a spa at the end of it all). Anne Coldiron, Carol Mattingly, and Katrina Powell gave helpful feedback on several chapters. Jesse Gellrich, Malcolm Richardson, Michelle Zerba, and the late Gale Carrithers supported their junior colleague in many ways. Lisi Oliver provided advice and humor in generous measure; she also transcribed a rare martyrology for me, suspending her own research to do so. Colleagues across campus, especially Andreas Giger, Suzanne Marchand, Victor Stater, and the MARIS (Medieval and Renaissance Interdisciplinary Studies) faculty have made LSU a warm academic home. Albert Watanabe carefully checked my translations from Latin. Courtney George and Elizabeth Cowan were outstanding research assistants. Students in my graduate seminars on Reformation literature and culture energized me with their enthusiasm and dedication; I thank them warmly.

Many others offered helpful comments at conferences and through other venues, including Deborah Burks, A. Leigh Deneef, Lori Anne Ferrell, Thomas S. Freeman, Achsah Guibbory, Graham Hammill, Chris Hassell, Heather Hirschfeld, Adam Kitzes, Daniel Lochman, Scott Lucas, John McDiarmid, and Rebecca Wagner Oettinger. Audiences at meetings of the RSA, SAA, MLA, and SCSC gave thoughtful responses to my work. Heather King and Cristine Varholy helped me greatly through this project's early stages. I owe a special debt to Robert M. Kingdon, David Loewenstein, Andrew Weiner, and Susanne Wofford for their insight, encouragement, and rigor. I have been the very fortunate beneficiary of Heather Dubrow's great generosity and capacious knowledge; she represents the best of our profession. Two anonymous readers offered invaluable feedback; Sarah Stanton and

Rebecca Jones were patient and efficient editors. Naturally, any remaining errors are my responsibility.

For supporting my research, I thank the Huntington Library, the University of Wisconsin-Madison, the Woodrow Wilson National Fellowship Foundation, the Louisiana State University Council on Research, and LSU's Department of English and College of Arts and Sciences. I thank the staff at the following libraries and archives: UW-Madison's Memorial Library, LSU's Troy H. Middleton and Hill Memorial Libraries (especially Elaine Smith), Huntington Library, Harry Ransom Humanities Research Center, British Library, Bodleian Library, York Minster Library, the Institute of the Blessed Virgin Mary, Bar Convent (York), Cambridge University Library, Inner Temple Library, Lambeth Palace, and Durham Cathedral Library. Portions of chapter 6 appeared previously in *The Sixteenth Century Journal* 34 (2003), 107–21, and *English Literary Renaissance* 30 (2000), 262–83; I am grateful to the editors of these journals for permission to reprint revisions of that material here.

My family (Lynn and Werner Haney; Stacy, David, and Becket O'Brien; Samantha Brietz; Samuel and the late Bonnie Brietz; Denise Jenkens and family; Dorothy and the late Charles Temple) encouraged me with humor and wisdom. Louis, Dorothy, and Peter Monta have cheerfully supported their in-law's rather peculiar preoccupation with martyrs. My two sons' daily escapades are a source of much-appreciated amusement. I must also thank the women who helped me care for my sons while I wrote this book; they gave me nothing less than peace of mind. I dedicate this book to Anthony Monta, who keeps me fed, grounded, and confident enough to write. His love, intelligence, and generosity constitute my greatest debt.

# List of Illustrations

# Introduction:
## conflicting testimonies

During the Reformation era, England witnessed religious persecutions of unprecedented intensity.[1] Under Henry VIII numerous reformers suffered, and Mary I's heresy proceedings against Protestants represented the most concentrated persecution of religious dissidents in England's history. Catholics too were threatened with hardship and death under Henry VIII, while in the late sixteenth and seventeenth centuries they endured further periods of intense persecution.[2] Those who suffered were celebrated as martyrs for their particular causes. Yet as a Protestant minister arguing with the recusant Catholic Margaret Clitherow notes, "In the tyme of Queen Marie were many put to death, and now also in [Elizabeth's] tyme, of two severall opinions; both these cannot bee martyrs."[3] The minister's comment identifies the crucial Reformation-era problem on which this book focuses: how to interpret martyrdom in an age of warring truths.

Competing martyrologies had a much wider, more pervasive influence on English literature and religious culture than is usually acknowledged. The sheer volume and popularity of texts about martyrs suggests their importance to early modern culture. Nine complete editions of John Foxe's Protestant *Book of Martyrs* were produced by 1684 (six of these by 1610) and over 50 works concerning the persecution of Catholics in England were published between 1566 and 1660.[4] Yet martyrologies deserve attention not only for their widespread popularity but also because martyrology is a key genre through which early modern writers grappled with religious change and conflict. Martyrological controversies and literary reactions to them focus crucial Reformation-era questions: questions concerning authority and resistance, the nature of the church, religious subjectivity, justification and sacrament, and historical continuity (or discontinuity). Martyrological controversies led writers to imagine the delineation of individual and corporate religious identities as a competition between variant forms of steadfastness, resolve, and sacrifice.

1

Examining in detail both Catholic and Protestant martyrological texts, I trace the literary impact of the Reformation era's complicated plurality of testimonial voices. I focus on areas of conflict and overlap between Protestant and Catholic martyrological discourses, broadly understood, because early modern martyrologists usually portrayed the religious world in these (admittedly simplified) terms. Even in the face of significant intra-Protestant or intra-Catholic fissures, most Protestant and Catholic martyrologists are reluctant to admit intra-faith divisions and instead labor to rally their co-religionists into an integrated opposition to a clearly demarcated religious Other. While I acknowledge and attend to divisions within Protestant and Catholic traditions, I focus primarily on the literary effects of interconfessional martyrological controversies. This wider perspective shows that in the early modern period the generic separation Protestant and Catholic martyrologists attempted to effect was difficult, imprecise, and incomplete. Martyrologies, texts seeking to draw firm boundaries between saint and sinner, often overlap uncomfortably with their polemical opposites in their rhetoric, conventions, and assumptions. Early modern martyrological writing both wishes to draw firm distinctions based on religious differences and, in its controversial context, reveals the considerable difficulty of doing so. This prolonged struggle to delineate different religio-literary traditions using an inherited generic arsenal warns us against adopting models of early modern culture that presume stable religious identities and representational habits.

My study's chronological limits highlight the main conflicts I trace: the book focuses on material written between roughly 1540 and 1650. In this period, even as magisterial Protestant martyrology (especially that associated with John Foxe) established itself, it underwent significant challenges from the conflicting testimonies offered by contemporary Catholic martyrologists. Simultaneously, both Protestant and Catholic martyrologists struggled to unite their often fractious co-religionists behind the causes for which their martyrs died. By the mid-seventeenth century Protestant unity was, of course, a distant dream; the use of martyrological tropes in Protestant nonconformist writing flourished alongside the *Eikon Basilike*'s rhetoric of martyrdom.[5] Still, I show that even martyrological texts at the end of my chronological range use the persistent allure of simple, binary oppositions between sharply demarcated "Protestants" and "Catholics" for particular religious and/or political purposes.

Throughout this book, I read Protestant and Catholic martyrological discourses against each other. A side-effect of my comparative approach is to give the Catholic presence in early modern literature more attention than is usual in most current studies.[6] Further, my approach imitates the way many early modern authors read martyrological texts. Patrick Collinson has argued that we do not yet fully understand how the Protestant martyrologist John Foxe was read.[7] I present evidence for one important way that contemporary authors read Foxe and other martyrologists: in the context of their competition. Each of the authors I discuss demonstrates awareness of Protestant and Catholic martyrological efforts; each shows the increasing strain competing martyrdoms placed on common hagiographical conventions and assumptions. Anthony Munday, Thomas Dekker, and Philip Massinger drew on Catholic and Protestant martyrologies for their plays. William Shakespeare's (and possibly John Fletcher's) *Henry VIII* adapts Foxe's *Actes and Monuments* and yet in doing so places Foxean martyrological conventions in tension with overlapping Catholic ones. John Donne's prose and poetry show his familiarity with Protestant and Catholic martyrologies. Robert Southwell's prose attacks Protestant claims about martyrdom and his poetry, often taking suffering as its subject matter, proved popular with Protestant and Catholic readers. Book I of Edmund Spenser's *Faerie Queene* is informed both by Caxton's *Golden Legend* and Foxean martyrological paradigms, while Anthony Copley's *A Fig for Fortune*, a Catholic rewriting of Spenser, responds both to Spenser's poem and to Catholic martyrologies.

As these cross-confessional reading habits suggest, if we do not consider martyrological discourses in the context of their competition we oversimplify early modern religious culture. Although literary scholarship on martyrologies has taught us a great deal, literary studies to date have focused on single confessional strands and influences, such as John Foxe's importance for nonconformist writing or the influence of rhetorical training on Catholic martyrologies.[8] Yet martyrologists were intensely aware of the competition's efforts. To be a martyrologist was also to be a polemicist; a martyr's biography in early modern England is essentially dialogical, not just encomiastic. A central claim of this book is that conflicts between Protestant and Catholic martyrological writing helped to produce, not merely to record, religious divisions. If we pursue only single-sided studies of martyrological discourse, we adhere to the lines martyrologies themselves helped to draw and may obscure a primary function of those texts: to wrest discrete religions from a shared (if sometimes only partially or half-heartedly embraced) generic inheritance.

Yet even as martyrologies undertake their work of sifting true from false witnesses, persistent, uncomfortable overlaps in their testimonial strategies and epistemological assumptions suggest the messiness of the very distinctions martyrologies tried to foster. Martyrologists' competitive zeal is aroused largely because, across religious lines, early modern martyrologies share the same primary concern: how to interpret particular lives and deaths as confirmation for abstract belief systems. John Foxe prints a letter from the Marian martyr George Marsh in which Marsh writes that he is willing "to confirm and seal Christ's gospel" with his blood.[9] Insisting that the charismatic Jesuit Edmund Campion (*d.* 1581) died a martyr to the truth, Father Henry Walpole, S.J., claims that Campion's "death confirmes his doctrine true."[10] Both the Protestant Foxe and the Catholic Walpole assume that the words, actions, and sacrifices of individual believers may witness to religious truth. This assumption reflects the etymology of "martyr," an etymology that suggests the epistemological issues at stake (pun intended) in martyrological discourse. In classical rhetoric the term "martyria" refers to a witness who confirms something by virtue of his/her own experience.[11] In religious discourse the word "martyr" has come to mean a person whose words, actions, and death offer authoritative testimony. As a friend of Foxe's martyr Joyce Lewes tells her, "Mistres Lewes, you have great cause to praise God, who will vouch-safe so speedely to take you out of thys world, & make you worthy to be a witnes to his truth, and to beare record unto Christ that he is the onely Saviour."[12] Lewes's friend makes a claim that is both conventional and remarkable: her death will point to and uphold religious truth.

The notion that individual testimony may confirm a body of religious precepts is one that many contemporary academics might well question. Indeed, literary critical paradigms have done more justice to the contours of religious ambiguity, equivocation, and irony than to representations of unshakeable faith. My approach to martyrological controversies corrects a tendency in some forms of literary scholarship to gloss passionate commitment to religious belief systems as the effect of political or ideological manipulation.[13] It is not helpful to impose the effects of twenty-first century skepticism on another culture with quite different methods of reading the world. To take seriously what early modern martyrological discourse purports to be about – the role of the individual subject in ascertaining and testifying to religious truth – is to embark on a study of historical epistemology, to uncover ways in which early modern people thought one might come to know what beliefs were true. The epistemologies of martyrdom are adapted and redeployed by writers of various religious persuasions as they reflect upon achingly similar problems: how truth may be confirmed by subjective testimonies in an age when so many suffer for different causes.

While my book focuses at different moments on various martyrological conventions and arguments, they all bear on this central assumption that martyrs could be used to confirm religious truth. Under the force of this central claim, martyrological writing had a particular impact on certain areas of literary production: on the imagining of history, on the formation of subjectivity in religious lyric, on the representation of corporate bodies of believers, and on the conception of forms of passive yet potent resistance to established ecclesiastical and political bodies. Discussion of each particular area does not appear in every chapter; the material is too varied to permit a neat march through the evidence. Nevertheless, these literary reactions to competing testimonies all indicate the difficulties of interpreting martyrdom and suffering in the early modern period. Some texts mourn persistent problems in interpreting testimonies. Others reveal a range of compensatory literary strategies that competing testimonies provoked. Still others show that these compensatory strategies could become so strained that they were not capable of papering over the growing faultlines in martyrological discourse, or of reconstituting its effectiveness in the service of a particular religio-political agenda.

The book is divided into two parts. The first highlights martyrologists' efforts to delineate distinct religions still newly separating and thus still using several uncomfortably overlapping (though certainly not identical) means of verifying martyrs' truth claims. Here, I give martyrologies sustained attention. They deserve it: they are of literary interest, by which I mean not that they are fictional (many are generally reliable), nor that they are exemplars of a particular martyrologist's rhetorical habits or prose style (many are formulaic and are not authored exclusively by the martyrologist whose name became associated with them). Instead, they are of literary interest because of their focus on hermeneutics. Early modern martyrologists are aware that they must foster particular methods of reading and interpretation in order to render their martyrs persuasive. The simple presentation of testimony is no longer, in an atmosphere of intense religious conflict, enough.

In Part I, I examine how Protestant and Catholic martyrologists try to establish interpretive frameworks that promote particular readings of martyrs' testimonies even as they counter polemical attacks and competing sets of martyrs. This part's three chapters explicate the logic of martyrology and show by a cross-confessional approach that that logic is put under severe pressure by the period's competing martyrdoms. Part I's title, *Non poena sed causa*, echoes the common argument that the cause, not the death, determines whether a particular person was a martyr. Given this assumption, it should be relatively easy to distinguish representations of martyrs in Protestant and Catholic martyrologies: the cause for which martyrs died should shape representations of martyrs' lives and deaths. This is sometimes the case. For instance, Catholic martyrologies uphold traditional reverence for relics by investing their martyrs' material remains with sacred power. Yet I show that complications arise and persist because Protestants and Catholics also share, often uncomfortably, similar assumptions about the best ways to authenticate their martyrs' testimonies. For example, the cross-confessional elevation of a martyr's conscience, the importance of an unbroken history of martyrs' testimonies, and the common belief in providential retribution against persecutors complicate representations of martyrs for different causes. Finally, the phrase *non poena sed causa* begs the question of how one determines what a good cause would be. Too often, martyrologies' rather circular answer is that the good cause is the one reinforced with the best martyrs. Because of uncomfortably overlapping assumptions and conventions, early modern martyrologies do not permit the tidy separation of suffering and doctrine, the *poena* and the *causa*, nor are the problems of competing martyrs easily resolved. Read against their polemical opposites, early modern martyrologies suggest the complex interaction between theology and representational habits, between splintering religious factions and a shared reverence for the Christian tradition of martyrdom.

In Part II, each chapter pairs texts influenced by both Protestant and Catholic martyrological material; each pairing is focused around a martyrological strategy shared in some fashion across religious lines. I have selected particular texts not out of an effort to be complete or even broadly representative – an impossible task, given martyrologies' wide reach – but rather on the basis of those texts' engagements with both Protestant and Catholic martyrological arguments. These chapters give sustained attention to the texts in question because the complex ways martyrological arguments are implicated in the texts I have chosen reward careful scrutiny. Chapter 4 shows that Book I of Spenser's *Faerie Queene* and Anthony Copley's *A Fig for Fortune* reveal the pressure competing martyrdoms exerted on early modern understandings and reworkings of Revelation's allegory. Chapter 5 explicates martyrology's powerful claim that those who suffered could be assured they were of God's flock and argues that that claim influences much of the prose and poetic work of John Donne and Robert Southwell. Chapter 6 examines a common guarantor of martyrological testimony, the claim that a martyr testifies in accordance with his/her conscience, as it is negotiated in *The Book of Sir Thomas More* (Anthony

Munday, *et al.*) and *Henry VIII* (Shakespeare and, possibly, Fletcher). In chapter 7, I argue that the interpretive habits martyrologists tried to foster persisted into the mid-seventeenth century, shaping the ways contemporary conflicts were understood. Dekker and Massinger's *The Virgin Martyr* (1620) and Catholic martyrologies published in Latin during the 1640s simplify seventeenth-century conflicts into a stark confrontation between right religion and idolatry or heresy; yet they also acknowledge new military and political realities by incorporating more active forms of resistance into their representations of martyrs.

As I show, martyrology is crucial to literary history not simply as a popular body of literature but for its pervasive influence on many central representational concerns of early modern religious writing, broadly construed. Competing martyrologies pressured early modern authors to represent the search for religious truth as essentially agonistic and as taking place in a world in which a true martyr could look disturbingly similar to a false heretic or a damnable traitor. It is no wonder that Spenser's Una is veiled as she wanders the world, or that Milton's Truth is herself a martyr.

## NOTES

1 Although religious persecutions in England never reached the intensity of continental persecutions, the sixteenth century saw a clear, traumatic break from earlier, comparatively scattered executions for heresy. There were at least 53 executions of Protestants for religion in England and Scotland between 1527 and 1546 (excluding those executed as Anabaptists, such as the ten executed in 1535), at least 282 executions during Mary Tudor's reign, and at least 300 English Catholics executed between 1535 and 1680 (Brad Gregory, "The Anathema of Compromise: Christian Martyrdom in Early Modern Europe," Ph.D. dissertation, Princeton University, 1996, 13). See also Geoffrey P. Nuttall, "The English Martyrs 1535–1680: a Statistical Review," *Journal of Ecclesiastical History* 22 (1971), 191–7; A. G. Dickens, *The English Reformation* (London: Batsford, 1964), and F. H. Hansford-Miller, *The 282 Protestant Martyrs of England and Wales, 1555–1558* (London: Hansford-Miller, 1970).

2 The worst were during Elizabeth I's and James I's reigns, the 1640s, and the Titus Oates plot.

3 John Mush, *The life and Death of Mistris Margarit Clitherow*, Bar Convent (York) MS, 97.

4 On recusant Catholic publication, see Brad Gregory, *Salvation at Stake: Christian Martyrdom in Early Modern Europe* (Cambridge, MA: Harvard University Press, 1999), 4; *A Catalogue of Catholic Books in English Printed Abroad or Secretly in England, 1558–1640*, ed. A. F. Allison and D. M. Rogers (London: W. Dawson, 1964); and *The Contemporary Printed Literature of the*

*English Counter-Reformation between 1558 and 1640*, ed. Allison, Rogers, and Wolfgang Lottes, 2 vols. (Aldershot: Scolar Press, 1989–94, works in English and in other languages). I discuss important post-1640 publications on Catholic persecutions in chapter 7.

5 The dynamics of seventeenth-century intra-Protestant martyrological controversies have been well addressed by John Knott in *Discourses of Martyrdom in English Literature, 1563–1694* (Cambridge: Cambridge University Press, 1993).

6 A notable exception is Alison Shell, *Catholicism, Controversy, and the English Literary Imagination, 1588–1660* (Cambridge: Cambridge University Press, 1999).

7 "John Foxe and National Consciousness," in *John Foxe and His World*, ed. Christopher Highley and John N. King (Aldershot: Ashgate, 2002), 25–6.

8 I am indebted to Knott, *Discourses*, and Ceri Sullivan (*Dismembered Rhetoric: English Recusant Writing, 1580 to 1603*, London: Associated University Presses, 1995).

9 *Actes and Monuments* (London, 1563), 669.

10 The line is from the poem "Why do I use my paper, inke, and pen?," published in Thomas Alfield's *A True Report of the Death and Martyrdome of M. Campion Jesuite and prieste, & M. Sherwin, & M. Brian priests* (London, 1582).

11 Nancy Wright discusses the term in "The *Figura* of the Martyr in John Donne's Sermons," *English Literary History* 56 (1989), 293–306.

12 *Actes and Monuments* (London, 1583), 2014.

13 Some scholarship on martyrologies tends to read through or past (and implicitly demote) their religious concerns. Hence in her theoretically sophisticated book Megan Matchinske nevertheless often reads past religion in martyraccounts to posit supposedly secular forms of resistance (*Writing, Gender, and State in Early Modern England: Identity Formation and the Female Subject*, Cambridge: Cambridge University Press, 1998). As Claire McEachern has recently argued, religion is not something to be read *through* but is "something in and of itself" (*Religion and Culture in Renaissance England*, ed. Claire McEachern and Debora Shuger, Cambridge: Cambridge University Press, 1997, 7).

# PART I

# Non poena sed causa: martyrdom and the hermeneutics of controversy

Most simply, the martyrologist's task is to show that the lives and deaths of particular witnesses confirm the beliefs they held. In the Reformation era, competing sets of steadfast, devoted martyrs complicated this task considerably. To resolve the dilemma competing martyrs posed, martyrologists proposed that the cause, not the death, makes the martyr (*non poena sed causa*). A letter from a Catholic man (named only "J. A.") who witnessed the martyrdom of Thomas Cranmer, sometime Archbishop of Canterbury, gives us a rare glimpse of a writer attempting to use this dictum to resolve his conflicting feelings about the good death of a supposed heretic. Under intense pressure from Marian authorities, Cranmer had recanted his religious beliefs, only to recant his recantation in spectacular fashion at the stake.[1] J. A.'s letter records that after denouncing his earlier recantation, Cranmer held his right hand, which signed that recantation, steadily in the fire so that it might burn first: "he put furth hys Ryghte hand & hild yt styll therein a good space before the fyre came to hys body, & so dyed paceintly & never stered or cryed." Impressed by Cranmer's steadfastness, J. A. calls him an "Image of sorowe" and arranges to have a "dirige" sung for him at an Oxford church. Yet he laments that this good death was for error:

hys pacience . . . hys corage in dyeyng, yf yt had byn token ether for the glory of god, the welth of hys countriy, the testimony of truth, as yt was for a pernycious error, & subversion of true Rilygion, I could worthily have commended the example . . . but . . . seing it [is] not the death, but cause . . . thereof, [that] commendyth the . . . sufferer: I cannot but moche dysprase hys obstinante stubbirnes & sturdie[nes] in dying in specially in so evell a cause.[2]

With startling candor, J. A. acknowledges that heretics and martyrs may look very similar, that Cranmer's behavior resembles the ideal behavior of one who dies for the glory of God (or country). Yet the traits J. A. admires – Cranmer's patience, steadfastness, and bravery, all traits Christian martyrs traditionally exhibited – are precisely those he must disparage in order to reconcile his admiration for this heretic's good death with his own faith. Patience becomes obstinacy, courage stubbornness. Significantly, he distinguishes martyrs from heretics only by using his religious predilections to turn a would-be martyr's ideal behavior into its dark opposite. He formulates an interpretational distinction, in other words, not one based upon any formal variation in what a martyr should do or say.

While prioritizing the cause helped J. A. resolve his conflicting feelings about Cranmer's patient/obstinate death, it could also work against persuasiveness. If the cause, not the death, makes the martyr, then martyrologies become mostly reflexive or circular confirmations of the causes readers are already inclined to endorse. Thus, although martyrologists frequently assert that the cause should determine whether a person died a martyr, in practice martyrologists also used martyrs' lives, words, and dramatic self-sacrifices to argue that their martyrs died for truth. Many early modern writers attributed considerable persuasive force to martyrs. Though he often repeats the mantra that the cause, not the death, makes the martyr, John Foxe also argues explicitly that the manner of one's death reveals the rightness of one's beliefs. Foxe added a section to the second (1570) edition of his work detailing the joyful, steadfast deaths of Protestant martyrs and the shameful deaths of Catholic persecutors for just this reason: "what greater proufe can we have to justifie their cause and doctrine agaynst the persecutyng Church of Rome, then to behold the endes of them both."[3] Recusant Catholic martyrologists also highlight the persuasive force of martyrs' deaths. In a letter describing the deaths of English martyrs, William Cardinal Allen writes, "Loud, indeed, is the cry of sacred blood so copiously shed. Ten thousand sermons would not have published our apostolic faith and religion so winningly as the fragrance of these victims, most sweet both to God and men."[4] The deaths are superior to discourse itself; martyrdom alone has "published" the Catholic faith.

Furthermore, the priority of the cause for people like J. A. should not blind us to the fact that a good death could lead witnesses to embrace the martyr's beliefs.[5] This proved true for Joyce Lewes, who embraced Protestant beliefs after hearing of Laurence Saunders's martyrdom, and for Henry Walpole, who converted to Catholicism after witnessing Edmund Campion's death.[6] Even persecuting authorities recognized the persuasive force of a good death. In 1546 Stephen Gardiner, leader of Henrician conservatives, wrote that reformers' "wilful death in obstinacie" might "serve for an argument, to prove the truth of their opinion."[7] Walsingham echoed this complaint under later, different circumstances; in a note dated December 1586, he writes that the "execution of [Catholic priests], as experience showeth, in respect of their constancy or rather obstinacy, moveth men to compassion and draweth some to affect their religion, upon conceipt that such an extraordinary contempt of death cannot but proceed from above, whereby many have fallen away."[8] Repeated assertions that the cause, not the death, makes the martyr would not have been necessary if many people had not believed the opposite.

Martyrologists wish above all to make their martyrs' deaths persuasive. Yet conceptions of a good death were by and large inherited from Christian tradition and were generally shared cross-confessionally, as the remarks of J. A., Walsingham, and Gardiner indicate: martyrs should be brave and patient, composed, long-suffering, even joyful. In this section, I trace the beginnings of a separation between Protestant and Catholic discourses of martyrdom: theologically distinct causes shape representation so as to effect some differences between depictions of Catholic and Protestant martyrs. Though differences in Protestant and Catholic martyrological discourses begin to develop during the sixteenth century, however, martyrologists of different religious commitments tend to privilege similar means of authenticating their martyrs' testimonies. Despite their attempted simplification of the religious landscape into godly martyrs and devilish persecutors, when read cross-confessionally martyrologies demonstrate compellingly that early modern religious writing resists easy categorizing. While there are distinctions between Protestant and Catholic martyrologies, they are often distinctions in the making, not ones already made, and they are frequently troubled by uncomfortably overlapping means of authenticating religious testimony. Literary criticism of martyrologies has tended to focus on questions of convention and rhetoric and to attempt to categorize martyrological discourse according to formal techniques (e.g., the claim – an erroneous one – that Catholic martyrologists use miracles and wonders while Protestant writers do not).[9] Yet martyrological conventions are not neatly divisible into distinct Protestant and Catholic discourses. Instead, distinctions were formed as much by interpretational imperatives and habits as by rhetorical conventions *per se*. The uneasy or surface similarities between representations of Protestant and Catholic martyrs mean that martyrologists must ask their readers to look closer, to read and interpret more carefully in order to perceive the martyrs' truths.

To demonstrate the complex ways in which common means of authentication were wrested to the support of differing causes, I read martyrologies along three major axes of persuasive force: the persuasiveness of individual martyrs' claims to adhere to their consciences and inward convictions; the persuasiveness of communities of martyrs; and the persuasiveness of material, marvelous, or miraculous testimonies. In order to facilitate distinction, martyrologists elaborate theories of interpretation derived from the beliefs their martyrs endorse. They work to shape reading communities that will celebrate their martyrs, effecting a sort of evangelism of interpretation. At the same time, martyrologists remain aware of the vexing interpretive problems caused by the multitude of opinions for which early modern martyrs suffered. Martyrologies thus hold considerable interest for literary history because they are deeply and self-reflexively concerned with interpretational frameworks, with the processes of reading and interpretation upon which early modern martyrology increasingly depended for its impact.

### NOTES

1 On Cranmer's recantations and execution, see David Loades, *The Oxford Martyrs* (London: Batsford, 1970), and Diarmaid MacCullough, *Thomas Cranmer* (New Haven: Yale University Press, 1996).
2 London, British Library, Harley MS 422, 49r-v. The letter survives in Foxe's papers, though Foxe puts its information to a celebratory use.
3 *Actes and Monuments* (London, 1570), 2301.
4 *A briefe historie of the glorious martyrdom of the twelve reverend priests*, ed. J. H. Pollen (London: Burns & Oates, 1908), ix.
5 Importantly, Ceri Sullivan urges critics not to focus on the martyr's pathos but on the beliefs which he or she upheld. Still, in the persuasive economy of martyrologies impersonal dogma and subjective testimony are deeply intertwined ("'Oppressed by the Force of Truth': Robert Persons Edits John Foxe," in *John Foxe: an Historical Perspective*, ed. David Loades, Aldershot: Ashgate, 1999, 154–66).
6 *AM* (1583), 2012; on Walpole's conversion and life, see *John Gerard: Autobiography of an Elizabethan*, trans. Philip Caraman (London: Longmans, 1951), 105, and Diego de Yepez, *Historia Particular de la Persecucion de Inglaterra* (Madrid, 1599), book 5, ch. 9.
7 *A detection of the Devils Sophistrie* (London, 1546), 92r; Alec Ryrie, "The Unsteady Beginnings of English Protestant Martyrology," in *John Foxe: an Historical Perspective*, ed. Loades, 52–66, brought this tract to my attention.
8 In Conyers Read, *Mr. Secretary Walsingham and the Policy of Queen Elizabeth*, vol. 2 (Oxford: Clarendon Press, 1925), 312–13.
9 John Knott, "John Foxe and the Joy of Suffering," *Sixteenth Century Journal* 27 (1996), 721–34; Arthur Marotti, "Manuscript Transmission and the Catholic Martyrdom Account in Early Modern England," in *Print, Manuscript, and Performance: the Changing Relations of the Media in Early Modern England*, ed. Michael D. Bristol and Marotti (Columbus: Ohio State University Press, 2000), 181; James Truman, "John Foxe and the Desires of Reformation Martyrology," *English Literary History* 70 (2003), 37.

# CHAPTER I

## *Controverting consciences*

Pervasive in both Protestant and Catholic martyrologies is the insistence that martyrs testify according to their consciences. Importantly, Reformation-era martyrologists usually invoke conscience not merely as the repository of personal beliefs but as an interface with the divine. In line with traditional hagiography's epistemic force, a martyr's revelations of conscience are typically presented as compelling evidence not just of a believer's earnestness but of the fundamental truth of his/her beliefs. The claim that a martyr's words and behavior reveal his/her conscience functions as a sort of epistemological trump card, the ultimate guarantor of martyrological testimony.[1] Indeed, it is clear that martyrs themselves recognized that onlookers would infer their inwardly held beliefs from their external performances; martyrs scripted their words and behavior, surely not insincerely, to persuade others (and perhaps even themselves) that they died for true religion's sake.[2] Yet even as martyrologists claim that martyrs' testimonies reveal their consciences' firmly held (and thus, the reasoning goes, true) convictions, martyrologists also recognize the difficulties of rendering interior constructs into discourse: may conscience and conviction remain persuasive once translated into interpretable, controvertible words? Those difficulties are exacerbated because the rhetoric of conscience is valued across religious lines. To overcome these problems, martyrologists encourage particular methods of reading internal convictions through martyrs' words and behavior, methods which should yield a correct reading of a martyr's sacrifice and of the doctrines that sacrifice was to confirm. To authenticate their martyrs despite competing claims to the authority of conscience, martyrologists encourage the habits of reading implied in the beliefs for which martyrs died, so that readers' interpretive habits and martyrs' doctrinal convictions are sufficiently aligned to enable leaps of faith.

LOOKING INWARDLY INTO SPIRITUAL THINGS: FOXE'S
MARTYRS AND THE COMFORTING OF CONSCIENCES

The rhetoric of conscience undergirds the most important English Protestant martyrology. The *Actes and Monuments* contains material collected by various editors and written by numerous authors.[3] The strongest shaping hand was John Foxe's; his name appeared on the title page and the work became known as "Foxe's" *Book of Martyrs*. Foxe's martyrology chronicles the sufferings of Marian Protestants as well as of early church and medieval martyrs whom Foxe considered Protestantism's spiritual predecessors. In making the case for its martyrs, Foxe's work asks readers to follow an interpretational paradigm similar to that outlined in a sermon Foxe preached at St. Paul's on Good Friday, 1570. In that sermon Foxe claims that "albeit [papistes] professe the whole history of Christs passion as we doe, yet . . . they goe no further then the outward history." He asks his audience instead to "looke inwardly with a spirituall eye into spirituall thynges,"[4] to perceive the spiritual, inward reality not readily apparent in outward history, for true interpretation discerns inward, spiritual things. Similarly, his massive martyrology implicitly asks its audience to link "outward history" to inner promptings. The work attempts to demonstrate the veracity of its martyrs' testimonies and to shape how readers understand "spirituall thynges," including the spiritual testimonies of their own lives. A type of hermeneutic circle is clearly at work, as the *Actes and Monuments* labors to consolidate the reading habits most consonant with the beliefs for which its martyrs died.

Adapting martyrology to Protestant concerns, the *Actes and Monuments* revises traditional emphases on a martyr's conscience. The work uses martyrs' testimonies of conscience to suggest their certainty in the convictions for which they die and to confirm the truth of those convictions. This alignment of the rhetoric of conscience, confirmation, and certainty, traditionally used to reinforce a martyr's steadfastness and reliability as a witness, is also adapted to show readers how to attain what Protestant writers called a "good" conscience, one confirmed and certain in its owner's salvation. The work thus tackles one of the most difficult questions arising from mainline Protestant theology – how may one be sure one is of the elect? – by modeling how answers might be found at moments of persecutory crisis and then by insisting that the processes which lead martyrs to their answers should be followed in readers' spiritual lives.

The prioritizing of faith over works in magisterial Protestant thought implies that outward histories should testify to inward, spiritual things. For

Luther and Calvin, the elect are "saints" who enjoy comfort and assurance in their spiritual security, a security founded not on outward works or on individual will but on God's will alone.[5] Foxe's translation of a sermon entitled *An Instruction of Christen Fayth howe to be bolde upon the promyse of God and not to doubte of our salvacyon* by the German reformer Urbanus Regius reveals the tautology of this understanding of religious comfort: "he that doubteth of the wyl and favore of god, and is not assured that he wyll be mercyful to hym for Christes sake and that all his synnes be pardoned in hym, he is no trew christiane, and in his incredulitie can not be but condemned."[6] Roughly, then, certainty is the key to being certain; since election is already settled, believers by definition cannot be incredulous. Works are valuable not because they procure or in any way induce justification but because they testify to one's elect status. The sermon clarifies works' function: they "exercise oure faith, that they may be testimones of oure belev, and thus do they profyt both me and my neybour."[7] Adapting this idea, John Bradford, one of the more prominent Marian martyrs, claims that Abraham and Job were tested so that "their faith whiche before laye hid almost in their heartes, might bee made knowne to the whole world to be so stedfast and stronge."[8]

Foxe attempts to demonstrate both the martyrs' works and what lies behind them, the "testimonies of oure belev." Foxe writes that George Tankerfield, a humble cook, was "a very papist" until he witnessed Catholic "crueltye" under Mary I. Tankerfield then "began (as he said) in his heart to abhorre them." The juxtaposition of "(as he said)" with "in his heart" both indicates and bridges the potential gap between inner conviction and perceivable testimony. Tankerfield himself desires inner confirmation of these early misgivings; he prays that if the Mass is indeed evil, God might "open to him the truth, that he might be thorowly perswaded therein, whether it were of God, or no: If not, that he might utterly hate it in his hearte." Soon Tankerfield feels "daily more and more in him to detest and abhorre the same." He experiences other inner changes, being "moved to read the Testament, whereby (as is sayd) the Lord lightened his minde with the knowledge of the truthe...thys lively faith, sayd he, kindled such a flame in him, as would not be kept in, but utter it selfe by confession therof."[9] The inner flame Tankerfield feels is soon fanned into a martyr's fiery sacrifice. Tankerfield's actions witness to and confirm his earlier inner motions, which Foxe's narration has opened for the reader. Sometimes even martyrs themselves model how to read from outer deeds to inward states. Bradford evaluates his own actions in order to ascertain his inner state as his martyrdom approaches:

Brad. I thought this night that I had bene sent for, because at a 11 of the clocke there was such rapping at the dore. Then answered a maid, and sayd: why then I perceive you were afrayd... Brad. "Ye shall heare how fearefull I was. For I considered that I had not slept, and I thought to take a nap before I went: and after I was a sleepe, these men came into the next chamber, and sang, as it was tolde me, and yet, for all my fearefulnes I heard them not: therefore belike I was not afrayd, that slept so fast.[10]

Bradford interprets his deep sleep as meaning that he was prepared to face death boldly and calmly; he shapes the interpretation of his behavior to suit traditional expectations about martyrs' fearlessness.

Foxe's text weaves together the martyr's conventional confidence with predestinarian emphases on certainty in salvation. A debate Bradford held with a Spanish friar evinces this conjunction. The friar urges Bradford to open his mind: "you must be as it were a neuter, and not wedded to yourself, but as one standing in doubt. Pray and be ready to receive what God shall inspire." Bradford emphasizes both his extant and increasing certainty in his religion:

Syr, my sentence, if you meane it for Religion, must not be in a doubting or uncertain, as I thanke God I am certayne in that for which I am condemned: I have no cause to doubt of it, but rather to be most certayne of it; and therfore I praye God to confirm mee more in it. For it is his trueth, and because it is so certayne and true that it may abide the light, I dare be bold to have it looked on, and conferre it with you, or any man.[11]

Because testifying is a means to still greater certainty, the beleaguered Protestant minister lays claim to the martyr's traditional steadfast confidence. For Bradford and his martyrologist, the elect's certainty pits them irreconcilably against those who wish them to be "neuter," for to admit that one is uncertain, or, indeed, even persuadable, is to admit the possibility that one's election is unsure. As Bradford indicates, the ideal life-pattern is one of increasing confirmation (though, importantly, a believer's growing confidence in salvation does not mean he/she will cease to struggle with sin, a point Bradford's writings bring out).[12] Challenging the circular argument that the key to being certain in one's salvation is being certain in one's salvation, sixteenth-century Catholics asserted that the doctrine of predestination could lead to despair and that the doctrine of assurance, of certain confidence in an eternally predestined salvation, was presumptuous. Hence the Council of Trent anathematized the proposition "That a man reborn and justified is bound by faith to believe that he is assuredly in the number of the predestinate."[13] Catholic interrogators bring these objections into the

*Actes and Monuments*'s pages as they criticize martyrs like Bradford for over-confidence. For Bradford and Foxe, of course, there is no such thing as over-confidence in what is "certayne and true." Ostensibly, then, elect readers have no need to be persuaded of the martyrs' truths; they only need, like Bradford, to be further confirmed in them.

Yet the *Actes and Monuments* not only exemplifies the progressive self-confirmation implicit in predestinarian theology; it also focuses its persuasive efforts (for, *contra* Bradford, the text does attempt persuasion) on encouraging its less-confident readers. This is evident in the stories of two brothers, Robert and John Glover. In a note added to the end of the 1563 edition (subsequently incorporated into the main text of later editions) Robert Glover, imprisoned for his faith and condemned to burn at the stake, seeks reassurance that he is chosen for a martyr's crown for he has "felt no strength nor comfort in hym selfe to dye" such as the elect should feel. As Robert goes to the stake, Augustine Bernher, a follower of Hugh Latimer and Glover's counselor, labors to comfort Robert, who still "founde hym selfe very infirme."[14] Bernher remains confident that God will comfort him and asks Robert to "shew some signification therof, that he myght wytnesse with hym to the same." As Robert goes to the stake, he "sodenly [was] mightely replenyshed with Gods holy comfort" and "cryed out . . . 'Augustine, he is come, he is come.' "[15] Robert's enthusiastic words testify to the surge of comfort and confidence he has at last received. His brother John seeks desperately for similar assurance. Foxe terms John a "double martyr" because, though spared literal martyrdom, he suffers greatly from his lack of confidence in his salvation: "what and how muche more grevous pangs, what sorrowfull tormentes, what boyling heates of the fire of hell in hys spirit inwardly he felt and sustayned, no speech outwardly is able to expresse." Foxe's reading of Glover's inner torments qualifies the Regius sermon's insistence that those who doubt "in [their] incredulitie cannot be but condemned":

I have greatly wondered oftentymes at the mervailous workes and operation of Christ shewed upon hym, who unlesse he had relieved betymes his poore wretched servant so far worne, with some opportune consolation, now and then betwixt, it could not possible bee, that he should have susteined so intollerable paynes and tormentes . . . we see common among holy & blessed men, how the more devout and godly they are . . . the more suspition and mistrust they have of them selves: whereby it commeth to passe, that often they are so terrified & perplexed with small matters, as though they were huge mountains: where as contrary others there be, whom most hainous & very sore crimes in deed do nothyng touch or stirre at all.

In a benevolent predestinarian catch-22, Foxe claims that John's self-doubts testify to his fear of God *and* that his endurance despite tormenting doubt means that he must have sometimes enjoyed that all-important comfort, election's sure sign. In subsequent editions of the *Actes and Monuments,* Foxe explains why he discusses John's struggles: "as concernyng his spirituall conflicts, and the Lordes gracious workyng in him, because the consideration thereof, is both worthy of memory, and the example may worke experience peradventure to the comfort of the godly, it shal not be hurtful to reherse some part of the same."[16] John Glover's account should comfort those who, like him, have unsettled or uncertain consciences, those who, though not in danger of literal burning, are at risk of a psychologically excruciating double martyrdom.

Indeed, much of Foxe's work exhibits a pastoral awareness that readers whose consciences are not yet convinced of their election need extra comfort.[17] The dedicatory epistle to Foxe's 1570 sermon begins, "To all them that labour and be heavy laden in conscience, John Foxe wisheth hearty comfort." In his preface to a translation of Luther's commentary upon fifteen psalms, Foxe hopes that the commentary will give "true comfort and spiritual consolation to such weake minds as in cases of conscience are distressed, and wrastle in faith."[18] Similarly, Foxe's martyrology seeks to demonstrate that reading about martyrs "do[es] not a little avayle to the stablishing of a good conscience";[19] owners of anxious consciences could turn for comfort to its pages. Perhaps it seems odd that a book about people suffering and dying painfully might have been meant for comfort. Nevertheless, Foxe explicitly claims that martyrs' stories may confirm and comfort readers, for if martyrs could persist amid tortuous flames, then readers may persist through their own more mundane trials of faith. Martyrs' stories should also lead readers to perceive what Robert Glover saw – the workings of God through the sacrifices of martyrs – for good consciences should align with one another. Readers' own convictions become evidence for the truthfulness of the martyrs' testimonies of conscience and, conversely, the martyrs' sure convictions comfort readers' consciences. The claim that martyrs' revelations of their consciences can comfort other, troubled consciences thus has polemical, spiritual, and testimonial resonances. It asserts a key Protestant doctrine against Catholic objections and disseminates the intense scrutiny of one's own testimonial narrative which becomes such a marked feature of Protestant spirituality. It also functions to create the sorts of reading habits that will most confirm the martyrs' truths.

The doctrine of predestination and the reading habits it implies – reading one's life for increasing confirmation of one's status and to ward off doubts and temptations to sin – are thus crucial to Foxe's *Actes and Monuments.* But if readers feel that they do not belong in that increasingly more confident interpretational circle, Foxe wants to bring them in. This is evident in Foxe's commentary on one of Bradford's letters. The letter is addressed to two friends struggling to understand the doctrine of election. Bradford explains his perspective:

> Thus doe I wade in Predestination . . . I am sure, that warely and wisely a man maye walke in it easely by the light of God's spirite, in and by his woorde, seeing this Faith not to be geven to all men . . . but to suche as are borne of God . . .[whose] wil we may not call into disputation, but in trembling and feare submit our selves to it as to that whych can will none otherwise then that whych is holy, righte, and good, howe farre soever otherwise it seeme to the judgement of reason, which must needes be beaten downe to be more careful for Gods glory, then for mannes salvation.[20]

Bradford's theological system must cohere at all costs; if God is holy and omnipotent, then we must submit to his predestinating whims regardless of reason's objections. Yet Bradford's own adverbs (how may a person walk both warily and easily?) suggest the difficulty of embracing both abject submission to a hard doctrine and "easy" confidence in one's salvation.

Foxe's commentary on this letter demonstrates his awareness of both the comfort and the anxiety that predestination and its correlative doctrine of assurance might provoke. Foxe's remarks link his thoughts on predestination to the epistemology of testimony. His work repeatedly claims that martyrs wish to "certify" their beliefs with their deaths. Similarly, faith's presence "certifieth" election: "Not that faith is the cause efficient of election, being rather the effect thereof, but is to us the cause certificatory, or the cause of our certification, wherby we are brought to the feeling and knowledge of our election in Christe."[21] To ascertain whether one has this faith, Foxe advises looking for internal evidence: "Who soever desireth to be assured that he is one of the electe . . . lette him not clyme up to heaven to knowe, but let hym descende into hym selfe, and there searche hys faith in Christe . . . whyche if hee finde in hym not fained, by the working of Gods holy spirite accordingly: thereupon let hym staye, and so wrappe hym selfe wholely both body and soule under Gods generall promise, and cumber hys head with no further speculations."[22] Foxe offers a model of the Protestant saint: one who descends into him/herself, tests his/her own faith and, finding that faith strong, persists in it. Yet should the reader not feel this faith, Foxe urges him/her to exercise humility until it is discovered: "if ye feele not this fayth, then know that predestination is to high a matter for you to be disputers of, untill you have been better scholers in the schoolehouse of repentance and justification."[23] Foxe instructs readers who do not feel faith to continue on a journey of faithful practice and study anyway. His commentary tries to accommodate those who, despite searching inwardly, cannot find the clarity towards which his martyrological accounts drive.

Foxe's work fosters methods of interpretation that confirm both the Protestant elevation of faith over works for which his martyrs died and, hopefully, readers themselves as self-assured claimants to the martyrs' faith. Further evidence supports this reading, for Foxe was recognized as an expert in comforting people with regard to the doctrine of election. To *The Treasure of Trueth, touching the Grounde Worke of Man His Salvation*, a translation of a Latin tract by Theodore Beza, the translator John Stockwood appends two additional treatises: one of these is the commentary Foxe wrote on Bradford's letter with all references to Bradford excised. The title page advertises that Foxe is a good popularizer of this difficult doctrine: "the chiefest poyntes of the doctrine of God his Election, are so plainely set foorth, as the verie simplest may easily understande it, and reape great profite thereby." The title page describes the other additional treatise, by Anthony Gylbie, quite differently: in it "the doctrine of God his Election and Reprobation is both Godly and learnedlie handled."[24] The role of the *Book of Martyrs* in elucidating and popularizing this doctrine becomes Foxe's own.

Late sixteenth- and early seventeenth-century evidence indicating how and why the *Actes and Monuments* was read underscores the book's role in helping those struggling towards certainty in faith. Foxe's extant papers contain a large number of letters written to the martyrologist. Several of these suggest that he was seen as an expert on how to settle consciences and foster confidence. One Thomas Dolman, writing with a heavy heart ("subit animum dubitatio"), pleads for Foxe's help: "good mr. foxe for criestes sake resolve in these doubtes & praye to your Cr my Cr all owre lorde Jesus that in mercye he will strengthen me & other his servantes withe the invincible force of his grace agaynste the maliciouse assawltes of sathan."[25] Another writer asks Foxe to help him resist a temptation to despair: he writes "to have your advise howe if you were so provoked your self with . . . temptacion of blasphemye what yowe wuld do & howe yowe wuld overcome it & be thorowlie comforted & quyeted . . . what yowe wold do if in suche sorte yowe shold offende as god firbydd for to dispeyre . . . this is the hevist burdyn that ever was to be in such a fere."[26] In another letter, a worried writer anxiously searches his life for evidence of Christ within. He prays that Christ "of hys great mercy" will preserve him "from desperation byinge wonderfully appawled to se no frewt to follow the herynge gods word . . . but rather wexhethe worse & worse" and begs Foxe "to remember me In your dayly prayers."[27] The letter-writers poignantly lay bare their unsettled consciences and fervently hope that the martyrologist could prescribe some remedy. This hope in the martyrologist's spiritually curative powers was apparently widespread: Simeon Foxe, John Foxe's son, wrote in his biography of his father that "there repaired to him, both Citizens and strangers, Noblemen, and Common-people of all degrees, and almost all for the same cause; To seek some salve for a wounded conscience."[28] The confirming, comforting effect of reading about martyrs is transferred to the man most identified with the dissemination of their stories.

An early, popular abridgement of Foxe's text further indicates that martyrology's emphasis on confidence and certainty was thought helpful for those suffering from unsettled consciences. The title page for Cotton Clement's *The Mirror of Martyrs* advertises that it includes both a "*Short View*" of the martyrs and "two godly Letters written by M. Bradford, full of sweet consolation for such as are afflicted in conscience."[29] The letters occupy 40 pages or roughly 20 per cent of the book and emphasize assurance and certainty. Bradford writes that doubt comes "undoubtedly" from the devil, and that good deeds and assurance spring from "certaien perswasion and faith."[30] The somewhat circular process of attaining certainty is juxtaposed with the insistence (on the title page) that this process is "full of sweet consolation." The emphases of Clement's abridgement suggest both the awareness that assurance ought to come with faith as well as the reality that believers often needed encouragement before they could lay hold of a martyr-like confidence. These texts underscore one reason for the popularity of texts about martyrs who with great certainty confessed their consciences to the bitter end: they show readers possible ways to wrest assured stability from the hard doctrine of predestination, articulated amid the sixteenth century's religious turmoil. Most importantly, Protestant martyrological discourse's simultaneous insistence that martyrs can provide comfort and that good readers ought already to hold faith in their hearts represents a wish both to seal off readers and martyrs in a self-reflexive hermeneutic of increasing confirmation and clarity and to preserve martyrdom's persuasive force by bringing others into that interpretive circle who, when looking inwardly into spiritual things, see only darkness.

## "AN OPEN PROTESTATION OF INWARD JOY": CATHOLICISM, TREASON, AND THE RHETORIC OF CONVICTION

The rhetoric of conscience, comfort, and certainty was no less important to recusant Catholic martyrologies. In language similar to that of Foxe's commentary on Bradford's letter, William Cardinal Allen urges readers of his *Defense and Declaration of the Catholic Church's Doctrine* to search within themselves for confirmation of the faith to which he clings: "Grope with owte flattery of thyselfe, the depthe of thyne owne conscience...Touche once the hemme of Christes garment, adore his foutstoole, cleave unto the altarre, and if thowe finde not comfort of conscience, ease of heart, and light of trueth, never credet me more."[31] Allen maintains that readers may find comfort in searching their consciences and that martyrs' testimony inspires such searches while giving those basic contentions a Catholic emphasis: his readers should derive comfort from an inner image of Christ and his altar imagined in intensely visual and tactile ways. In *An Apologie and True Declaration of the Institution and Endevours of the Two English Colleges* (Rheims, 1581), Allen specifies the effects martyrs' testimony may have on others' inner convictions. He urges Catholics to be meek, patient, and steadfast in order to "stirre up the mindes of al men, inwardly and in conscience, to consider the cause of your afflictions, and give them such sense, reason, and religion, that they may acknowledge your undeserved calamities."[32] If Catholics behave like martyrs, in other words, all consciences, theirs and those of "al men," will align behind the proper interpretation of the disasters befalling them. These "undeserved calamities" derive from the Elizabethan government's persecution of recusant Catholics under charges of treason.

Catholics used the language of conscience and certainty to argue that Catholic martyrs were no traitors, despite the declarations of Elizabethan treason laws.[33] Political, controversial, and historical circumstances thus exerted as much influence on recusant Catholic martyrology as specific theological formulations. During the 1560s and early 1570s, Catholic recusancy was at a relatively low level because many Catholics chose to conform and because many authorities did not pursue recusant Catholics vigorously.[34] A number of circumstances contributed to increasing religious polarization, including the 1569 northern rebellion, the papal bull *Regnans in Excelsis* (1570) excommunicating Elizabeth and absolving Catholic subjects of loyalty to her, the imprisonment and eventual execution of Mary, Queen of Scots, and the launching of a Catholic missionary effort from continental English Catholic colleges. Increasingly harsh treason legislation gave these missionaries a bitter welcome. In 1571, it became treason to import, publish, or put into effect any bull or writing from Rome. In 1581 reconciling others to the Catholic Church or being reconciled oneself was declared treason, while in 1585 the Act against Jesuits and Seminarians declared English Catholic priests found on English soil *de facto* traitors.[35] The first Elizabethan priest to suffer a traitor's death was Cuthbert Mayne in 1577. A recusant martyrological literature quickly sprang up to celebrate him and his co-sufferers.

Elizabethan treason discourse challenged encomiastic interpretations of Catholic martyrs' consciences. Catholic martyrologists valorize the consciences and inward convictions of people who, they say, die only for religion; Protestant propagandists open a chasm between martyrs' rhetoric of conscience and their inner purposes, insisting that recusant Catholic martyrs hide traitorous intentions beneath religion's guise. Cecil's apology *The Execution of Justice in England* argues that only traitors would sneak about and refuse openly to declare their identities. *Ergo*, Catholic priests must be traitors: "Let it be answered why they came thus by stealth into the realm. Why they have enticed and sought to persuade by their secret false reasons the people to allow and believe all the actions and attempts whatsoever the pope hath done or shall do to be lawful. Why they have reconciled and withdrawn so many people in corners from the laws of the realm to the obedience of the pope."[36] The geography of recusancy, as Julian Yates terms it, is well established in the official imagination; priests operate by stealth in the realm's corners and even their reasons in support of their faith are "secret."[37] A 1593 law codifies such rhetoric; it provides "for the better discovering" of those who "terming themselves Catholics, and being indeed spies and intelligencers . . . and hiding their most detestable and devilish purposes under a false pretext of religion and conscience, do secretly wander and shift from place to place within this realm, to corrupt and seduce her majesty's subjects, and to stir them to sedition and rebellion."[38] Catholics hide their true intentions behind a smokescreen of faith and conscience, that guarantor of religious honesty used so frequently by Foxe; Protestant controversialists take it upon themselves to expose the supposedly treasonous intentions masked by the rhetoric of conviction.

In contrast, Catholic writers claim that their martyrs' true inner convictions are plainly visible to all, a claim that adapts contemporary Catholic theology to martyrological discourse's controversial and celebratory needs. Most significant are Counter-Reformation reaffirmations of Catholic thought concerning transubstantiation and the honoring of saints, issues central to the *Actes and Monuments*'s anti-Catholicism. Foxe's martyrs charged that the Mass idolatrously usurped the honor due Christ's original sacrifice. In contrast, the declaration of Session XXII of the Council of Trent stresses that Christ's sacrifice is easily seen in the sacrifice of the Mass: "The fruits of this (the bloody) oblation are perceived most fully through this bloodless oblation; so far is it from taking any honour from the former." Similarly, Session XXV of the Council of Trent asserted that honoring saints and their images cannot be idolatrous as that honor is readily transferred to God who is glorified through them.[39] For the Tridentine divines, the holy lives of saints, their images, and their relics easily point to, not obscure, the divine.

To counter treason discourse and to deploy this sacred sign theory, recusant martyrologists frequently claim that their martyrs' subjectivities are transparent: the martyrs reveal clearly to all but the willfully stubborn the faith to which they testify. The fullest Catholic response to Foxe was the martyrology *Concertatio Ecclesiae Catholicae in Anglia*, designed to broadcast English Catholics' sufferings to a continental audience who then might support the English mission and/or Catholic military intervention.[40] First published by John Gibbons, S.J., and the Rev. John Fenn in 1583, it was greatly expanded in 1588. It repeatedly emphasizes, *contra* Elizabethan propaganda, the clarity of the Catholic testifying subject. For instance, the text claims that when John Munden (or Mundyn) was condemned on 6 February 1584, he responded by singing *Te deum* and "could not help, indeed, but project that joy poured forth from his inner man even into his countenance, voice, and every bearing of his body."[41] The priest cannot hide his "inner man"; he reveals in every possible way the joy of a true martyr.

Since Catholics died under treason charges and were targeted by polemicists imagining secretive, hidden traitors, their martyrologists focus insistently on questions of truth and distortion, inwardness and authenticity. Published illegally at Smithfield in 1582, Thomas Alfield's *A True Report of the Death and Martyrdome of M. Campion Jesuite and prieste, & M. Sherwin, & M. Brian priests* uses a poetic of transparent plainness to open the martyrs' mouths, mouths shut by government cruelty and distorting propaganda.[42] Prefaced with a statement by its editor Stephen Vallenger, the tract contains Alfield's narration of the deaths of three Catholic priests, Vallenger's attack on Anthony Munday, a playwright and polemicist who wrote a tract attacking Edmund Campion, and several verses on Campion, the most prominent of the tract's martyrs.[43] These texts labor to make testimony readable despite Protestant efforts to suppress or distort correspondences between conscience and outward protestations. Alfield claims that he will avoid arguments about "how truth is made treason, religion rebellion" and will instead simply record an eyewitness account: "What he [Campion] spake openly, that my meaning is to set down truly, my self being present."[44] Yet government attempts to silence Campion and the others, and to distort what they do say, mean that recording what a martyr speaks openly is no longer, in the early modern controversial climate, enough.

Controversy erupted over determining the inward state motivating the priests' open protestations. In the exchange between Munday and Alfield over Campion's final moments, what Campion actually did and said are not at issue but rather what those words and actions might reveal or conceal.[45] Both record that Campion acknowledges Elizabeth as his lawful Queen. Yet Munday claims that behind that serene acknowledgement lurked an inconstant, wavering self: "there somewhat he drew in his woords to himselfe, whereby was gathered, that somewhat hee would have gladly spoken, but the great timeritie and unstable oppinion of his conscience, wherein he was all the time, even to the death, would not suffer him to utter it." Munday infers a fearful, unstable conscience and recasts Campion's eloquence as deception: "the outward protestations of this man, urged some there present to teares, not entring into conceyte of his inward hipocrisie."[46] In an implicit criticism of the suspicious scrutiny to which Munday subjects Campion, Alfield encourages readers to attend to the most apparent signification of the martyrs' words and actions, to their "outward protestations" and "plain disclaiming."[47] Yet his text is repeatedly concerned with the martyrs' ability to speak at all, for all three are silenced as they try to make their final confessions of faith. Not able to declare "openly" all that they wish, they require the services of a martyrologist to open and display their hearts.

For instance, the first remarks Campion attempts at his execution site, an explication of I Corinthians 4:9, are quickly stifled:

"*Spectaculum facti sumus deo, Angeli et hominibus* saying, These are the wordes of S. Paule, Englished thus: We are made a spectacle, or a sight unto God, unto his Angels, and unto men: verified this day in me, who am here a spectacle unto my lorde god, a spectacle unto his angels, & unto you men." And here going forwarde in this text, was interuptid & cut of by Syr Frauncis Knowles and the sheryfs.[48]

This verse's place in martyrological discourse is longstanding (Origen uses it in his *Exhortation to Martyrdom*, for instance).[49] Campion's words connect his death to martyrological tradition; the executioners cannot, therefore, allow him to proceed. A poem in Alfield's volume entitled "What yron hart that wold not melt in greife?" incorporates the verse; at the martyrs' deaths, "a pacient spectacle was presented then, / in sight of God, of angels, saints, and men."[50] The poem speaks for Campion when he cannot, elaborating his status as a martyr. Foxe also records instances of silencing. Before his burning Bradford began to rail against idolatry and "false antichrists." When the attending sheriff threatens to bind his hands, Bradford stops his jeremiad but manages a few pithy sentences before dying. Representations of sixteenth-century recusant Catholic martyrs do not usually claim that they spoke as provocatively as did Bradford. Although both Alfield and Foxe use the silencing of martyrs to build sympathy for them and to condemn the cruelty of executioners, Alfield dwells more on the problem of silencings than does Foxe; it becomes more urgent given anti-Catholic propaganda about sneaky, subtle traitors afraid to declare themselves by light of day.[51]

The poetry in Alfield's volume shares this focus on the mouth stopped in mid-confession. "Why do I use my paper, inke, and penne" (probably by Henry Walpole, himself executed in 1595) concerns the extent to which martyrs are able to speak for themselves.[52] The poem first wishes to find a language worthy to represent the martyrs:

> Why doo I use my paper inke, and penne,
> and call my wits to counsel what to say,
> such memories were made for mortall men,
> I speak of Saints whose names can not decay;
> an Angels trumpe were fitter for to sound
> their glorious death, if such on earth wer found.    (sig. E2r, 1–6)

The lines celebrate Campion and yet place him and his testimony above the controversial fray. Representation is unnecessary, for saints' names are already inscribed in a "register" which "remaineth safe above" (8), beyond controversy. Yet with full awareness of the climate in which recusant authors wrote, the poem quickly takes up controversial issues. It laments, for instance, the government's misnaming (and prosecuting) religious practices: "Religion there was treason to the queene, / preaching of penance warre against the lande, / prests were such dangerous men as have not bin . . . / so blind is error, so false a witnes hate" (55–7). The poem both inscribes Campion in a realm beyond controversy and reinserts him in that controversy in order to reverse its terms.

The poem, like Alfield's text, emphasizes Campion's triumph over attempts to silence him and to distort the meaning of his death. Renowned for eloquence, Campion is even more effective after suffering in relative silence. Before his arrest, "With tung & pen the truth he taught & wrote"; after his capture, "his patience then did worke as much or more, / as had his heavenly speeches done before" (31, 35–6). Foxe prints a ballad on Bradford's death that makes a similar point:

> And where you would not gyve hym leave
> His mynde foorth for to break

> All men of God will him beleve,
> Thoughe little he did speake.
> In going to the burning fire,
> He talked al the waye:
> The people then he did desyre
> For him that they would praye.[53]

The "little" Bradford was able to speak nevertheless is enough for "All men of God" to believe in him (and he speaks, and invites more speech – in the form of prayers – on the way to his execution). In Walpole's considerably more skillful poem, Campion's silence is even more thoroughly overcome through the materiality of his martyrdom. The poem declares that the government has amplified an eloquence that cannot be stifled:

> You thought perhaps when lerned Campion dyes,
> his pen must cease, his sugred tong be still,
> but you forgot how lowde his death it cryes,
> how farre beyond the sound of tongue and quil,
> you did not know how rare and great a good
> it was to write his pretious giftes in blood.　　(sig. E4r, 109–114)

The executioners perform the writing they thought they were erasing, translating the body of the martyr into a text whose meaning is starkly apparent. Attempts to silence martyrs fail spectacularly as the truth is everywhere proclaimed; the martyrs' triumph has already been inscripted in spaces and texts outside governmental control. Like the ballad on Bradford, the poem notes the expansion of the martyr's influence despite his executioners' cruelty. Yet the poem also deftly reasserts recusant claims to an authentic inwardness:

> Living he spake to them that present were,
> his writings tooke their censure of the viewe,
> Now fame reports his lerning farre and nere,
> and now his death confirmes his doctrine true,
> his vertues now are written in the skyes,
> and often read with holy inward eyes.　　(sigs. E4r–v, 115–120)

The lines contain a paradox increasingly common in early modern martyrological discourse: Campion's virtues are widely proclaimed – "written in the skyes" – and yet accurately read only by "holy inward eyes," by readers predisposed to interpret public declarations properly. The plain truth depends on the eyes of the holy beholder.

Alfield's book descants on the few words these martyrs managed to speak. The next major English-language treatment of Catholic martyrs,

William Cardinal Allen's *A Briefe Historie of the Glorious Martyrdom of Twelve Reverend Priests, Father Campion & His Companions*, seeks both to present transparent testifying subjects and to protect Catholic consciences from undue government scrutiny. His text thus focuses the influence of both theology and political exigencies on martyrology. First published in 1582 and incorporating much of Alfield's text, Allen's work was to serve as the definitive Catholic version of disputed events, the execution of twelve Catholic priests in England between 1577 and 1580.[54] Sometimes characterizing martyrs in sacramental language, Allen's text associates them with the sort of clear image outlined in Tridentine discussions of the Mass. In a letter of Campion's which Allen reprints, the martyrs' deaths are figured as sacrificial offerings: "Very many, even at this present, being restored to the Church, new souldiars geve up their names, whiles the old offer up their blood. By which holy hostes and oblations God will be pleased."[55] Most dramatically, Allen asserts that everything to be known about Campion and his conscience has already been revealed through his insistence that he dies not for treason but for religion. No government probing could ever reveal otherwise: "The meaning of the wordes he both then and afterward, as wel at the barre, as at his death uttered most sincerely: and for the rest if they had torne him in ten thousand peeces or stilled him to the quintessence, in that holy breast they should never have found any peece of those fained treasons."[56] Campion's body itself would refuse attempts to invest it with the government's symbolism of the secretive traitor dismembered and exposed; ultimately there is nothing within which is not already apparent from his words.

Yet even as he proclaims Catholic subjects' openness, Allen also argues that Catholics should be able to reserve their consciences from interrogation provided their actions are not treasonous.[57] Allen insists that in pursuing the so-called "bloody question" (whether, if the pope should amass an army to invade England, one would assist the invasion), the English government goes where angels fear to tread:[58]

God him self that doth above mans law punish the trespasses even of our hart, which are as open and subject to his sight and judgement as external actes be to men: yet chargeth no man nor searcheth any man for the time to come, nor for sinnes that he would have committed, or might, or were like to have committed if he had lived, or had had such occasions, provocations or tentations as other men, or he might have had. But now confessing the Prince to be our liege and soveraine . . . onely not making her our God, yet we must be farther demaunded by authoritie, othe or torment, what we wil do in such & such cases to come.[59]

Allen's sidenote proclaims that such questioning constitutes an "unreasonable search of mens consciences"; these interrogations "rack not our bodies only, but our very consciences."[60] Intrusion into unrealized potentialities produces what the government purports only to find: "by othes, interrogatories, and other indewe meanes, [they] purposely drive simple plaine meaning men, that never offended their lawes in word, deed, nor thought, into the compasse of their treasons . . . This is to make traitors and not to punish treasons."[61]

Allen's narration of the priest Thomas Cottam's story is a microcosm of his martyrology's dual claims that its martyrs are open, nontreasonous men and that Catholics should be able to protect their consciences from official scrutiny. Before his death Cottam offers two slightly different versions of his subjectivity, one that implies his right to reserve his conscience from government scrutiny and another that insists on his conscience's utter clarity. He first attempts to separate faith from politics: " 'unles it be for my conscience and faith I never offended her maiestie.' " Later Cottam claims that " 'My conscience giveth me a clear testimonie, that I never offended her.' "[62] First separating his conscience from political duty, Cottam now makes his clear conscience available to all who listen. Wishing to enclose and disclose, to allow Catholics to testify to and to reserve their consciences, the narrative exhibits the complications resulting from the subjection of martyrology's "open protestations" to the pressures of Elizabethan recusancy.

Responding to Foxe's influential bid to inherit martyrological discourse's authority, recusant martyrologies are concerned with ways to authenticate religious truth when that truth is expressed not primarily or only through doctrinal pronouncement but through individual testimony. Because Foxe typically defends his martyrs against heresy charges, his martyrology emphasizes doctrinal tenets more than do recusant Catholic martyrologies, which defend primarily against treason charges. In fact, recusant Catholic martyrologists often explicitly distinguish between their texts and doctrinal debate, differing markedly from Foxe's lengthy reprintings of interrogations over theological points. Still, to reclaim the language of conscience and conviction so integral to Foxe's *Book of Martyrs*, recusant martyrologists assert that their martyrs' inward states are plainly observable and convincing, a project that overlaps with Catholic doctrinal formulations and owes its challenges to religio-political circumstances. In authenticating rhetorical proclamations of inwardness, recusant Catholic martyrology wrestles with problems of self-disclosure – how disclosure ought to be read, how it ought to be represented, the extent to which it needs extra confirmation. Because the issue of self-disclosure is itself inflected by controversy, recusant Catholic martyrological writing often complicates its own claims to reveal straightforwardly martyrs' "outward protestations" of "inward joy."[63]

As Protestant and Catholic martyrologists adapt the rhetoric of conviction to support different causes, they expose how a common generic inheritance was contested in the early modern period. Martyrologists attempted to write religious separation, starkly distinguishing devious persecutors from martyrs acting transparently and only upon their consciences. Yet people who differed from each other violently in terms of doctrinal precepts held in common key conceptual vocabularies: consciences are repositories of truth; confident martyrs offer believable testimony. Martyrologists' persistent attachment to common rhetoric warns against overly rigid formal distinctions (e.g. "Protestant martyrologists emphasize conscience while Catholic martyrologists stress conformity to church discipline"). Rather, martyrologists more typically weave common conventions into the fabric of theological specificities and controversial exigencies. Thus Protestants ask readers to scrutinize martyrs' consciences as made manifest in their words and actions, in keeping with the habit of self-scrutiny for signs of election; thus Catholic writers urge readers to believe that Catholic martyrs are what they claim to be, that their martyrs' claims to suffer for conscience and religion function as true images do, to point towards, not to obscure, the truth. The perceived link between inner conscience and broader truths is precisely the one that controversy tended to weaken and that martyrologists tried to reinforce. Because the rhetoric of conscience was valued cross-confessionally, martyrologists must strive to meet interpretive challenges even as they seek to expose, with seemingly straightforward plainness, their martyrs' hearts: they must simultaneously shape the hearts and consciences of their readers.

## NOTES

1 See Katharine Eisaman Maus, *Inwardness and Theatre in the English Renaissance* (Chicago: University of Chicago Press, 1995), on the epistemological challenges the privileging of inwardness presents, though I disagree with her statement that those challenges do not apply to martyrs (18–19); see also Elizabeth Hanson, *Discovering the Subject in Renaissance England* (Cambridge: Cambridge University Press, 1998).
2 On the dynamics of scaffold performances, see Peter Lake (with Michael Questier), *The Antichrist's Lewd Hat: Protestants, Papists, and Players in Post-Reformation England* (New Haven: Yale University Press, 2002), chapter 8.

3 Patrick Collinson, "John Foxe and National Consciousness," in *John Foxe and His World*, ed. Christopher Highley and John N. King (Aldershot: Ashgate, 2002), 12–17. I use "Foxe" as a term of convenience, not as an indication of sole authorship.

4 London, 1570, c1. Seven editions were printed by 1609.

5 See, e.g., Luther from *The Bondage of the Will*: "the Christian's chief and only comfort...lies in knowing that...His will cannot be resisted, altered or impeded" (*Martin Luther: Selections from His Writings*, ed. John Dillenberger, New York: Doubleday, 1962, 185). Foxe's martyrology clearly endorses predestination. On the struggle between predestinarians and free-willers in Marian Protestantism, see David Loades, *The Oxford Martyrs* (London: Batsford, 1970), 175–6; Andrew Penny, *Freewill or Presdestination? The Battle over Saving Grace in Mid Tudor England* (Woodbridge: Boydell Press, 1990); and M. T. Pearse, *Between Known Men and Visible Saints: a Study in Sixteenth-Century English Dissent* (Madison: Farleigh Dickinson University Press, 1994).

6 *An Instruction of Christen Fayth*, trans. John Foxe (London, 1550), Aᵛ.

7 *Ibid.*, Bii.

8 *AM* (London, 1583), 1848. Bradford was a fellow of Pembroke College, Cambridge, and prebendary of St. Paul's under Ridley.

9 *AM* (1583), 1689.

10 *Ibid.*, 1623.

11 *Ibid.*, 1618.

12 Cf. Luther's *Commentary on Galatians*: saints "be not stocks and stones (as the monks and schoolmen dream) so that they are never moved with anything, never feel any lust or desires of the flesh" (*Martin Luther*, 153).

13 Reprinted in *Documents of the Christian Church*, ed. Henry Bettenson (Oxford: Oxford University Press, 1963), 263. On whether predestinarian thought encouraged comfort or anxiety, see Richard Strier (*Love Known: Theology and Experience in George Herbert's Poetry*, Chicago: University of Chicago Press, 1983), who emphasizes the former position, and John Stachniewski (*The Persecutory Imagination: English Puritanism and the Literature of Religious Despair*, Oxford: Clarendon Press, 1991), who stresses the latter.

14 On Bernher see Loades, *Oxford Martyrs*, 171.

15 *AM* (1563), 1733.

16 *AM* (1583), 1709.

17 Collinson, "John Foxe and National Consciousness," 25.

18 *A commentarie upon the Fiftene Psalmes...very frutefull and comfortable for all Christian afflicted consciences to reade*, trans. Henry Bull (London, 1577), Preface, vii.

19 Preface, "The Utilitie of this Story," *AM* (1583), 1. The 1563 preface reads "do much prevayle for the attaining of a good conscience"; subsequent editions have the same wording as the 1583 edition. I do not read Foxe's change to this preface as a weakening of the link between martyrs and good consciences given the rest of the evidence I discuss.

20 *AM* (1583), 1657.

21  *Ibid.*, 1657–8.
22  *Ibid.*, 1658.
23  *Ibid.*, 1657.
24  *The Treasure of Trueth* (London, 1576).
25  London, British Library, Harley MS 416, 116.
26  *Ibid.*, 131.
27  *Ibid.*, 120.
28  *AM* II (London, 1641), B2r.
29  *The Mirror of Martyrs* (London, 1613). This text enjoyed multiple editions. On its printing history see David Scott Kastan, "Little Foxes," in *John Foxe and His World*, ed. Highley and King, 123.
30  *Ibid.*, 186.
31  Antwerp, 1565, 288. On Allen, see A.C. Southern, *Elizabethan Recusant Prose, 1559–1582* (London: Sands & Co. Publishers, 1950), 49–50, and Eamon Duffy, "William Cardinal Allen, 1532–1594," *Recusant History* 22 (1995), 265–90. Protestant inwardness is a critical commonplace, but numerous Counter-Reformation practices testify to the importance of inwardness in Catholic experience. Michael Questier highlights the role of introspection in Jesuit conversion techniques (" 'Like locusts all over the world': Conversion, Indoctrination, and the Society of Jesus in Late Elizabethan and Jacobean England," in *The Reckoned Expense: Edmund Campion and the Early English Jesuits*, ed. Thomas M. McCoog, S.J., Woodbridge: Boydell Press, 1996, 265–84).
32  *An Apologie* (Rheims, 1581), 105a–b.
33  Foxe celebrates some who died under treason charges (e.g. George Eagles); still, the main charge Foxe's martyrs counter is heresy.
34  John Bossy, *The English Catholic Community, 1570–1850* (London: Darton, Longman, and Todd, 1975); Leslie Ward, "The Treason Act of 1563: a Study of the Enforcement of Anti-Catholic Legislation," *Parliamentary History* 8 (1989), 289–308; Arnold Pritchard, *Catholic Loyalism in Elizabethan England* (Chapel Hill: University of North Carolina Press, 1979), chapter 1; Alexandra Walsham, *Church Papists: Catholicism, Conformity, and Confessional Polemic in Early Modern England* (Woodbridge: Boydell Press, 1993).
35  Pritchard, *Catholic Loyalism*, chapter 1.
36  William Cecil, *The Execution of Justice in England*, ed. Robert M. Kingdon (Ithaca: Cornell University Press, 1965), 37.
37  "Parasitic Geographies: Manifesting Catholic Identity in Early Modern England," in *Catholicism and Anti-Catholicism in Early Modern English Texts*, ed. Arthur F. Marotti (New York: St. Martin's, 1999), 63–84.
38  35 Eliz. c. 2, reprinted in *Documents of the Christian Church*, 243.
39  *Ibid.*, 265.
40  On Catholic martyrology in international propaganda efforts, see Anne Dillon, *The Construction of Martyrdom in the English Catholic Community, 1535–1603* (Aldershot: Ashgate, 2002).
41  *Concertatio Ecclesiae Catholicae in Anglia* (Trier, 1588), 140v.

42 On Alfield's life see Southern, *Recusant Prose*, 35–6, 53. On his book's circulation see *Unpublished Documents Relating to the English Martyrs*, Vol. 1, *1584–1603*, ed. John Hungerford Pollen, S.J. (London: Catholic Record Society, 1908), 26–30. Alfield was executed on 6 July 1585 on treason charges. For a hostile account, see *The Life and Death of T. Awfeeld a Seminary Priest and Thomas Webley a Dyers Servant* (London, 1585).

43 See Munday, *A Discoverie of Edmund Campion, and his Confederates, their Most Horrible and Traiterous Practises, against her Majesties Most Royall Person, and the Realme* (London, 1582). On Campion's prominence and textual afterlives, see Helen C. White, *Tudor Books of Saints and Martyrs* (Madison: University of Wisconsin Press, 1963); Thomas McCoog, S.J., "'The Flower of Oxford: the Role of E. Campion in Early Recusant Polemics," *The Sixteenth Century Journal* 24 (1993), 899–913; Michael E. Williams, "Campion and the English Continental Seminaries," in *The Reckoned Expense: Edmund Campion and the Early English Jesuits*, ed. Thomas McCoog, S.J., (Woodbridge: Boydell Press, 1996); and Scott Pilarz, " 'Campion dead bites with his friends' teeth': Representations of an Early Modern Catholic Martyr," *John Foxe and His World*, ed. Highley and King, 216–231.

44 *A True Report*, B4r.

45 Brad Gregory, *Salvation at Stake: Christian Martyrdom in Early Modern Europe* (Cambridge, MA: Harvard University Press, 1999), 20.

46 *A Discoverie of Edmund Campion*, G1v.

47 *A True Report*, B2r.

48 *Ibid.*, B4v–C.

49 White, *Tudor Books*, 220. The text is ubiquitous: Bishop Challoner notes that Thomas Tunstal began to speak on the verse at his 1616 execution but was interrupted (*Memoirs of Missionary Priests*, rev. and ed. John H. Pollen, London: Burns and Oates, 1924, 80–1); Henry Burton invoked the verse as he awaited punishment (the loss of an ear) for defying the Laudian regime (*A Briefe Relation*, London, 1638, 48–9).

50 In *A True Report*, F2.

51 This emphasis is widespread in Catholic martyrologies; Diego de Yepez, *Historia Particular de la Persecucion de Inglaterra* (Madrid, 1599), stresses attempted silencings of priests, e.g. in his account of John Cornelius (639).

52 Anthony Raspa notes the likely authorship in *The Emotive Image: Jesuit Poetics in the English Renaissance* (Fort Worth: Texas Christian University Press, 1983), ix-x. Pilarz records that Walpole's poem also circulated in manuscripts, "four of which survive" ("'Campion dead bites with his friends' teeth,'" 223). Munday parodied the poem in *A briefe Aunswer made unto two seditious Pamphlets* (London, 1582).

53 *AM* (1563), 1216.

54 Allen omits three men Burghley discusses, two of whom apparently recanted (Southern, *Recusant Prose*, 276).

55 *A Briefe Historie of the Glorious Martyrdom of Twelve Revered Priests* (1582), E7.

56 *Ibid.*, dviv.

57 This was the sticking point, of course. Kingdon (*The Execution of Justice*, Introduction) and Duffy ("William Cardinal Allen") note Allen's involvement in various plots; White writes that Allen's and Persons's activities did not "reassure anybody" that English Catholics were nontreasonous (*Tudor Books*, 255).

58 Patrick McGrath, "The Bloody Questions Reconsidered," *Recusant History* 20 (1991), 305–19.

59 *A Briefe Historie*, C3.

60 *Ibid.*, Cv.

61 *Ibid.*, C4v.

62 *Ibid.*, B8. Recusant Catholic martyr accounts challenge common understandings of scaffold speeches as recusant martyrs neither confess the crime for which they are executed nor uphold the state as a just executor. See Peter Lake and Michael Questier, *The Antichrist's Lewd Hat: Protestants, Papists, and Players in Post-Reformation England* (New Haven: Yale University Press), 229–80.

63 John Geninges, *Life of Mr. Edmund Geninges, Priest* (St. Omer, 1614), 84.

# CHAPTER 2

# Too many brides:
# the interpretive community and ecclesiastical
# controversy

The most readily visible manifestation of a faith is its institutional incarnation. For early modern Catholics, the witness of their church across time guarantees their faith's truth. That witness is, in the Jesuit Robert Persons' words, "ever more visible & notoriously known in time of affliction and persecution, then in peace."[1] Conversely, it was imperative for Protestant martyrologists to demonstrate the transhistorical presence of their faith to counter Catholic charges of novelty. For mainline Protestants, the visible church is not necessarily coextensive with the true church, for the visible church is a site of struggle between elect and reprobate;[2] still, the true church can be perceived in moments of persecution. The rhetoric of these ecclesiastical arguments, often invoking vision and/or visual perception, is formative for martyrological discourse which depends so heavily on the spectacular for its impact. Theories of the true church that relied on persecution to identify her were complicated, however, by the fact of competing martyrdoms. Protestant martyrologists acknowledge that not all readers are able to perceive the true church even as they try to make martyrs' corporate testimony visible and persuasive. Catholic martyrologists must adjust to both inter- and intra-religious controversy by, for instance, including ideal readers within their texts who interpret properly the testimony their martyrs offer. Both approaches to some extent concede, even as they attempt to resolve, the increasing complexity of identifying the true bride of Christ.

## "LIKE AS IS THE NATURE OF TRUTH": PROTESTANT
## COMMUNITY AND THE INTERPRETATION OF MARTYRDOM

The four English editions of the *Actes and Monuments* published during Foxe's lifetime (in 1563, 1570, 1576, and 1583) appeared as the English nation continued to debate what it meant to be "Protestant." The text's different versions reflect ongoing struggles over the Elizabethan settlement, ranging from the 1563 edition's hope for further reformation to the 1583 edition's worry over growing faultlines in English Protestantism. The differences in the prefatory material to these editions reflect Foxe's shifting conception of the audience he addresses. The 1563 prefatory material exhibits optimism about the prospects for reform in the English church. Catholic and intra-Protestant attacks on the *Actes and Monuments* (such as criticisms that Foxe's "Kalendar" was too popish) together with setbacks in the progress of reform contributed to the 1570 edition's more defensive tone and imagining of a more exclusive audience.[3] The 1570 edition opens with a new preface (subsequently included in the 1576 and 1583 editions) entitled "To the true and faithful congregation of Christes universall Church, with all and singular the members thereof, wheresoever congregated, or dispersed through the Realme of England." Here, the true congregation has no explicit institutional identity but is identified instead by its faithfulness to Christ.[4] Yet the preface's running title is "A Protestation to the whole Church of England." The preface's conflicting titles exhibit a tension between identifying true godly readers and representing the Church of England itself as a united, godly reading community.[5] More broadly, Foxe's text alternately imagines itself as speaking to an established community of godly readers (in keeping with Protestant theories of the invisible church, composed of elect members) and as actively shaping such a community through martyrs' testimony.

The 1570 preface's struggle to identify the proper readership is also a struggle to identify the true church. From the first English edition, Foxe demands that the true church not be equated with the visible church of Rome. In his commentary on Thomas Becket in his 1563 edition, Foxe defines the true church instead in spiritual terms:

> If the cause make a marter (as it is saide) I see not why we shulde esteme Thomas Becket, to die a martir, more then any other, whom the princes sworde dothe here temporally punish for their temporall deserts. To dye for the churche, I graunt, is a glorious matter. But that churche as it is a spirituall not a temporall church: so it standeth upon causes spirituall, and upon an heavenly foundation, as upon faith, religion, true doctrine, sincere discipline, obedience to Gods commaundementes, &c., not upon thinges pertening to this world.[6]

The 1570 preface "To the True and faithfull congregation of Christes universall Church" also identifies the true church as spiritual: it is "neglected in the world, nor regarded in histories, & almost scarce visible or knowne to worldly eyes." As the martyr John Philpot stresses, the visible church contains the good and the bad, but "the invisible church is of the electes of God onely."[7]

How may an invisible church lead others to truth? Robert Persons charges that Protestants "seeke to assigne such a Church, as no man can tell where to find it; for that it is rather imaginary, mathematicall, or metaphysicall, then sensible to mans eyes, consistinge (as they teach) of just and predestinate men only, whome, where, or how to find, yow see how uncertayne and difficult a thing it is, in this mortall life."[8] The difficulty Persons identifies is somewhat ameliorated by the persecutions Foxe documents. In a 1530 letter to Henry VIII Hugh Latimer argues that persecution points to truth: "where the word of God is truely preached, there is persecution, aswell of the hearers, as of the teachers: and where as is quietnesse & rest in worldlye pleasure, there is not the trueth."[9] John Warne, an upholsterer burned in London on 30 May 1555, wrote a confession of his beliefs which explicated the apostle's creed. He defines "the holy Catholike church" as "an holy number of Adams posteritie, elected, gathered, washed, and purified by the bloud of the Lambe from the beginning of the world, and . . . dispersed through the same, by the tiranny of Gog and Magog, that is to say, the Turke and his tiranny, and Antichrist, otherwyse named the Bish. of Rome and hys aungels."[10] Warne's catholic church of the elect is illuminated by the fires of persecution.

Yet persecution is not an unproblematic marker of the true church in an era in which both Protestants and Catholics suffered. The 1583 edition's title page is the first to claim that the *Actes and Monuments* documents "*true* Martyrs" (emphasis added) rather than simply "martyrs." By 1583 the execution of Catholic priests and the writing of recusant Catholic martyrologies had begun; perhaps Foxe and his publisher John Day found it necessary to clarify matters a bit.[11] Within the work, a theory of the true church as the elect means that the true church may be seen only by those predisposed to see her: "For although the right Church of God be not so invisible in the world, that none can see it: yet neither is it so visible agayne that every worldly eye may perceave it. For like as is the nature of truth: so is the proper condition of the true Church, that commonly none seeth it, but such onely as be the members and partakers therof."[12] The epistemological assumptions here are breathtaking: truth is visible only to those who already possess it.

Debates over the visibility and identity of the true church on earth were central to many examinations printed in the *Actes and Monuments*.[13] Bradford's account, for instance, posits a closed circle of interpretation in which the church is seen by its members.[14] Bradford claims that identifying the true church requires the proper vision: "to see her wee must put on such eyes, as good men put on to see & know Christ when hee walked here on earth" – that is, eyes informed by the word of God.[15] As his interrogations wear on, Bradford repeatedly characterizes the true church as visible only to a limited few. He tells the Archbishop of York: "The fault why the Church is not seene of you, is not because the Church is not visible, but because your eyes are not cleare inough to see it."[16] The ability to perceive the communion of true believers is dependent upon true belief. One of Foxe's sidenotes extends this ecclesiastical circularity in its conception of the Eucharist: "He must be in Christes body that must receive Christes body."[17] This account reforms the mystery with which traditional hagiography is infused into the invisibility of the true church to all but those who already contain the mystery of faith within themselves.

This circularity of interpretation is both irrefutable – for those who question it are clearly not of the true church – and also potentially unpersuasive. Yet of course Foxe's mammoth text is designed to serve as a powerful, visible witness to the supposedly invisible church and to try to confirm readers in it. A number of Foxe's martyrs seem presciently aware of the need to provide testimony around which a godly reading community may coalesce. Early in his account, George Marsh is concerned with various possible interpretations of his choice to stay in Marian England and brave persecution:

my weak flesh would gladly have consented [to flee], but my spirit did not fully agree: thinking and saying thus to my selfe, that if I fled so away, it would be thought, reported, and sayd, that I did not onely flie the countrey and my nearest and dearest frendes: but much rather from Christes holy worde, according as these yeares past I had with my hart, or at least with mine outward living professed, and with my mouth & word taught.[18]

Marsh's worries are resolved through communal intervention. As he prays for guidance, a friend encourages him to "abide & boldly confesse the fayth of Jesus Christ." Marsh then declares himself "so confirmed and established in my conscience" that he remains. Before this confirmation, he was tormented by an unquiet conscience; afterwards, he declares himself "merry and in quiet estate."[19] These struggles are not included in the 1563 edition, as Marsh's own account of his ordeals was apparently not yet available to Foxe. In the 1570 and subsequent editions, this account was printed, including Marsh's account of why he decided to write:

there be divers and sondry reportes, and opinions of the cause of mine imprisonment . . . some saying it was onely because I would not do open penance, and some because I could not agree with my Lord and his councell concerning the sacrament of Christes body and bloud, and the maner of Christes presence there: some because I woulde not graunt it sufficient and according to Christes institution the lay people to receave the sayd sacrament under the one kinde onely, I thought it good, dearely beloved in Christe...to certifie you by mine owne hand writing...the certaynty of those thinges as neare as I could...not omitting any thing at al concerning Religion.[20]

Marsh "certifies" proper interpretation through his writing and fixes the conclusions readers should draw from this martyr's testimony.

The account of the gentlewoman Joyce Lewes suggests a similar concern with a martyr's ability to unite a godly interpretive community. Fellow Protestants exerted careful control over this female martyr's conscience. Yet Foxe also suggests that this woman's steadfast martyrdom – a surprise to Catholic authorities who assume she will weaken when she must stand on her own – provides a powerful model for the Protestant community and other women in particular. After Laurence Saunders was martyred (he was the second, after John Rogers, to suffer the Marian fires), Lewes inquired about the beliefs for which he died. After receiving instruction from John Glover, she refuses her husband's command that she go to Mass and he turns her in to authorities.[21] In prison, Lewes seeks counsel about the best ways to bear witness, to behave like a martyr: "shee consulted [with friends] how shee might behave her self, that her death might be more glorious to the name of God, comfortable to his people, and also most discomfortable unto the enemies of God."[22] The bond between would-be martyr and her encouragers is, Foxe claims, what her enemies hope to destroy: "Well, tomorrow her stoutnes will be proved and tryed. For although perhaps shee hath now some frendes that whisper her in the eares, tomorrow will we see who dare be so hardy as to come neare her." Lewes's execution scene is initially scripted against her: "the Papistes had appointed some to rayle upon her openly, and to revile her, both as shee went to the place of Execution, and also when she came to the stake." Nevertheless Lewes takes control of the moment's drama. At the stake she raises a cup a friend gave her, saying "I drynke to all them that unfaynedly love the Gospell of Jesus Christ and wish for the abolishment of Papistry. When she had dronken, they that were her frends dranke also. After that a great number, specially the women of the towne dyd drynke wyth her." Foxe notes that some women were put to open "penaunce" and that authorities later sought out but never found other supporters present at her execution.[23]

Yet this community of godly women was not so steadfast as Foxe might have hoped; there was more inconsistency and wavering in interpretations of martyrdom than his vision of an elect church would suggest in theory. In this instance, Foxe suppresses evidence that some of those watching Lewes's death explicitly recanted their interpretations of her demise. Foxe had a copy of – but chose not to print or specifically refer to – the recantation of Agnes Glover (the wife of John Glover, who had counseled Lewes). The list of Protestant errors Agnes Glover recanted includes the following: "I have beleved and sayed that Joyce Lewes late of the parrshe of Mancester condempned by the lawe and our mother holy churche for heresye and burned for the same, that she dyed well, wisshing that I might dye as she dyd, and Saying that though her carcas suffred, yet god Receaved her soule." Glover, or at least the document written for her (she signed it only with the mark of a cross), specifies that after receiving "trewe and faithfull instruccion" she now believes "that the forsayde Joyce Lewes Late of Mancester was an obstinate and arrogant heretike, and that she woorthely and justly according to thorder of the Lawe was putte the execucion of Death by fyer for her hereticall and Devlishe belief against the Sacrament."[24] The document suggests the pressure Agnes Glover must have felt as the wife of one of Lewes's counselors. Most importantly, its suppression illuminates Foxe's efforts to present a Protestant community unified in their understandings of Protestant martyrs' sacrifices, despite evidence that some sympathizers were far from steadfast.

Of course, the pressure Catholic authorities exerted on Agnes Glover was not always needed to break up Protestant interpretive circles. Fissures in Protestant communities may be seen from the earliest English Reformation martyrologies. In the introduction to his 1546 edition of Anne Askew's first examination, Bale compares Askew to Blandina, an early church martyr. Askew herself, however, chooses Stephen as her model, insisting in the first comment she makes in her text that she models herself on this martyr-preacher.[25] While Bale insists that Askew, like Blandina, is a mother of martyrs, Askew seems rather to wish to be a father. Further, Bale's move replaces Askew's comparatively more radical reliance on the Bible alone with a reference to early church persecutions. Thus, Thomas Betteridge argues that Bale co-opts Askew's text for a magisterial Protestant project: locating mainline Protestantism as the descendant of a continuously present, faithful, and suffering church.[26] Askew's comparative radicalism is suppressed in favor of her status as a proto-martyr for mainline English Protestantism, at least as Bale understands it.

Given the potential fractiousness of a Protestant community that both insists on the laity's right to interpret scripture and attempts to fix what correct interpretation would be, Foxe's stress on a circularity of interpretation seems partly defensive, an attempt to hold together a Protestant community always threatening to break apart. In a sidenote on John

Philpot's examinations, which center on the nature of the true church, Foxe declares that "The end of all controversies is to know the true church."[27] The difficulty for Protestants is that their true church was not always so clearly defined in practice as in theory. The Catholic polemicist Miles Huggarde levels a common charge: "if these good fellows will needs be of Christ's church, as arrogantly they presume by their own confession; They must have one unity of doctrine as the church hath, which surely they have not."[28] A ballad written by Richard White, a recusant Catholic martyr, and entitled "The Church of God is One" argues that "If two have agreed in their midst, / On points of new doctrine, / Myself would ever bear their praise, / And be a third [amongst them]."[29] Particularly sensitive to this argument, Foxe works to unify Protestant doctrine despite his martyrs' sometimes differing beliefs.[30] Henry Ramsey, burned at Smithfield on 12 April, 1557, was one of those Foxe's 1563 edition termed "silly sheep," comparatively uneducated martyrs whose sometimes confused responses to questioning needed a bit of explanation. In the 1563 edition, Foxe includes a preface to Ramsey's story urging his readers to consider that while Ramsey and his companions showed ignorance on some theological points, "in the chiefe and principall grounde and foundation of their religion and faythe, they swarved not, laying Jesus Christ for their corner-stone."[31] In subsequent editions this apology is cut, perhaps for fear of protesting too much. Still, in each of the four editions published during his lifetime, Foxe feels compelled to explain their confusion about the number of sacraments (they include matrimony as a third sacrament, which "undoubtedly was done rather of simple ignoraunce then of any willful opinion") as well as their response to their interrogators' charge that they rejected the faith of their baptism when they rejected the Church of Rome.[32] Somewhat befuddled by the interrogators' logic, the martyrs agree that they had indeed rejected the faith of their baptism. Foxe explains that they did not as they still held the faith of the Trinity, in which form they were baptized. Similarly, in reporting Ramsey's reply to his interrogators' questions about the true church, Foxe finds it necessary to clarify Ramsey's imprecise words: " 'there are two Churches upon the earth, and we, (*meaning him selfe and other true Martyrs and professours of Christ,*) be of the true Church, and ye be not' " (emphasis mine).[33]

The need to elaborate who exactly "we" happens to be haunts the inheritance of the *Book of Martyrs*. The martyrs' sharp distinctions between true and false churches imbue the invisible English church with, in Richard Helgerson's words, "a strongly oppositional identity . . . founded on suffering and resistance and profoundly antithetical to the hierarchical order of the English state."[34] Thomas Betteridge and Jesse Lander have both found that the 1583 edition urges Protestant unity and solidarity; what Betteridge calls the "historicization of martyrdom" in the 1583 edition works to unify Protestant history and shut down contentious debates.[35] This drive towards historicization was particularly urgent as English Catholic martyrologies began to be printed. Despite this attempt to close the book on martyrdom, so to speak, and despite Foxe's hermeneutics of a self-confirming elect church, martyrdom's oppositional identity held the potential to splinter English Protestantism.

This potential was recognized as early as 1589, the year of the first abridgement of Foxe's *Book of Martyrs*. The Martin Marprelate controversy was in full swing, and the Marprelate tracts attempted to use the authority of the Marian martyrs to make their case. Thus *Theses Martiniae* claims that "this wicked governement of bishops was an especiall point, gainesaid by the servants of God, in the time of King Henrie the eight, and Q Marie; and in the withstanding whereof they died, the holie martires of Christ Jesus."[36] During their earlier controversies Whitgift and Cartwright had both appealed to Foxe. Now, in response to the Marprelate furor, Whitgift chose a strategy of abridgement. Damian Nussbaum has shown that Timothy Bright's 1589 abridgement of Foxe's text was part of "a concerted effort by the authorities to have Foxe's work disseminated in a more congenial form." Bright's abridgement stressed England's role as an elect nation, cast the English episcopacy in an unfailingly positive light, and told the story of Bishop Hooper, the "*locus classicus* of opposition to wearing vestments," so as to imply that Hooper's scruples about wearing vestments had been satisfied.[37] Despite this effort, separatists, Presbyterians, and congregationalists continued to use the *Book of Martyrs* to authenticate their struggles against the established church. The Elizabethan separatist Henry Barrow (hanged at Tyburn on 6, April 1593) claimed the authority of an invisible church, based on apostolic practice, whose members were the true faithful scattered throughout the world, "a companie called from the world, as were Christ's disciples, and the faithfull in all places at the first gathering of the church."[38] The Foxean martyrs' rhetoric of seeing, perceiving, invisibility and enlightened vision thus both addressed and potentially exacerbated difficult interpretive problems. This complex dynamic comes under additional pressure given that the rhetoric of visibility Foxe uses to foster the identification of the elect church was so highly prized that recusant Catholic martyrologists, too, attempted to wrest it to their cause.

In *A Treatise of Three Conversions* (St. Omer, 1603–4), an anti-martyrology designed to counter *Actes and Monuments*, Robert Persons cites St. Gregory's remark that the world is full of martyrs.[39] The implication is that witnesses to the Catholic Church are convincing in their plenitude. Yet in the early modern period, the surplus of martyrs testifying to different causes resulted in another sort of fullness, less amenable to a clear vindication of one faith. For Catholics, the Roman succession demonstrates the historical continuity and coherence of true Christian community. The Jesuit Superior Henry Garnet argues that the true church is visible to all who look: "Calvin dreameth out a Church invisible, and manifest onely unto the eies of God. Of this Church if you desire to be, you may easely dreame it; but then are you not of the trew Church, but of a dreamed Church...the trew Church of God is visible it selfe."[40] While for Catholics the church's historicity and interpretive authority are of paramount importance, martyrs' testimonies figure so prominently that even in his doctrinal defense Allen emphasizes personal testimonies to the detriment of more abstract argumentation. His readers may dismiss or "Take away all these arguments"; the Church will still be adequately defended by "the noble army of Martyrs, the holy company of Confessors, the glorious train of so many blessed, wise and learned Doctors, of many thousand saints that ever accompany her majesty."[41]

Yet Foxe's assertion of a competing army of martyrs complicates matters. At one moment in John Mush's account of the recusant Catholic Margaret Clitherow, two Protestant ministers are culling biblical examples to bolster their doctrine. Frustrated with what they call Clitherow's obstinacy, they demand to know why she refuses to come to their church since they have "soe plaine and sure testimonies to showe on our syde for the truth." The statement is of course ironic: the insistence that there are "plaine and sure testimonies to show on our side for the truth" is recorded in a martyrology that seeks to provide "plaine and sure testimonies" for the Catholic cause.[42] Still, the juxtaposition of the phrase "our syde," an almost schoolyard-level taunt, with the insistence on a truth that transcends sides – "plaine and sure testimonies" – points to the epistemological crises brought on by the simultaneous evocation of transcendent truth and the polemical assertion of "our side." Catholic martyrological representations of religious certainty in an age of conflicting truths mean that, increasingly, claims that Catholic martyrs participate in the true church's visible community need further bolstering.

Persons's *A Treatise of Three Conversions* echoes Allen's and Alfield's arguments about the Catholic Church's clarity while also acknowledging the difficulty of perceiving – in the sense of understanding – that clarity. Engaging in ecclesiastical controversies, Persons's tract combines a defense of the Catholic Church with an extended, almost martyr-by-martyr refutation of *Actes and Monuments*.[43] Persons wishes to clarify true religion for those who "imagine by the multitude of contradictions, which they see and heare everywhere, that it is a hard matter to discerne, which party hath the truth, or where that certainty lyeth."[44] He vigorously challenges Foxe's claims that the authentic church is invisible and yet has visible witnesses: "if the Church of Christ be invisible, how can Fox or the Magdeburgians write so greate & large stories therof? ... [Foxe] cometh forth with a new opinion never heard of perhaps before: affirming that the true Church of Christ is both visible and invisible, to witt, visible to some, and invisible to others; visible to them that are in her, & invisible to them that are out of her."[45] In contrast, the Catholic Church is "most cleare & evident to all them, that have eyes of understanding to see, and grace to consider the truth."[46]

Those eyes of understanding can, however, be manipulated. In an extended metaphor, Persons accuses Foxe of literally pulling the wool over readers' eyes:

the difference betwene us and him [Foxe], and his ... is not much unlike to that of two cloth sellers of London, the one a Royall marchant, which layeth open his wares cleerely, geveth into your hands the whole peece of cloth at midday, willeth yow to view and behold yt in the sunne, removeth all veyles, pentices and other stoppings of light that may give obscurity, or impediment to the manifest beholdinge, handlinge and discerninge therof. Whereas contrariwise the other, being a crafty broker or poore pedler, havinge noe substantiall wares indeed to sell, but such as is false made and deceytfully wrought, and taken up also for the most part of the others leavings, seeketh by all meanes possible to sel in corners, and to shut out the sunne that it be not well seene, or to give yow a sight therof by false lights only, neyther will he deliver yow the whole peece into your hand to be examined thorowly by your selfe, but sheweth yow one end therof only, different from the rest which he suppresseth.[47]

The economic metaphor suits martyrologies' persuasive agenda, their need to sell particular theories about which church is true. In this ecclesiastical economy the visual trick, the possibility of manipulating readers to see incorrectly, concerns Persons. The "invisible" church is so because evidence for it is tattered and loosely woven. Persons's metaphor likens Protestants to the deceitful, tricky recusants familiar from government propaganda and aligns Catholics with royalty. What Protestant martyrologies make visible is the shabby fabric of a religion always in turmoil, whose witnesses testify merely to their own contradictory, individual views: each "sectary" under Henry VIII "held what himselfe thought best, of things invented by themselves, every one cited scriptures, and interpreted them as he listed, without authoritie, president or example of former ages."[48] Catholics make visible a different sort of church: "By all that hitherto hath byn wrytten and discoursed (good Christian Reader)...I do not doubt, but that of thy prudence thow hast observed a farre different course holden by us that are Catholicks, and our adversaryes in this behalfe, we seeking to make matters playne, evident, easy, perspicuous & demonstrable (so farr as may be ) even to the eye yt selfe."[49]

Yet the demonstration of Catholicism's visible truth "so farr as may be" relies at least partly on the interpretive work of the reader. As Persons knew well, the English Catholic community was far from united. The English Catholic community is best characterized as dispersed along a continuum ranging, roughly, from sympathy towards the Church of Rome to church papistry to staunch recusancy, and including a spectrum of political opinion as well. At some points, such as the intense persecutory period of the late 1580s, the Catholic community tended to coalesce behind its more evangelical factions; when persecution ebbed, as in the mid-1590s, divisions resurfaced.[50] Aware that readers' eyes are predisposed to interpret in a variety of ways, Persons' text aims to unite fragmented reading communities. His three volumes contain dedicatory epistles devoted to three different groups: English Catholics, English Protestants, and the community of saints. Each epistle intertwines the language of visibility, history, and community in a bid to resolve the problems spawned by competing martyrologies and conflicting intra- and inter-religious interpretive communities. The epistle to Catholics, prefacing the first volume, encourages Catholic readers to see and lay claim to their inheritance of the true church, visible throughout history: "Which tradition being sett downe, prooved and declared most cleerlie in this ensuinge woork, I do by offering the same unto you, but present you with your owne, to wit, the history of your owne house, the records & chronicles of your owne family, the pedigree and genealogie of your owne forefathers, the antiquity and nobility of your owne progenitors, together with your just title & clayme to their inheritance."[51] Invoking economic privilege in its metaphor of inheritance, Persons envelopes his Catholic readers in circular self-shaping in an attempt to unify their perspective: they inherit what is already theirs, see what they already know. The epistle to Protestants stresses the value of belonging to a community of good readers and martyrs precisely because the martyrologies one reads have shaping power over the reader and his/her community. Persons asks the "moderate and discreet *Protestant*" not to commune visibly with the wrong sort of martyr: "yf the prudent & judicious Protestant . . . will open his eyes of understandinge, and without passion behold these things, he cannot of his wisdome, but discover the manifest iniurie and dishonour, which is offered both to him and his Religion, by this association with so notorious wicked people."[52] Protestants must open the "eyes of understandinge" to overcome the misleading "passions" Protestant martyrologies arouse. While admitting that martyrologies shape what one sees, Persons wishes to retain a Catholic ecclesiastical emphasis on seemingly objective, convincing visibility. Thus in his epistle to the community of saints, he claims that the contrast between them and Protestant martyrs is clear; all he need do is present contrasting calendars of martyrs. He wishes seeing and understanding to be aligned against Protestant pseudo-martyrs and yet acknowledges throughout the potent challenge Foxe has launched to that alignment.

Recusant Catholic martyrologists are also aware that even within the Catholic community seeing and proper understanding may be misaligned. Divisions in the Catholic community over whether to conform or not, over the controversies between Jesuits and secular priests, and over the relative merits of loyalism and resistance meant that support for the martyrs was far from uniform.[53] Clitherow's martyrologist and confessor John Mush is eager to use her life to unify a Catholic community divided over whether to conform outwardly (so-called church papistry) or to imitate Clitherow's recusancy and willingness to suffer. He records that a Catholic man urged Clitherow not to shelter priests in her home for fear of increasingly harsh treason legislation; in response to Mush's counsel that she should continue to do so, Clitherow expressed "great dislike" for "such timorous Catholicks, which would not onely, through worldly fear, slack their own Christian duty, but would also be an instrument of the devill and hereticks to discomfort and terrify such as would gladly do well."[54] Still, despite Mush's claim that she was totally "Innocent and blamelesse," her virtues "would noe more staie the rancour of envious harts and sclanderous tongues, in some foolish Catholicks, then her constant faith staied the furious rage of hereticks."[55] Mush gradually makes criticisms of Clitherow as a saintly model tantamount to heresy, claiming that even those Protestants "(. . . who saw this Martyrs behaviour in death) witnes freely her constant vertue; and saie, she was a rare woman in mortification to the world, and the pleasures thereof; and that nothing wanted to make her a true Martyr, but onely a true faith."[56] If even heretics read her behavior as virtuous, Catholics surely ought to be able to interpret well enough to move from her "outward behavior" to her "Inward intention."[57]

Thomas Worthington uses similar interpretive modeling in his account of Catholics executed in 1600.[58] His text devotes over half its space to one martyr, the layman John Rigbie. Worthington first distinguishes his narrative's clear testimony from controversial arguments:

> ...for avoiding of al partialitie, I wil omit other proofes of our Religion...and simply...touch those onlie points which concerned the necessarie knowledge of [Rigbie's] person, and pertained directly to the cause of his death: and then set before your eyes the whole processe, as it passed before manie witnesses, in forme and shew of publiq injustice. The divulging wherof in print, no resonable men, and namely the Magistrats and others that concurred in this action, can not dislike, nor possibly be offended therwith, except their consciences accuse them.[59]

Our "eyes" should look beyond the show of (in)justice and the cacophony of controversy to the true reasons Rigbie suffered. Worthington's text, however, reveals the deep involvement of martyrology in early modern controversy, as he devotes nearly half his text to the controversial issues he says he will avoid.[60] Most significantly, in narrating Rigbie's life and death Worthington uses audiences within the text as model readers, to shape what readers' eyes perceive.

Anticipating his readers' need to probe conventional, contested martyrological language, Worthington uses the skepticism and inquiries of audiences represented within the text to authenticate correspondences between Rigbie's conscience and his suffering. When two riders, an earl and a captain, pass by just before Rigbie's execution, they question him about his status and character. He politely apologizes for not removing his hat (his arms are tied) and tells them that he is to die simply because he was reconciled to the Catholic Church and would not attend Church of England services.[61] The captain remarks that it is odd anyone should die for such a reason. Because various audiences are convinced of the martyr's honesty and merit – the earl and captain are "much astonished at his courege and constancie" – they model appropriate responses for Worthington's readers.[62] Simultaneously, these moments of interrogation suggest a complexity to martyrological testimony not fully acknowledged by Worthington's claim to narrate simply a martyr's death: he anticipates his readers' need to probe beyond surface appearances and provides opportunities for further disclosure in order to authenticate Rigbie as a martyr.

Worthington's final comment on Rigbie's death blurs the lines between supposedly simple narration and the narrator's attempts to guide inter-pretation: "Thus you have a plaine and sincere narration of this mans death, and of the cause therof. Which was, as you see, for being reconciled and for refusing to go to the Protestants Church."[63] Despite plain, sincere narration, Worthington still feels pressed to identify the cause for Rigbie's death; in turn, the articulation of that cause is fashioned as a simple mirroring of the audience's perception: "as you see." After digressing into controversial issues, Worthington emphasizes that the purpose of the Rigbie story is to uphold strict recusancy:

al that looke to have feloship with Christ and his members in his bodie and blood, must flie from the feloship of al infidels . . . And in nowise conforme them selves to these new procedings, by going to their Churches, which is the *proper marke of their societie*. And therfore most constantly refused by this glorious Martyr, so manfully fighting this good fight (emphasis mine).[64]

Worthington's admonition reminds his readers of the lesson he taught through his own representational tactics: the need to align oneself with the right community. His text is designed to authenticate Rigbie as a true martyr and to encourage English Catholics towards strict recusancy, to ensure that they do not commune visibly with the wrong "societie."

John Wilson's *The English Martyrologe* (first published in 1608) and the Protestant response to it, *The fierie tryall of Gods saints, as a counterpoyze to J. W., Priest, in his English Martyrologe* (London, 1611), crystallize one inevitable response to a world too full of martyrs: what one sees is pre-dicated upon what one wishes to see. Not engaging at all with Protestant martyrs, Wilson's tract simply presents a calendar of traditional saints and martyrs of England, Scotland, and Ireland. Drawing on sources including Worthington's martyrology and *Concertatio Ecclesiae Catholicae in Anglia*, Wilson also appends a list of Catholic martyrs who suffered from Henry VIII's time forward, including the two priests caught up in the Gunpowder Plot, Henry Garnet and Edward Oldcorne. He dedicates his tract to Catholics who suffer for honoring saints and martyrs; they are included in his implicit chronology of continued persecution, the "certaine inher-itance" of Catholicism and Catholic witnesses.

In countering Wilson, *The fierie tryall* does not bother engaging Wilson's readership. The anonymous author (possibly Francis Burton) claims he will not try to convert Catholics but only to prevent the conver-sion of weak Protestants and to defend Queen Elizabeth and King James from false accusations. Because "It is not the punishment, nor the place, but onely the cause that maketh a man . . . loved of God for his owne free graces, or hated of God and good men for their villannies," and because the author does not wish to defend doctrine, he is reduced simply to proclaiming "that the Gospell which we now in England professe is the Truth, and hath for truth beene confirmed with the bloud of many more Martyrs (in lesse then sixe yeares space) then this Popish Priest in his Martyrologe with any shew of truth can (though falsely) pretend to have suffered in England for Religion in 50. yeares since."[65] Playing a numbers game, he assumes a readership already committed to his interpretation of true martyrdom's "cause," to his view of "Truth." His refutation comprises simply Wilson's list of sixteenth- and seventeenth-century English martyrs printed under a derisive heading: "A Beadroll of all such traiterous Priests, Jesuits, and Popish Recusants, as by J. W. priest in his English Martyrologe are recorded for Martyrs." In this tangle between Wilson and his adversary, one either sees or does not see the "truth" to which martyrs testify. An almost inevitable result of arguments over whose martyrs are genuine is the calcifying of confessional boundaries and interpretive communities.

Indeed, although martyrologists recognize the importance of interpretive communities and attempt to shape them, they also write as though those communities are increasingly self-enclosed and self-sustaining. Sir Thomas Tresham (1543?–1605), a prominent lay Catholic, kept extensive notes on points of controversy to prepare for interrogation. In those notes, Tresham reveals the entrenchment that was often the result of controversies such as those over whose martyrs were true ones: "Hereticks are to be forsake[n] and Catholiques to be belived . . . Though yet ye geve proves yet we be Catho: . . . yt folowth that we have the truth the whole truth and noth. but the truthe."[66] "Proves" or proofs are of no avail; counter-arguments succumb to what one already believes. Such calcification of interpretation is not absolute, of course; there are many instances of converts who, moved at the spectacle of a steadfast martyr, embrace a new faith.[67] Further, martyrologists frequently claim that the crowd gathered before a martyrdom pities the martyr and reconsiders the cause for which he or she died. Still, the desideratum of a visible, united, persuasive tradition of martyrs is somewhat compromised by martyrologists' intense awareness of the controversial environment in which they write, by the challenges overlapping rhetorics produced, and by martyrologists' own tendency to insist that the church is visible mostly to those who have good vision. Ecclesiastical theories of a continuous tradition of persecuted witnesses made visible in martyrological narration become complicated by the exigencies of controversy, by the pressures of multiple brides competing for the hand of Christ.

## NOTES

1 Persons, *A Treatise of Three Conversions* (St. Omer, 1603–4), 269.

2 David Loades, *The Oxford Martyrs* (London: Batsford, 1970), 22ff.; cf. John Philpot's argument that the true church exists alongside the false: "always from the beginnying there hath been joyned to the same true church, a false church, adversarie to the true" (*AM*, 1583, 1818).

3 Cf. Thomas Betteridge, *Tudor Histories of the English Reformations, 1530–83* (Aldershot: Ashgate, 1999), 189, and Susan Felch, "Shaping the Reader in the *Acts and Monuments*," in *John Foxe and the English Reformation*, ed. David Loades (Aldershot: Scolar Press, 1997), 52–65. Thomas Freeman finds that most of the material urging Elizabeth I to godliness was inserted in 1570 or later, suggesting that Foxe did not feel the queen was pursuing reform as she ought ("Research, Rumour and Propaganda: Anne Boleyn in Foxe's 'Book of Martyrs,'" *The Historical Journal* 38 [1995], 797–819).

4 Thus the 1576 title simply reads: "To the Christian Reader." See John Knott, *Discourses of Martyrdom in English Literature, 1563–1694* (Cambridge: Cambridge University Press, 1993), on the tension in Foxe's work between the church as a persecuted, godly people and as an authoritative establishment.

5 Patrick Collinson, "John Foxe and the National Consciousness," in *John Foxe and His World*, ed. Christopher Highley and John N. King (Aldershot: Ashgate, 2002), 27.

6 *AM* (1563), 46; the passage appears in all four early editions.

7 *AM* (1570), iii; *AM* (1583), 1824.

8 *A Treatise of Three Conversions*, 643.

9 *AM* (1583), 1753.

10 *Ibid.*, 1581.

11 Copies of Campion's "Bragge" survive in Foxe's papers and Foxe definitely read Catholic counter-martyrologies, such as Nicholas Harpsfield's *Dialogi Sex*.

12 *AM* (1570), iii.

13 Geraldine Thompson argues that a debate over the Eucharist forms the central pattern of the *Actes and Monuments* ("Foxe's 'Book of Martyrs': A Literary Study," Ph.D. dissertation, University of Oregon, 1974). Yet debates about the visibility of the church appear as frequently and hold important implications for interpretive authority.

14 Mark Breitenberg argues that the text's circularity implies both its openness to the Protestant community and its closed ideological space ("The Flesh Made Word: John Foxe's *Acts and Monuments*," *Renaissance and Reformation* 13 [1989], 381–407).

15 *AM* (1583), 1613.

16 *Ibid.*, 1616.

17 *Ibid.*, 1620.

18 *Ibid.*, 1561.

19 *Ibid.*, 1562.

20 *Ibid.*, 1564. Compare *AM* (1563), 1120.

21 *AM* (1583), 2012.

22 *Ibid.*, 2012.

23 *Ibid.*, 2013.

24 London, British Library, Harley MS 421, 85.

25 On this point, see my "The Inheritance of Anne Askew, English Protestant Martyr," *Archive for Reformation History* 94 (2003), 134–60.

26 Betteridge, "Anne Askew, John Bale, and Protestant History," *Journal of Medieval and Early Modern Studies* 27 (1997), 265–84.

27 *AM* (1583), 1852.

28 *The displaying of the Protestantes* (London, 1556), 12.

29 In *Unpublished Documents Relating to the English Martyrs*, Catholic Record Society, vol. 1 (London: J. Whitehead and Son, 1908), 90.

30 D. R. Woolf writes that for Foxe "unity is the watchword of the Reformed, division...that of Rome" ("The Rhetoric of Martyrdom: Generic Contradiction and Narrative Strategy in John Foxe's *Acts and Monuments*", in *The Rhetorics of Life Writing in Early Modern Europe: Forms of Biography from Cassandra Fedele to Louis XIV*, ed. Thomas F. Mayer and Woolf, Ann Arbor: University of Michigan Press, 1995, 259).

31 *AM* (1563), 1567.

32 *AM* (1570), 2159–60.

33 *Ibid.*, 2161.

34 Helgerson, *Forms of Nationhood: the Elizabethan Writing of England* (Chicago: University of Chicago Press, 1992), 217.

35 *Tudor Histories*, 209; Lander, " 'Foxe's' *Books of Martyrs*: Printing and Popularising the *Actes and Monuments*," in *Religion and Culture in Renaissance England*, ed. Claire McEachern and Debora Shuger (Cambridge: Cambridge University Press, 1997), 69–92.

36 *Theses Martiniae* (Wolston, 1589), Biir.

37 "Whitgift's 'Book of Martyrs,' " in *John Foxe: an Historical Perspective*, ed. David Loades (Brookfield, VT: Ashgate, 1999), 150, 144.

38 Leland Carlson, ed., *Elizabethan Nonconformist Texts* (London: Allen and Unwin, 1951–70), vol. 5, 161. On Barrow, see Helgerson, *Forms of Nationhood*, 271; B. R. White, *The English Separatist Tradition: from the Marian Martyrs to the Pilgrim Fathers* (Oxford: Oxford University Press, 1971), 2–3, 12–15, 160; and Knott, *Discourses of Martyrdom*, 119–34.

39 *A Treatise of Three Conversions*, 62.

40 *An Apology Against the Defence of Schisme* (London, 1593), 91.

41 *Defense and Declaration of the Catholic Church's Doctrine* (Antwerp, 1565), 50.

42 John Mush, "The life and Death of Mistris Margarit Clitherow," Institute of the Blessed Virgin Mary, Bar Convent (York) MS, 95.

43 Persons had an annotated copy of the *Actes and Monuments* (Christopher Highley, "Richard Verstegan's Book of Martyrs," in *John Foxe and His World*, ed. Highley and King, 187), probably from the 1596 edition.

44 *A Treatise of Three Conversions*, preface, vii.

45 *Ibid.*, 292–3.

46  *Ibid.*, 484.
47  *Ibid.*, 629–30.
48  *Ibid.*, 253.
49  *Ibid.*, 627–8.
50  Peter Lake and Michael Questier, *The Antichrist's Lewd Hat: Protestants, Papists, and Players in Post-Reformation England* (New Haven: Yale University Press, 2002), 285ff.
51  *A Treatise of Three Conversions*, +4.
52  *Ibid.*, +2v, ++4v.
53  See Lake and Questier, *Lewd Hat*, chapter 8; see also Arnold Pritchard, *Catholic Loyalism in Elizabethan England* (Chapel Hill: University of North Carolina Press, 1979).
54  "The life and Death of Mistris Margarit Clitherow," 36.
55  *Ibid.*, 70–1.
56  *Ibid.*, 118.
57  *Ibid.*, 70.
58  Worthington held the presidency of Douai College from 1599 to 1613 and wrote numerous devotional and doctrinal works (Southern, *Recusant Prose*, 24).
59  Worthington, *A Relation of Sixtene Martyrs* (1601), 5.
60  These include controversies over toleration and over the appointment of an archpriest. On the archpriest controversy see Pritchard, *Catholic Loyalism*.
61  *A Relation of Sixtene Martyrs*, 29.
62  *Ibid.*, 31.
63  *Ibid.*, 33.
64  *Ibid.*, 44–5.
65  *The fierie tryall of Gods saints, as a counterpoyze to J. W., Priest, in his English Martyrologe* (London, 1611), 41.
66  London, British Library, Add. MS 39830, Tresham papers, vol. 2, 86. Brad Gregory observes that "over the long term, martyrdom militated against conversion and reinforced confessionalization" (*Salvation at Stake: Christian Martyrdom in Early Modern Europe*, Cambridge, MA: Harvard University Press, 1999, 340).
67  Converts include Margaret Clitherow, Joyce Lewes, and Henry Walpole.

# CHAPTER 3

# Material witnesses

To proclaim their martyrs' authenticity in an era of competing Christianities, both Protestant and Catholic martyrologists adapted hagiographic tradition to argue that the metaphysical could penetrate, if only briefly, the material world and offer compelling, marvelous evidence. These marvels include providential interventions to protect a would-be martyr or to punish persecutors; wonders or marvels attending the martyr and/or those who honor the martyr; and the wonder of the death scene itself, showcasing the martyr's spiritual commitment despite seemingly unbearable pain. Though many Protestants criticized the miracles recorded in many medieval saints' lives, Protestant martyrologists use wonders to compete more effectively, so to speak, with other martyr traditions, while Counter-Reformation caution together with Protestant polemics influenced many Catholic writers to qualify their uses of miracles somewhat. Theological viewpoints are thus refracted by, not simply reflected by, martyrological writing and the controversies in which it was inevitably caught up. Although the ways marvels are rendered in martyrological writing evince particular theological viewpoints, so that there certainly are representational differences between Protestant and Catholic martyrologies, those differences are not particularly clean-cut; often they are more in the way of emphasis, and only sometimes of kind. Like common appeals to inwardness and continuous communities, appeals to material testimony indicate martyrologists' longing to turn martyrs' deaths into absolutely clear testimonies. Martyrologists use martyrs' lives and spectacular deaths to articulate subtle theological distinctions while drawing on powerful generic traditions to invoke marvels and wonders as seemingly irrefutable evidence.

## REFORMING MIRACLES

It is almost a critical truism to assert that Protestants eschewed miracles while Catholics embraced them.[1] Yet while writers like Foxe are critical of miracles in traditional saints' legends, they are willing to use strange or "marvelous" occurrences to confirm Protestant testimony, as Catholic controversialists realized. In partial response to Foxe's 1563 edition of the *Actes and Monuments*, Thomas Stapleton published a new translation of Bede's *Ecclesiastical History* in 1565.[2] Stapleton wrote a lengthy preface defending Bede's use of miracles, decrying Protestant attacks on miracles, charging Foxe with hypocrisy for using miracles, and arguing, for good measure, that Protestants have no real miracles anyway. Stapleton insists that if Bede's accounts of marvels are to be derided, so should Foxe's: "if all this suffiseth not to defende this history from the cavilles of protestants, bicause of the miracles here reported, then let them shewe a reason why the Actes and Monuments of M. Fox, deserve not the lyke. Are there not also in that donghell heaped a number of miserable miracles to sette forth the glory of their stinking Martyrs?"[3] Those "miserable miracles" are caught in a bind which Stapleton heatedly identifies between Protestant criticisms of traditional hagiographic miracles and the desire to offer marvelous testimony on Protestant martyrs' behalf.

The common assertion that Protestant martyrologists rejected the miraculous stems from Foxe's own rhetoric. Recounting Saint Alban's legend, Foxe carefully separates the martyr's admirable life from his legend, rich with miraculous occurrences.[4] Foxe wishes "that the stories both of him, and of al other Christian Martyrs, might have bene delivered to us simply as they were, without the admixture of all their Abbeylike additions of Monkish-miracles."[5] The scorn Foxe heaped on traditional hagiographers should not lead us to assume, however, that he rejects all sorts of wonders and marvels. Instead, Foxe desired both to use dramatic testimony and to distinguish his work from that of the traditional Catholic hagiographers he frequently disparaged. In his 1570 narrative of William Tyndale, Foxe includes a story that demonstrates both Protestant caution towards miracles and a lingering fascination with them:

There was at Antwerpe on a tyme, amongst a company of marchauntes as they were at supper, a certaine juggler, whiche through his diabolicall inchauntements or Art Magicall, would fetch all kindes of viandes, and wyne from any place they would, and set it uppon the table incontinent before them, with many other such lyke thinges. The fame of this judgler beyng much talked of, it chaunced that as M. Tyndall heard of it, he desired certaine of the Marchauntes, that hee might also be present at supper, to see hym play his partes. To be brief, the supper was appointed, and the Marchauntes, with Tyndall were there present. Then the juggler beyng required to play his feates, and to shew his cunnyng, after his wonted boldnes began to utter all that he could do, but all was in vayne. At the last, with hys labour sweating & toyling, when he saw that nothyng would go forward, but that all his enchauntmentes were voyde, he was compelled openly to confesse that there was some man present at supper, whiche disturbed and letted all his doinges. So that a man even in the Martyrs of these our days cannot lacke the miracles of true fayth, if miracles were now to be desired.[6]

In claiming for Tyndale the "miracles of true faith" Foxe does not deny the presence of miracles in true martyrs' lives. He instead refigures miracles so as to chasten magical excess – here represented by the juggler – and to harness marvelous testimony for the Protestant cause. The changes Foxe made to this narrative in the 1570 edition highlight the ambivalence implicit in Tyndale's miraculous confutation of false miracles. In the 1563 edition, the story closes with the words "if miracles are to be desired."[7] In 1566, Nicholas Harpsfield had attacked Foxe's credibility, including his use of dubious miracles; the Tyndale story was a particular target.[8] In the 1570 edition, Foxe seems to respond: the story ends in the subjunctive, "if miracles were now to be desired," implying that miracles are no longer necessary even while relating one. The 1563 edition introduces the anecdote with much fanfare: "among all other testimonies of his godly life, there is none more famous and worthy of remembraunce then this." The 1570 edition retreats from florid rhetoric; among other stories of Tyndale's virtues, this one "semeth . . . worthy of remembraunce, [so that] I thought not in silence to overpasse [it], which hath unto me credibly bene testified by certaine grave Marchauntes, and some of them also such as were present the same tyme at the facte, and men yet alive. The story wherof is this."[9] The tale once decreed most famous now merely seems worthy of recounting (and needs further support not just from the 1563 edition's single source for this anecdote, one "grave marchaunt," but from several willing "grave" witnesses).

Foxe's text thus tries to use some of traditional hagiography's spectacular resources without running afoul of Protestant attacks on superstitious miracles. Foxe's translation of the Regius sermon theorizes true miracles as deriving from the flesh's subjugation to religious imperatives: to "mortefye" the "flesshe" reveals "trewe and lyvely faythe" which in turn produces "miracles and thynges farre passynge the possibilitie of naturall workynge."[10] Protestant theologians frequently associate the "flesshe" with concupiscence.[11] Importantly, this emphasis on mortifying and transcending the flesh should not be taken to mean a dualistic denial of the body *per se*;[12] instead, mortifying the flesh is shorthand for controlling sinfulness. The *Actes and Monuments* literalizes this figure to make the controversial point that Protestants are superior in the mortification arena. Of course, Catholic

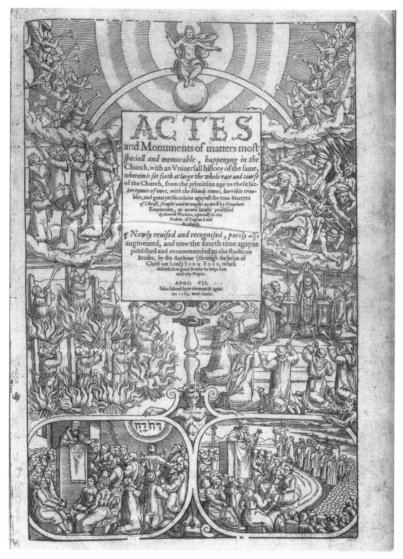

1 Title page from *Actes and Monuments* (1583), John Foxe.

martyrologists also claim that their martyrs subjugate the flesh, as in the case of the virginal middle-aged martyr John Rigbie (discussed above); Foxe's claim is clearly polemical and is staked immediately, on his title page (Figure 1). The top of the illustration shows Christ seated as if on judgment day. To his right is a series of pictures depicting Protestants and on his left a series depicting Catholics, whose fates are markedly different. The bottom pair of pictures opposes Catholic forms of devotion – e.g., praying the rosary – to a Protestant service in which worshippers listen attentively, Bibles open, and others kneel before the tetragrammaton. The next pair opposes the centerpiece of the Catholic liturgy, the elevation of the host just at the miracle of transubstantiation, to the central witness of Foxe's text: the burning of martyrs, sacrifices for truth. The figures in the Mass scene kneel in adoration of the sacrament and face the priest, ignoring the divine judge at the woodcut's top. Directly opposite, martyrs, tied to stakes and engulfed by flames, face upward. They represent in iconographic form the true miracle of fleshly mortification, which points towards and does not usurp God's glory in idolatrous and ineffective attempts to repeat Christ's sacrifice. The pictures at the top show the results of these differing sacrifices. The Protestants stand robed, wearing the martyr's crown and holding the martyr's palm of victory. Meanwhile Catholic figures still gaze downwards while devils clutch at their robes. The title page argues that the sacrifice of the martyrs' flesh replaces the Mass's central miracle because their mortification of the flesh powerfully reveals the "trewe and lyvelye faythe" for which the martyrs suffer.[13]

As the title page intimates, Foxe's death scenes are precisely the moments in which many of his wonders appear. In the martyrs' death scenes Foxe maintains, though in chastened, subtle forms, many traditional hagiographic emphases (on the saints' mortifying of the flesh; on last-minute marvels). The death scenes combine the emphases of the title page, in which martyrs' deaths are opposed to the Mass's idolatrous, pseudomiraculous sacrifice, with the residue of traditional saints' stories, in which death scenes were redolent with marvels and exhibited the martyr's subjugation of the body to testimonial imperatives. Foxe's martyrs often state their desire to overcome the "flesh." Rawlins White, an illiterate but charismatic Welsh fisherman, uses the word "flesh" to mean not only his body but also those with whom he shares a bodily connection: his own family. Seeing his family as he is led to the stake, he struggles with himself: "Ah flesh, stayest thou me so? wouldest thou fayne prevayle? Well, I tell thee doe what thou canst, thou shalt not, by Gods grace, have the victory." His fear of the flesh's power is so great that he gives the executioner special instructions: "I praye you good frend knocke in the chayne fast, for it may be that the fleshe would strive mightely: but God of thy great mercy geve me strength & pacience to abide the extremity." After a gruesome depiction of his death, Foxe insists, remarkably, that White felt little pain. In fact, Foxe claims that White undergoes something of a transfiguration; going to his death, White, a stooped old man, suddenly stands upright and reportedly looks sturdier, more vibrant; his hair, usually grey, looked white instead so that he appeared "altogether angelicall." His final mortification of the flesh produces a wondrous revitalization of the body, spectacular confirmation that his flesh was at last brought under the control of grace.[14] The claim that Foxe rejects miracles, then, needs qualification. Foxe's death scenes exhibit his interest in revealing the spectacular triumph of the martyr through final, material testimony; he lays claim to the traditionally persuasive force of marvels even as, in keeping with the Regius sermon, he recasts marvels as the result of fleshly mortification.

In revising his account of another martyr, Julius Palmer, Foxe adds a wondrous resuscitation or "notable spectacle" to underscore Palmer's persistence despite intense suffering. In 1563, Foxe writes only that Palmer (who suffered with two others) "being resolved into ashes, yelded unto God as joyful a soule, (confirmed with the swete promises of Christ) as any one that ever was called beside to suffer for his blessed name."[15] The 1570 and subsequent editions insert a marvel before this benediction:

after their three heds by force of the ragyng and devouryng flames of fire were fallen together in a plumpe or cluster, which was mervailous to behold, and that they all were judged already to have geven up the ghost, sodainly Palmer, as a man waked out of sleep, mooved his tongue and jawes, and was heard to pronounce this word Jesu. So beyng resolved into ashes, he yelded to God as joyfull a soule ... [16]

The miracle's transience enacts the Tyndale anecdote's ambivalence: poised at the threshold of its own dissolution, the body offers final, marvelous testimony. The resolution of the wondrously speaking head into ashes leaves behind no material site for idolatrous worship, no relics which, traditional saints' legends claim, spread miracles wherever they are translated. Instead, Foxe theorizes a different sort of iteration, characterizing the elect's mortification of "the flesh" as reformed commemoration:

though we repute not their ashes, chaines and swerdes in the stedes of reliques: yet let us yelde thus muche unto their commemoration, to glorifie the Lord in his Saintes, and imitate their death (as muche as we maye) with like constancy, or their lives at the least with like innocencye. They offered their bodies willinglye to the rough handling of the Tormentours. Is it so great a matter then for our part, to mortifie our flesh, with all the members thereof?[17]

This understanding of relics responds implicitly to Catholic criticisms of some onlookers who sought physical relics from Protestant martyrs. Miles Huggarde insists that "because our heretikes wil nedes have their men to be taken for martyrs, some of them counterfayting the trade of the auncient state of the true churche, gather together the burnt bones of these stynking martyrs . . . to preserve them for relykes . . . when an heretike is burnt, ye shal see a route enclosing the fyer, for that purpose."[18] Marotti's assertion that Protestants dismissed relics needs slight refinement:[19] the reconceptualization of relics as imitative mortification of concupiscence is something the *Actes and Monuments* must argue for, not merely describe or record, as it encourages readers to admit both the wonder of Palmer's final word and its singular finality. The moment balances the desire to incinerate would-be relics with the desire to make the body a powerful site of witness; the body becomes a temporary, liminal site of testimony.

In attempting similar balances, other accounts indicate the relative sophistication of early modern martyrology as they acknowledge that even spectacular, marvelous testimony increasingly depends on proper interpretation. The martyr Thomas Haukes's friends "prively desired" that he would show them some "token" if the pain of the fire could be withstood with patience. Haukes promises to do so, and they "secretly" agree that if the pain of immolation were tolerable, Haukes would lift his hands towards heaven before dying. At his martyrdom, Haukes suffers incredibly but still gives the sign. In the 1563 edition, after everyone assumes he has died, Haukes,

mindeful of hys promis made, dyd lift up his hands halfe burned, & burning with heate above his head, to the living God, & even in a sodain, and with great rejoycing striketh them three tymes together: By which thing, contrary to all mens expectation beyng sene, there followed so great rejoycing and crye of the multitude gathered together, that you would have thought heaven & earth to have com together. But he straight way, as it wer sincking downe into the fyre, gave up his spirite . . .[20]

In this version, the entire multitude exclaims at the wonder as if it were like the transcendent conjunction of heaven and earth (what Catholic theologians claimed happened in the Mass); the marvel is seemingly universally acclaimed. Later versions somewhat qualify, however, the multitude's exclamations, imagining a more exclusive interpretive community:

the blessed servaunt of GOD, being myndfull of his promise afore made, reached up hys hands burning on a lyght fier (which was marveilous to behold) over his head to the living God, and wyth great rejoysing, as seemed, strooke or clapped them three tymes together. At the sight whereof there followed such applause &

outcry of the people, *and especially of them which understoode the matter,* that the lyke hath not commonly bene heard: And so the blessed Martyr of Christ, straight way sinckyng downe into the fire, gave up his spirite. (emphasis mine)[21]

Here the "token" is explicitly called "marvelous" but it is also slightly qualified. It no longer prompts a response as if "heaven and earth" had come together; Haukes's rejoicing is supposed ("as seemed"), not proclaimed definitively. Significantly, Haukes's clapping is most appreciated by "them which understoode the matter." The revision both invites readers to see what those who "understoode the matter" saw and suggests that the proper interpretation of marvels depends upon prior understanding. A woodcut included in all editions shows Haukes clapping his hands amid flames and crying, "O Lord, Receive my spirite" (Figure 2). These words, not recorded in the text itself, are an imitation of the protomartyr Stephen and an *imitatio Christi*; the woodcut is to place this marvelous death in Christian tradition.[22] That placement was challenged by Harpsfield, who mocked this clapping marvel, comparing it unfavorably with the miracles of hagiographic tradition.[23] Yet what most distinguishes Foxe's marvel from those in pre-Reformation hagiographic texts is not so much its type or quality but rather Foxe's keen awareness (spurred in part by Harpsfield's attack) that the right reading of marvels depends on properly ordered interpretive frameworks and communities ("those who understoode the matter").

Protestant martyrologists are well aware that questions of interpretive authority inhere even – perhaps especially – where marvels are concerned. In the 1583 edition Foxe adds material to George Tankerfield's account implying that Tankerfield (who, this additional material claims, struggled with his flesh like White did) felt little pain at his martyrdom: "embracing the fire he bathed himselfe in it, and calling on the name of the Lord Jesus he was quickely out of payne." Relative imperviousness to pain has a long lineage in martyr narratives;[24] the addition of this claim situates Tankerfield's death in this tradition. Yet Foxe also adds that several "superstitious old women" claim that he feels little pain because "the Devill was so stronge with him."[25] Foxe uses the combined force of gendered and religious derogation to discount these women's reactions, to dismiss the possibility that a marvel could reveal not godliness but devilish possession.

Confronting similar interpretive challenges in his commentary on Anne Askew's martyrdom, John Bale addresses Catholic arguments that Askew was no martyr because there were no miracles at her death. Bale first claims that Askew's perseverance is sufficient testimony: "Of hys owne chosen

¶ The Martirdome of Thomas Haukes in Essex, at a Towne called Coxhall. Anno. 1555. Iune. 10.

O Lord receiue my spirite.

In the which when he continued long, and when his speech was taken away by violence of the flame, his skin also drawen together, and his fingers consumed with the fire, so that now all men thought certainly he had bene gone

martyrs, Christ loketh for non other myracle, but that onlye they persever
faythfull to the ende."[26] Yet in his closing comments, Bale claims that
Askew's witness *was* confirmed by something wondrous. As the fire consumed her and her fellow believers,

the skye abhorrynge so wycked an acte, sodenlye altered coloure, and the cloudes
from above gave a thonder clappe, not all unlyke to that is written, Psal. 76. The
elementes both declared therin the hygh dyspleasure of God for so tyrannouse a
murther of innocentes, and also expreslye sygnyfyed hys myghtye hande present to
the confort of them whych truested in hym.[27]

Bale claims that the thunderclap clearly shows God's verdict. Yet his
subsequent remarks admit the various interpretations to which even things
"expreslye sygnyfyed" are subject. He records that some felt the thunder
signified Askew's damnation. This is clearly wrong, Bale says, because in
scripture thunder represents the voice of God.[28] When Foxe incorporated
this story into the *Actes and Monuments*, he tried to fix this marvel's
meaning firmly (Figure 3). The woodcut illustrating Askew's death conflates the thunderclap with a representation of a voice from heaven while
the soldiers executing her and her fellow martyrs wear Roman dress: the
thunderclap voices God's disapproval of revived Roman tyranny.

That thunderclap resounds throughout the *Actes and Monuments* insofar
as it features marvelous providential interventions to protect the godly or
punish their persecutors with grievous maladies. Although the closings of
Foxe's English editions saw many changes between 1563 and 1583, they all
emphasize, amid various notes and additional material, providential preservations and punishments. Freeman has argued that no other section of
Foxe's text received as much careful revision as his material on providential
retributions.[29] Foxe's determination to include providential wonders led
him (as Freeman shows) to insert at the front of the 1570 edition, apparently at the last minute, an anecdote about the marvelous escape of
William Laremouth from prison. Although he prefaces the anecdote with
a caution reminiscent of the 1570 version of the Tyndale wonder – he says
he is "loth to insert any thing in this booke which may seme incredible or
straunge to ordinary working" given "quarreling adversaries which do
nothing but spie what they may caveil" – Foxe nevertheless cites godly
witnesses to bolster the story that Laremouth heard, while in prison, a voice
twice telling him to arise and leave; upon arising Laremouth found that the
prison wall had collapsed and made his escape.[30] In later editions, this
anecdote was placed with Foxe's concluding material on providentialism.

## ❧ The order and maner of the burning of Anne Askew, John Lacels, John Adams, Nicholas Belenian, with certayne of the Councell sitting in Smithfield.

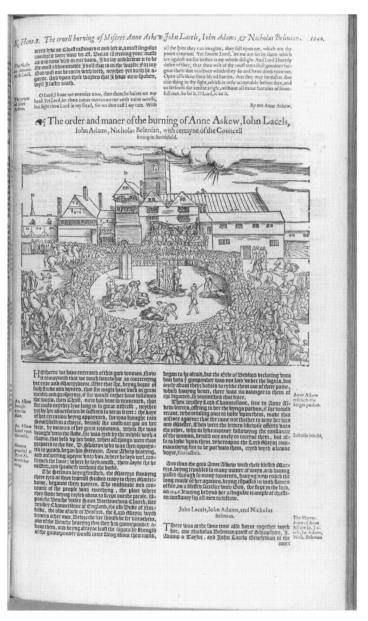

3 'Martyrdoms of Anne Askew, John Lasselles, John Adams, and Nicholas Belenian' from *Actes and Monuments* (1583), John Foxe.

Foxe's changes to George Marsh's account between the 1563 and 1570 editions suggest his determination to include wondrous occurrences despite doubts that arose over the supposedly providential punishment of Marsh's persecutor. In the 1563 edition, Foxe writes that,

by reason that the fier was unskilfully made, and that the wind dyd drive the flame to and fro, [Marsh] suffred great extremitie in his death, whiche notwithstanding he abode very paciently. Upon this many of the people said that he was a Martir, and died marvelous patiently and godlye. Which thing caused the bishop shortly after to make a sermon in the Cathedrall Church, and therein affirmed, that the said Marsh was an heretike, burnt like a hereticke, and was a fierbrand in hell.[31]

Foxe claims that God's judgment was soon visited upon this bishop for his "good and charitable sermon": through his shameful behavior he was "burned with a harlot, and died thereof, as credible report hath bene made." Changes made to the 1570 edition, however, suggest that this story had been questioned. Foxe's 1570 narrative of providential punishment is more cautious: "not long after [his sermon] he turned up his heales and dyed. Upon what cause his death was gendred, I have not here precisely to pronounce, because the rumour and voyce of the people is not allwayes to be folowed. Notwithstandyng such a report went in all mens mouthes, that he was burned of an harlot . . . " Foxe here questions a rumor suggestively; he goes on to state, as he did in the 1563 edition, that some of those who saw the bishop's body after his death could give evidence to support the rumor that his death was caused by whoring. Given the tempering of this providential revenge anecdote, it is particularly striking that in the 1570 edition Foxe actually adds a wonder to the story of Marsh's death. In the 1570 edition, after Marsh is supposed dead he suddenly spreads his arms and cries, " 'Father of heaven have mercy upon me!' . . . Uppon this, many of the people sayd that he was a martyr . . . "[32] In the 1563 edition, Marsh's patient suffering alone prompts the crowd's reaction. The 1570 revision interjects a wonder that compensates for Foxe's qualifications to the story of the bishop's death. The revisions to Marsh's account indicate Foxe's determination to use wondrous testimony despite the challenges such testimony could provoke.

Foxe does not, then, eschew the rhetorical power of marvels and wonders. To the contrary, his work seeks to redeploy the traditional hagiographic power of the marvelous without running afoul of Protestant attacks on late medieval hagiographic excesses. Although cavils by the likes of Stapleton and Harpsfield may have led Foxe to drop some marvels between the 1563 and 1570 editions,[33] in other instances he actually increased the

presence of the marvelous in his later editions, albeit with more defensiveness and caution. Foxe's revisions where marvels and miracles are concerned suggest that he became both more aware of the attacks these
wondrous instances could provoke and more defensively insistent upon
including at least some marvels. The arguments Foxe tries to build about
marvels and wonders respond in intricate ways to their controversial
environment. Indeed, what most distinguishes Protestant martyrologists'
uses of marvels from their medieval forerunners is not necessarily the type
used but the acknowledgment that marvels' persuasive force depends as
much on the reader's interpretive work as on the hagiographer's rhetorical
power. That acknowledgment surfaces as well in recusant Catholic martyrologies. A comparison of marvels and wonders in Protestant and
Catholic martyrologies produces fewer firm distinctions than we might
expect; it also reveals a shared awareness of the interpretive work to which
even seemingly irrefutable, marvelous testimony was subject.

## OPERA DEI ADMIRATIO NOSTRA

For recusant Catholic martyrologists, the question is not whether to use
wonders and miracles to authenticate their martyrs but rather what sorts of
material witnesses will be called upon and in what circumstances. Catholic
uses of miracles attempt to counter anti-Catholic polemic, challenge Foxe's
paradigms, and uphold Catholic theology; theologically driven emphases
are thus mediated by the literary fray over the martyrological genre. In fact,
the most striking feature of recusant Catholic martyrologies is their relatively restrained use of miracles, especially in comparison to late medieval
hagiographies. The most common marvel in recusant Catholic martyrologies (as in Foxe's more staid accounts) is the wonder of the martyr's joyful,
steadfast perseverance. A manuscript account of the martyr John Finch
claims that "the more his calamities encreased and the more they grew to
extremities, the more our mercifull God, by His internal and secret consolation, did supporte and supplye the want of external confort; in such
sort that His afflicted servaunt thyrsted every day more and more to dedicat
life and blod for God's honor and in ye defence of ye Catholike fayth."
After his condemnation, Finch's kinsmen and neighbors come to comfort
him "but they found hyme so merry in God and so ioyfull of the next dayes
banket (which he expected) that they were all mervelously comforted and
edified by his rare fortitude."[34] The "mervel" Finch's friends witness is his
calm cheerfulness before his impending butchering. The wondrous joyfulness of Catholic martyrs is sometimes portrayed with graphic vividness.

Jean Chiflet's *Palmae Cleri Anglicani* celebrates the seven martyrs it documents by inscribing joy in the martyr's willingly dismembered body: "Erepta laetis exta pectoribus vigent, / Spirantique venae, corq[ue] non pavidum salit" ("They thrive, their organs snatched from happy breasts; while the arteries yet breathe, the heart, not frightened, leaps").[35] The language implies, as do Foxe's accounts of White and Tankerfield, that the greatest marvel of all is the martyr's joyful triumph over excruciating pain.

When Catholic martyrologists choose to relate more spectacular miracles, they are keenly aware of the controversial environment in which they write. Consequently, they often emphasize proper methods of reading the physical world, inferable from Catholic theology's insistence that the transcendent and the material can and do touch. At the same time, however, what is perceptible in a recusant Catholic's execution is the bloody drawing and quartering of a traitor, meant to invert and parody gruesomely the traitor's intended dismemberment of the English state.[36] Catholic martyrologists use the physical world to challenge the bloody political theatre in which their martyrs played out their final moments. They strive both to affirm their own faith's insistence that the spiritual world is available through the physical and to offer solid reinterpretations of the most obvious meaning of their martyrs' final ordeals.

Perhaps the most consistent difference between recusant Catholic martyrologies and Foxe's *Book of Martyrs* is the way relics are conceptualized. The story of relics taken from William Davies exhibits both Catholic devotion to relics and the conviction that martyrs offered a bloody sacrifice not unlike that of the Mass:

[his] cassock and other clothes were brought by the hangman to the prison, to sell them to his companions, and they were laid, running with blood, on the table on which the Martyr used to say Mass. The clothes were divided amongst catholics, and 'the cassock, stained with blood, was kept in a certain part of the kingdom, that priests might with much devotion wear it under their priestly vestments, when they said Mass.'[37]

Instead of a hair shirt, the priests wear Davies's bloody cassock; it enhances their devotion and brings the remains of the martyr's sacrifice to the sacrifice the priests offer in the Mass. Indeed, contact between martyrs' blood and witnesses present at their executions was believed to prompt conversion: Henry Walpole converted after a drop of Campion's blood splashed on him.

Yet when no explicit physical transference between martyr and reader is possible, Catholic martyrologists argue for a more subtle interpretive one: they insist that Catholics can read wondrous signs while Protestants cannot.[38] In *A Briefe Historie*, Allen records that the martyr Thomas Cottam gave his hangman a parting word of advice: " 'Take example by the executioner of S. Paul, who during the time of his execution, a little drope of blood falling from S. Paul upon his garment, white like milke, did afterward call him to remembrance of himselfe, and so became penitent for his sinnes, and became a good man; whose example I pray God thou maiest follow."Cottam's words invoke the maxim that the blood of martyrs is the milk of the church. But the attending minister misunderstands his meaning and quibbles: " 'What, did milke fall from his breast?" Cottam patiently responds with a nuanced reading: "*Cottam.* No, blood fell from his necke or head, in likenes of milke. *Minister* ... What, do you say he was saved by that blood which fel upon him? *Cottam.* No. I marvel what you meane."[39] Allen characterizes Protestants as poor readers, entrapped in clumsy literalness, while Catholics move easily from the simile to its correct religious import.

Recusant martyrologists frequently insist upon the meaning of the wondrous sign alongside its sheer miraculousness. Contrary to what might be supposed, Catholic writers are generally cautious about using miracles, aware that traditional hagiographic miracles had come under heavy attack. That caution manifests itself in their insistence that marvelous signs correlate to, and derive value from, holy inner states. Occasionally, the inner state trumps any wondrous outward manifestations. Allen reprints a letter from a priest named Brian that depicts a miracle dependent upon inner perception, not outer spectacle, for its power:

Whether this that I will say be miraculous or no, God he knoweth: but true it is, and thereof my conscience is a witnesse before God ... in the end of the torture ... comforted, eased and refreshed of the greeves of the torture bypast, I continued still with perfect and present senses, in quietnes of hart, and tranquilitie of mind ... when I hearde them say [that the racking would resume] ... I did verily beleeve and trust, that with the help of God I should be able to beare and suffer it patiently. In the mean time (as well as I could), I did muse and meditate upon the moste bitter passion of oure Saviour, and how full of innumerable paines it was. And whiles I was thus occupied, me thought that my left hand was wounded in the palme, and that I felt the blood runne out, but in very deede there was no such thing, nor any other paine then that which seemed to be in my hand.[40]

Brian carefully links the incident to an explication of his inward state – his belief that God would help him suffer renewed torture patiently, his pious meditation on the passion – and stresses the inner sensation of the stigmata rather than any physical marks or wounds. The miracle privileges inward transformation and perception over any physical alteration.

Similarly, a manuscript about the martyr William Freeman records with many qualifications his prophetic dream about his own arrest:

his dreames . . . whether they were so indeed or [ra]ther revelacions . . . I will not much stand upon, but surely from God they may seeme to be probablie the event provinge the thinge trew. Emong others he would tell that both when he was scholler at Rheimes & also since his comminge thence he should dreame somtymes that he was apprehended, & evermore the one end of his dreame was that one Acton & another whose name I have forgotten, should be the causes of his death. This happened unto hym longe before he knew this Acton, & this would he report to some of his familiars longe before this matter fell out. In dreames I put no certaintie, knowinge that they are for the most parte illusions and deceites; yet no man doubteth but that some tyme yt pleaseth God to reveale his wille & future purpose to His servauntes by dreames, as He did to Joseph, Pharo, & others, & here not unlike to His designed martyr.[41]

The writer's defensiveness about dreams is striking: "surely from God they may seeme to be probablie." The writer insists that generally dreams cannot be given credence but also that the outcome of the martyr's arrest supports the dream's truth. Both Brian and this anonymous author recognize that prophetic dreams and marvelous stigmata could be challenged by skeptical Catholics and Protestant scoffers alike. For these writers, marvelous testimony is vulnerable to controversy and doubt; it must be bolstered in other ways, by the verification of the martyr's own conscience, in Brian's case, or by a cautious link to biblical precedent ("not unlike"), in the case of the author recounting Freeman's dreams.

Perhaps the most politically charged miracles are those linked with the execution and dismemberment of Catholic martyrs. In refuting the physical symbolism of the traitor dismembered, Catholic martyrologies offer a materially inscribed political revolution: the physical world itself refuses to endorse the traitorous inscription of Catholic martyrs' bodies. The insistence that the martyr's final moments resist the government's scripting finds a physical parallel in what I call miracles of preservation. Martyrologists sometimes claim that the quarters and/or head of a martyr do not rot away at their respective postings but are preserved whole and relatively free of decay for an extensive period of time. Through these miracles the martyr's desecrated body resists its traitor's punishment. Preservations also demonstrate that relics persist despite the multiple provisions (dismembering, quartering, boiling) for destroying the martyr's body. Building on Catholic veneration of relics, these wondrous preservations also inscribe relics with controversial purpose and political resistance. In a letter dated 21 October 1598, about the execution of a Franciscan named John Jones, Father Garnet records that Jones's head was set on a pillory but retained its natural color for two days. Some "officers... scratched, bruised and blackened it with powder" but, these efforts at disfigurement failing, finally had to take the head down.[42] A catalogue of martyrs executed from 1587 to 1594 includes many marvels, such as the claim that Robert Sutton (*d.* 1588) was seen to pray in a bright light the night before he suffered. When three of his quarters were taken down after hanging for a year, the index and thumb were "found whole and are so conserved."[43] This miracle of preservation asserts that the most essential physical remnant of a priest – the digits consecrated to touch Christ in the sacrament – survives despite the Elizabethan government's determination to root out and destroy men so consecrated.

The most famous preservation miracles are associated with the priests implicated in the Gunpowder treason, the thwarted plot to blow up Parliament in 1605. Henry Garnet, Superior of the English Jesuits, probably learned of the plot under seal of the confessional. Once captured, his explanation that he could not reveal information shared under a sacramental seal fell on deaf ears. Together with Father Edward Oldcorne, he was executed on 3 May 1606.[44] Perhaps because Garnet's ordeal was so notorious, his preservation miracles are particularly spectacular. His head was said to retain "the same hue and shew of life which it had before it was cut off"; for six weeks citizens flocked to see this "so strange and wonderful a spectacle."[45] Father Oldcorne too offers lingering physical resistance to his investment as a traitor: "when this holy martyr's intestines were thrown into the fire, according to sentence, they burned for sixteen days, the exact number of years he had worked in that country, kindling the fire of divine love and nursing it with his word and example."[46]

Most notoriously, a story quickly spread that Garnet's face appeared entire on a piece of straw on which his blood had splashed at his execution. The rumor of the miracle caused great consternation and affected both intra- and extra-Catholic politics.[47] After the Earl of Northampton, widely believed to be crypto-Catholic, had revealed the contents of a speech of his against Jesuits, "the miracle being divulged and hundreds having seen it, many in merriment said: 'A straw for my Lord of Northhampton's book.'"[48] Gerard claims that while Garnet's straw was at the Spanish

Ambassador's house, "there was such public resort of nobility and gentlemen, not only Catholics, but also schismatics and heretics to view it, that there wanted not those which continually entered for that purpose, and having seen it departed so confounded, edified, and comforted therewith, as with one accord they acknowledged it to be supernatural."[49] Gerard's claim that Catholics, "schismatics," and heretics alike believed in it is a hopeful elucidation of the miracle's intended reach, for despite the stir the straw caused it is evident that many Protestants and anti-Jesuit Catholics were dubious.[50] The Protestant pamphleteer Robert Pricket claimed the straw was painted; such "painted show" was typical of Rome's deceptions, to which Pricket contrasted God's providence in preserving Elizabeth I and James I and at the time of the Spanish Armada: "These miracles their truth doth farre surpasse."[51]

Yet *contra* Picket, Protestants seem to have had no monopoly on providential marvels. In one particularly dramatic instance, a calendar of Catholic martyrs represents those involved in persecuting Thomas Pilchard (*d.* 1587) as suffering providential retribution: many of the officers presiding at his execution "died presently crying out they were poisoned with the smell of his bowells" while the Keeper of the prison where Pilchard was held was haunted by his ghost and shortly became ill.[52] Another entry in the calendar describes the punishment inflicted upon Richard Daye's executioner, "whoe soone after was himself put to death for felonie, at what time he muche lamented that ever he had done so wicked a deede, for which fact he sayd he beleeved that God did nowe justly punishe him."[53] Because the recourse to providential retribution is shared cross-confessionally, Catholic martyrologists often bolster instances of retribution with interpretive guidance. Thomas Worthington's account of sixteen Catholic martyrs includes an anecdote about a judge who receives a severe punishment for his role in condemning two of them:

riding abroad for his pleasure, nere to his owne house with one man, sodainly in the plaine filde, [the judge] fel from his horse to the grounde, the horse not stumbling at al, but running away a greate pace, the servant stept quickly to his master, and assaying to help him up, found him dead . . . .

Worthington attributes this death to divine judgment, verifying his claims by presenting a village investigation of the judge's body, and, oddly enough, by relating the testimony of the judge's horse:

vewing the corps, they [the villagers] saw evidently, that a spirit and no man had donne this act. For they found part of his braines straingely comming forth, both at his nose and mouth, not having anie other hurt in his head, but towards the right side behind a great dimple or hole, wherin a child might have put his fist; neither his skinne, nor his hat broken at al, nor a heare of his head wanting to anie mans judgment. They found likewise his right shoulder sore scorched, like burnd leather, as blacke as pitch; and from thence along upon his arme a great gash, as it had bene made with a knife, but not deepe; and in the calfe of his legge on the same side, they found an other hole, about an inch broad, and three inches deepe, and (which is most strange) not so much as a threde of his hose, nor of his other aparel could be found to be broken. In the meane while, the horse that ranne away, with much ado was taken, but could by no meanes be brought nere to the place, where his master fel downe.[54]

Explaining what the villagers and the servant "saw evidently," the text uses the villagers' investigation to substitute for the readers'; all should read the judge's mangled body and his horse's odd behavior as convincing evidence of providential retribution.

John Geninges's *The Life and Death of Mr. Edmund Geninges, Priest* (St. Omer, 1614) highlights the problems facing Catholic writers who wish to use wondrous testimony in an age when controversial opponents both decry such testimony as superstitious and attempt to revise it for their own purposes. The work concerns the life and martyrdom of Edmund Geninges (John Geninges's brother), executed at London in 1591. It relies more than many other recusant Catholic martyrologies do on miracles and wonders. Yet although Geninges's work makes use of many wonders, those wonders are stealthy, almost unsure of themselves; they begin covertly and swell into an explicit refutation of treason charges. Geninges first emphasizes that he will relate only those admirable testimonies that are, to his mind, authentic:

What then will it profit me to seeke to honour a Martyr, by faygning and forging a lye? . . . Therfore to cleare my selfe from this suspition, I protest, that I will make mention of not one thing, which I have not eyther knowne to be true my selfe, or heard from his mouth whose life and martyrdome I write, or have not receyved as true, by relation from very honest, vertuous, and sufficient persons, whose tender and Catholike consciences (as may justly be thought) could not beare the burthen of uttering such untruthes.[55]

Geninges is not simply "romantic" as Sullivan suggests; he is keenly aware of controversies over miracles and of the need to verify the ones he uses.[56] He nevertheless persists in using them in order to make providential workings observable and because he believes people need such testimony given their imperfect judgments: a martyrologist writes so that "the secret and hidden decrees of God Almighty . . . might be made manifest . . . to convince . . . humane rash judgments, whose censures are commonly according to the outward apparence."[57] The difficulty of discerning God's workings should be mitigated by wonders.

The martyrologist wishes to make those workings clear primarily through the martyr's self-declaration; yet that self-declaration needs extra-ordinary support to persuade "humane rash judgments." At his execution, Edmund emphasizes that his only trespass has been for religion:

> If to returne into England Priest, or to say Masse be Popish treason, I heere confesse I am a traytour; but I thinke not so. And therfore I acknowledge my selfe guilty of these thinges, not with repentance or sorrow of hart, but with an open protestation of inward joy, that I have done so good deedes, which if they were to do agayne, I would by the permission and assistance of Almighty God accomplish the same, although with the hazard of a thousand lives.[58]

The source of evidence is the "I" who speaks; "I thinke not so" sets the martyr's self against the entire architecture of state and law. Yet Edmund's open protestation needs to be bolstered by other, more miraculous signs. In a chapter entitled "Of a certain miracle that happened at his death," Geninges insists that "the glory of his martyrdome was declared and confirmed by an evident signe."[59] This "evident signe" is a virgin's success-ful quest for a relic from the dead priest. The virgin follows the executioner who carries Edmund's body after it has been quartered and placed in a basket; the priest's right arm hangs over the basket's edge.[60] Worried about being caught, she nevertheless touches Edmund's right thumb, the thumb anointed at his ordination, consecrated to touch the sacramental host:

> taking the thumbe in her hand, by the instinct of Almighty God, she gave it a little pull, only to shew her love and desire of having it. The sequele was miracu-lous: . . . by the divine power, the thumbe was instantly loosed . . . she carryed it away safely both flesh, skinne, and bone without sight of any, to her great joy and admiration. O strange and miraculous separation! O benefit past all requitall! The thumbe of a man newly dead and quartered, to depart from the hand, as it were, *sponte sua*, of its owne accord . . . and . . . in the middest of so many hundreds of people, of a different Religion, yet not espyed by any.[61]

This miracle is open – and opened to us – through Geninges's narration. Yet an integral part of the miracle is its secrecy: the virgin is not spied by anyone else, and only those to whom she reveals the secret will know of it. The illustration accompanying the text emphasizes this secrecy; the "vir-gin" appears in the lower right-hand corner of the image, pulling covertly at the thumb as the public butchering proceeds all around her (Figure 4). The wonder invites readers to join a particular community, to align themselves with its perceptions and values: the marvel appeals to the desire to be in the know, so to speak, since those "of a different Religion" fail to perceive the miraculous "evident signe" in their very midst.

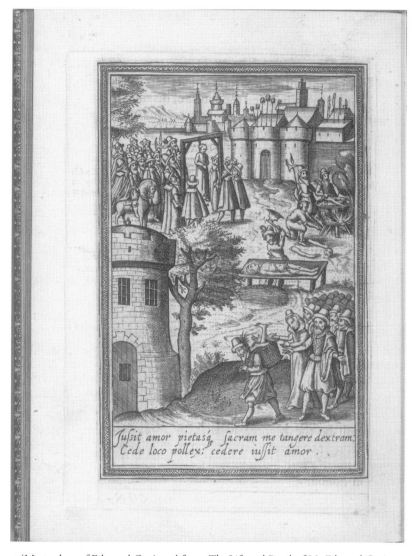

*Iußit amor pietasq̃, facram me tangere dextram;*
*Cede loco pollex; cedere iußit amor.*

4 'Martyrdom of Edmund Geninges' from *The Life and Death of Mr Edmund Geninges* (1614), John Geninges.

Geninges also, however, attempts to model for those of a different religion what their responses ought to be. Geninges describes his conversion to Catholicism as originating beyond himself, with his brother's intercessory prayers: "whosoever readeth" of his conversion "shall find the intercession of

this Saint to have bene the only cause (next after God) of all his good."
Referring to himself in the third person, John Geninges tells readers he had
actually "rejoyced" at the news of his brother's condemnation and refused to
see his brother in prison or at his execution.[62] Geninges then records a
miraculous change:

comparing the Catholike manner of living with his, and finding the one to desire
payne, the other pleasure . . . being stroken with exceeding terrour and remorse, he
wept bitterly, desiring God . . . to illuminate his understanding, that he might see
and perceyve the truth. O what gret joy & consolation felt he at that instant! Nay
what reverence on the suddayne began he to beare to the B. Virgin and the Saynts
of God, which before he had never scarse heard talke of! What strange motions, as
it were inspirations, with exceeding readines of will to chaunge his Religion,
possessed his soule![63]

Geninges's response to his brother's death testifies to the Catholic doctrine
of intercessory prayer and to his brother's status as true martyr. Well aware
of controversies over miracles, Geninges uses interpretive modeling to
clarify the proper response to his brother's testimony while reaching for
the persuasive force of seemingly irrefutable wonders.

As I have been suggesting, Catholic martyrologists' desire to use physical
witnesses to their martyrs' truths derives both from particular theological
predilections and the intensity of religious controversy. In an attempt to
distinguish one strand of Christianity from another, they use the most
powerful material at their disposal – wonders, marvels, the unshakeable
witness suffering joyfully through unbearable pain – and yet so do their
opponents. Like Foxe, Catholic martyrologists use wondrous tales of providential rescue and of punitive retribution redounding on persecutors'
heads; like him they grant martyrs a marvelous patience and constancy.
There are theological refinements, to be sure. Catholics celebrate physical
relics; Protestant martyrologies encourage readers to embrace only the
physical pages of books containing accounts of the martyrs' mortification
of the flesh and to imitate that mortification. Yet martyrologists share a basic
impulse to recruit testimony from the outside world that can somehow
overcome or outweigh controversies. Likewise, they share the awareness that
the reading of marvels – of the drop of blood that falls like milk, of the three
handclaps amid growing flames – depends as much on establishing proper
habits of interpretation as on the persuasiveness of the marvel itself.

Well aware of the apparent confusion which could ensue from a cacophony
of conflicting testimonies, martyrologists respond to the problem of competing martyrs by, in effect, asking readers to look more closely at the martyrs'
accounts and at their own hearts. As competing martyrologies reveal in

agonizing detail, in the Reformation era questions of interpretive authority and procedures were paramount. By working to link familiar rhetoric to particular theological stances and by trying to shape readers' interpretive habits according to those theological positions, martyrologists labor to enforce religious distinctions and to reclaim shared rhetorical territory for discrete causes. They elaborate theories of interpretation that celebrate both their own theological stances and the martyrs who died to establish those stances. Simultaneously, martyrologies remain self-consciously aware of the vexing interpretive problems caused by the multitude of opinions to which early modern martyrs testified and for which they sacrificed themselves.

As this section of the book has shown, early modern martyrologists worked to draw distinctions between religions, but they also deploy overlapping vocabularies of conscience, inwardness, historical continuity, visibility, and wondrous testimony that complicate neat divisions of martyrological discourse along Protestant and Catholic lines. The fact that rhetoric and conventions overlap even in a genre of religious writing devoted to drawing religious distinctions in blood suggests the relative instability of religious genres in the period, an instability fueled by the complexity of early modern religious cultures. Despite their ostensible purpose, then, of dividing religions firmly, martyrologies also impel us to think about religion and religious habits of representation cross-confessionally. Compelling moments of testimony – the recanting hand held steadily in the flame, the head that refuses to decompose, the inner strength that keeps a martyr firm despite unimaginable torment, the historical communities witnessable across time – are never articulated in religious isolation, but in full awareness of the conflicting testimonies voiced by competing, evolving traditions.

NOTES

1 John Knott, "John Foxe and the Joy of Suffering," *Sixteenth Century Journal* 27 (1996), 721–34; Arthur Marotti, "Southwell's Remains: Catholicism and Anti-Catholicism in Early Modern England," in *Texts and Cultural Change in Early Modern England*, ed. Cedric C. Brown and Marotti (New York: St. Martin's, 1997), 37–65.

2 On this publication's role in polemic about Anglo-Saxon culture, see Benedict Scott Robinson, "John Foxe and the Anglo-Saxons," in *John Foxe and His World*, ed. Christopher Highley and John N. King (Aldershot: Ashgate, 2002), 54–72.

3 *The history of the Church of Englande* (Antwerp, 1565), 8v–9.

4  Alban's legend was told by, among others, Gildas, Bede, a monk of St. Alban's named William, Jacobus de Voragine, and John Lydgate. With each retelling, more miraculous deeds were added. Lydgate's version was reprinted as late as 1534, 21 years before the burning of the first Marian martyr (see the introduction to Lydgate, *The Life of Saint Alban and Saint Amphibal*, ed. J.E. van der Westhuizen, Leiden: Brill, 1974).

5  *AM* (1583), 89.

6  *AM* (1570), 1230.

7  *AM* (1563), 520.

8  *Dialogi Sex* (Antwerp, 1566), 734.

9  *AM* (1563), 520; *AM* (1570), 1230.

10 *An Instruction of Christen Fayth*, trans. Foxe (London, 1550?), Dviv.

11 Luther links the "flesh" to remaining impurities and argues that "all the saints have had and felt" the "battle of the flesh against the spirit" ("Commentary on Galatians," in *Martin Luther: Selections from His Writings*, ed. John Dillenberger, New York: Doubleday, 1962, 151).

12 Thomas Betteridge, "Truth and History in Foxe's *Actes and Monuments*," in *John Foxe and His World*, ed. Highley and King, 145–59; Cynthia Marshall, *The Shattering of the Self: Violence, Subjectivity, and Early Modern Texts* (Baltimore: Johns Hopkins University Press, 2002), 91.

13 Janel Mueller argues that Protestant martyrs' sacrifices replace the transubstantiated flesh of the Mass with another "presence" of truth, though the tropes she identifies as central to this process derive from common martyrological rhetoric and are not unique to Foxe ("Pain, Persecution, and the Construction of Self in Foxe's *Actes and Monuments*," in *Religion and Culture in Renaissance England*, ed. Claire McEachern and Debora Shuger, Cambridge: Cambridge University Press, 161–87).

14 *AM* (1583), 1558–9.

15 *AM* (1563), 1541.

16 *AM* (1583), 1940. Compare *AM* (1570), 2123; *AM* (1576), 1846.

17 *AM* (1563), "A Declaration concerning the utilitie and profite of thys history" (sig. B6v); later editions retain this wording.

18 *Displaying of the Protestants* (London, 1556), 62. Loades (*The Oxford Martyrs*, London: Batsford, 1970, 161) cites evidence that Protestant martyrs' relics were sometimes sought; Pollen reprints documents suggesting non-Catholics sought relics from Catholic martyrs (*Unpublished Documents Relating to the English Martyrs*, CRS, vol. 1, London: J. Whitehead and Son, 1908, 390). See also Southwell's letter to Claude Aquaviva (26 August 1587), which claims that an English crowd sought relics from an executed heretic (reprinted in Philip Caraman, *The Other Face: Catholic Life Under Elizabeth I*, London: Longmans, 1960, 79).

19 "Southwell's Remains," 52.

20 *AM* (1563), 1162.

21 *AM* (1570), 1767.

22 See Betteridge, "Truth and History," on the function of Foxe's woodcuts.

23 *Dialogi Sex*, 736.
24 Numerous martyrs in the *Legenda Aurea* claim not to feel the pain of tortures (e.g., George, Agnes, and Dorothea).
25 *AM* (1583), 1690–1.
26 John Bale, *The Examinations of Anne Askew*, ed. Elaine Beilin (Oxford: Oxford University Press, 1996), 7.
27 *Ibid.*, 154.
28 *Ibid.*, 156.
29 Thomas Freeman, "Fate, Fact, and Fiction in Foxe's *Book of Martyrs*," *The Historical Journal* 43 (2000), 601–23.
30 *AM* (1570), D1.
31 *AM* (1563), 1122.
32 *AM* (1570), 1738.
33 Freeman, "Fate, Fact, and Fiction," 621.
34 Stonyhurst MS Anglia A1, n. 19; reprinted in *Unpublished Documents Relating to the English Martyrs*, ed. J. H. Pollen (London: J. Whitehead and Son, 1908), 84, 87. Compare *Concertatio Ecclesiae Catholicae in Anglia* (Trier, 1588), 164–71.
35 *Palmae Cleri Anglicani* (Brussels, 1645), 6.
36 Curtis Breight, "Duelling Ceremonies: the Strange Case of William Hacket, Elizabethan Messiah," *Journal of Medieval and Renaissance Studies* 19 (1989), 35–67; Stephen Greenblatt, "Murdering Peasants: Status, Genre, and the Representation of Rebellion," *Representations* 1 (1983), 1–29.
37 Pollen, ed., *Acts of English Martyrs* (London: Burns and Oates, 1891), 142. See also Diego de Yepez's *Historia Particular de la Persecucion de Inglaterra* (Madrid, 1599), 666.
38 Cf. Ceri Sullivan, *Dismembered Rhetoric: English Recusant Writing, 1580 to 1603* (London: Associated University Presses, 1995), 119.
39 *A Briefe Historie of the Glorious Martyrdom of Twelve Reverend Priests* (Rheims, 1582), B7.
40 *Ibid.*, 6v.
41 *Unpublished Documents*, 200.
42 *Ibid.*, 374.
43 *Ibid.*, 291.
44 For a decidedly pro-Jesuit view of the plot, see John Gerard, *John Gerard: Autobiography of an Elizabethan*, trans. Philip Caraman (London: Longmans, 1951), 199ff.
45 London, British Library, Add. MS 21, 203; cited in Gerard, *Autobiography*, 274.
46 Gerard, *Autobiography*, 202.
47 Alexandra Walsham, *Providence in Early Modern England* (Oxford: Oxford University Press, 1999), 243.
48 Gerard, *Autobiography*, 275.
49 *Ibid.*, 275.
50 Peter Lake and Michael Questier, *The Antichrist's Lewd Hat: Protestants, Papists and Players in Post-Reformation England* (New Haven: Yale University Press, 2002), 307.

51  *The Jesuits miracles, or new popish wonders* (London, 1607), B3v, E3r.
52  *Unpublished Documents*, 288–9.
53  *Ibid.*, 293.
54  *A Relation of Sixtene Martyrs* (Douai, 1601), 89–90.
55  *The Life and Death of Mr. Edmund Geninges, Priest* (St. Omer, 1614), 10–11.
56  Sullivan, *Dismembered Rhetoric*, 116.
57  *Life and Death of Mr. Edmund Geninges*, 14.
58  *Ibid.*, 85.
59  *Ibid.*, 90.
60  The (later, married) name of Geninges's "virgin" is given in the *c.* 1603 rough draft of this text as Mrs. Lucy Ridley (*Unpublished Documents*, 207).
61  *Life and Death of Mr. Edmund Geninges*, 93–4.
62  *Ibid.*, 96–8.
63  *Ibid.*, 98–100.

# PART 2

# Conflicting testimonies in the English literary imagination

The complex hermeneutics of early modern martyrdom – affected by uncomfortable cross-confessional overlaps in martyrological conventions and assumptions, and by martyrologists' tendency to acknowledge and attempt to direct readers' potentially varying interpretations – register in literary texts in other genres as those texts represent, explicitly or implicitly, competing or conflicting martyr-figures in order to invoke and wrestle with the complexities of Reformation-era religious culture. Most of the works I discuss below belong to relatively familiar literary genres and modes which need no lengthy introduction, including allegorical narrative, lyric poetry, sermons, prose polemic, and drama. These works use martyrological texts and controversies as source materials, subtexts, or points of departure; they set diverse claims to generic tradition against each other and struggle with points of conflict and overlap in competing martyrologies. But in negotiating those conflicts and overlaps, the works I discuss also invoke other discourses in which martyrology was implicated for, naturally, martyrology was not a world unto itself. It influenced and was influenced by other intertwining, developing discourses, including those of resistance, election, merit, historiography, treason, and apocalypse. The focus of this part is thus necessarily more diffuse, as I trace martyrology's imprint through the interstices of other genres and discourses in order to set in relationship a key body of religio-polemical literature, works in more traditionally recognized literary genres, and central Reformation-era concerns. My goal is to demonstrate that competing martyrologies provided writers with important conceptual (and, sometimes, stumbling) blocks for thinking through how the early modern period's religious upheavals affected representational habits in more familiar literary genres.

CHAPTER 4

# En route to the New Jerusalem: martyrdom and religious allegory

The earliest Protestant commentary on Book I of Spenser's *Faerie Queene* was penned by the Elizabethan John Dixon, whose annotations have saved him from anonymity. Dixon repeatedly reads Spenser's allegory as alluding to persecution, as in his gloss on I.iii.3 ("virgins love the Lambe Jesus, and Love none but him though persecuted too and froe").[1] Despite Dixon's energetic marginalia, scholars have not often placed Spenser's dreamy fairie world against the backdrop of the bloody religious persecutions discussed above.[2] Yet in its quest to become a "Legend of Holiness," Book I of Spenser's *Faerie Queene* repeatedly, albeit subtly, struggles with how to identify a true saint and how to differentiate the true from the false church. Foregrounded in martyrologies, these struggles also shape the rewriting of Redcrosse Knight into a Protestant St. George. Through his uses and revisions of traditional St. George materials, Spenser represents and attempts to resolve interpretational, historiographical, and epistemological problems exacerbated by contemporary martyrological controversies over the nature of true sainthood, the true church, and the recovery of early church history. These controversies and the interpretive challenges they posed are also formative for the first Roman Catholic response to Spenser's poem: Anthony Copley's *A Fig for Fortune*.

Spenser's and Copley's poems engage with two arguments also commonly made in martyrologies: that conflicts between suffering saints and persecutors on earth figure ultimate conflicts between true church and Antichrist and that the true church is made visible by its suffering. Protestant and Catholic martyrologists used Revelation's vocabulary and imagery to interpret contemporary martyrdoms as representing a transhistorical struggle of truth against falsehood, adapting Revelation's framework to distinguish firmly between true and false saints and churches. In Spenser's poem and in Copley's response to it, the keen competitive clarity of Revelation, with its good and bad women, its persecutory terrors and its ultimate triumphs, is achieved through invoking, directly or indirectly, suffering's clarifying force. The poems thus share with martyrologies the desire to effect distinction in a world of deceptive appearances and uncomfortable similarities. Yet in both poems the distinctions suffering was believed to draw may be realized only after an extended process of sifting through persistent, misleading forms of sanctity. Una as she wanders in the world remains a relatively shadowy figure for these poets, such that the unifying, even coercive drive of martyrologies to integrate disparate martyrdoms into an apocalyptic narrative of stark clarity is somewhat compromised. Copley and Spenser acknowledge that finding truth in an era of competing martyr-saints necessitates a lengthy, often painful quest. Transcendence is achieved only in isolated, temporary moments, moments hard-won through the protagonists' misinterpretations, missteps, and pain.

### EVERY SAINT HAS A PAST

Spenser's "Legend of Holiness" invokes martyrdom in several ways. At times, the poem alludes directly to Romish persecutions. When Duessa first appears, for instance, her garments are the "skarlot red" of the Whore of Babylon, a color the Geneva Bible's gloss (on Revelation 17:4) links to persecution (the whore's "crueltie and blood sheding is declared by skarlet"); Archimago's name echoes that of deceptive figures in Foxe's *Actes and Monuments*;[3] and when Arthur penetrates Orgoglio's dungeon he finds the floor soaked in martyrs' blood and strewn "new" with "sacred ashes," a probable allusion to Marian martyrs. In addition to such direct references, the poem invokes martyrdom more obliquely in its allusions to St. George's legendary sufferings. The George legend as Spenser knew it had two halves: George's dragon fight and his martyrdom. In Spenser's poem, the presence of the first half is obvious enough. Though its presence is more subtle, the legend's second half is also important. Spenser reworks both halves of the legend and their relationship to each other in order to negotiate the complicated past of his hero, a figure battered by Reformation iconoclasts and saddled with numerous legend-ary, saintly, and not-so-saintly incarnations. In Book I, the pre-Reformation past of St. George appears in echoes of various George legends that threaten or impede Redcrosse's quest. Hints of martyr-like suffering purge elements of George's legendary past from Redcrosse's legend and separate Spenser's reformed saint from his predecessors. Spenser thus reunites the two halves of George's legend often severed in other early modern English renditions which usually stress either his dragon-fighting prowess or his martyrdom but not both together.[4] In using suffering to reform St. George's legend. Spenser blends romance allegory's wanderings with Reformation-era concerns about reinterpreting the pre-Reformation past.

On a broader, almost methodological level, Spenser's simultaneous revision and restoration of George's past finds an analogue in the ways that Protestant historians and martyrologists claimed historical legitimacy: they worked to discover in the pre-Reformation past a continuous narrative of a true church that was constantly present but sometimes hidden, one most clearly visible in times of persecution. As part of this legitimating effort, writers like Foxe reread early church martyrs as Reformation Protestantism's spiritual ancestors, reinterpreting the past so it might figure a truth outside time. In their terms, certainly, that truth had always been present; only the corruptions of human error prevented its full recognition. Setting Spenser's recuperation of St. George against the discourses of martyrdom found in numerous George legends and in Foxe's *Actes and Monuments* reveals that Spenser shared with Protestant martyrologists the drive to reread the persecuted saints of the past so as to construct a historical narrative of a pure, continuous faith and to realize that faith more perfectly in the present. Indeed, the poem's structure demands that the reader's experience unfolds over time in a manner resembling the historical work martyrologists undertook: she must reread earlier episodes in light of later ones. This feature of Spenser's poetics, often discussed in terms of allegory, shares with Protestant martyrologists the insistence on rereading the past, uncovering a purer, continuous faith, and developing that faith more fully in the present.[5] The reader's own interpretive struggles as she is confronted with various facets of the George legend resonate with contemporary controversies over how to make sense of martyrs suffering for different causes and how to negotiate competing claims to martyrology's own generic history.

Just as important as this methodological parallel, however, are the ways in which the analogy between allegorical poet and martyrologist breaks down. Significantly, in Spenser's poem the sort of temporal resonance achieved in the culminating dragon fight, in which George's victory signifies not only his own sanctification but also alludes to final, apocalyptic triumph, is at best provisional, a temporary respite amid the reader's ongoing, difficult quest to identify a true saint. Shadowing in its doublings and wanderings the complexity of Reformation-era debates, Spenser's poem stresses the difficulty of identifying a valid model of sanctity more so than does Foxe's text, so stark in its polemic. Further, Spenser's allusions to martyrdom suggest both his indebtedness to Reformation culture and his relative religious moderation. Spenser is willing to retain more of his saint's legendary past than writers like Foxe; the comparison yields a more even-tempered Spenser than some scholarship on Spenser and iconoclasm might suggest.[6]

Most importantly, because Spenser insists on the initial difficulty of sorting true from false churches and true from false saints, his poem demands a more sympathetic, less sternly moralistic reading of Redcrosse than is often found in scholarship on *The Faerie Queene* in Reformation contexts. Both formalist and politically driven readings of Book I usually recognize that Redcrosse's ability to act ethically is limited by his necessary lack of knowledge about the constraints and conventions of the allegorical fiction he inhabits.[7] Yet scholars who read Redcrosse against a Reformation backdrop often do not sufficiently acknowledge this lack. Richard Mallette argues that Redcrosse "is a crude and naive literalist who prefers swords to words," while John N. King remarks that Redcrosse cannot interpret "the symbolic or theological dimension" of language and thus cannot uncover "concealed spiritual meanings."[8] These indictments of Redcrosse's reading skills belie the fact that he cannot know what would enable him to read his world well: he cannot know he is in an allegory, and he cannot know (as I argue below) that his foes represent aspects of his own legendary history.

The limitations Spenser places on his knight's horizons of knowledge resonate with the interpretive challenges Reformation-era confusions and controversies presented. To some extent, the allegory places the reader in a position of superiority to the knight, because we have access to information he does not and cannot have. But the allegory also depends on the fundamental analogy between his experience and ours, for the difficulties of Spenser's fiction are clearly meant to help the reader through the complexities of the Reformation-era world, with its competing churches, creeds, and martyrs.[9] If Redcrosse's confusions and imperfect struggles stem in part from the various and confusing echoes of differing, conflicting George legends in Book I, then he is our interpretational scapegoat, our stand-in martyr.[10] Watching and interpreting Redcrosse's misfires and sufferings, we are to begin to recuperate a story of holiness and *whole*ness from the cacophony of Reformation controversies.

Those controversies are most obviously present in Spenser's poem as he invokes competing versions of the George legend. St. George came to Spenser in numerous forms: in late medieval legendaries like Jacobus de Voragine's *Legenda Aurea*; in popular mumming plays; in stories of

George's miraculous appearances to medieval Crusaders; in some Protestant attacks on his legend; and in the Order of the Garter's chivalry and pageantry. Throughout Book I, echoes of earlier Georges recur as threats to Redcrosse's progress. His own cultural history is, quite literally, haunting him, a haunting that represents meta-fictionally the difficulty of shaping a valid saintly model amid competing hagiographic paradigms. While scholars have focused on details Spenser might have borrowed from the *Legenda Aurea* and other late medieval George legends, the differences are just as telling.

An overview of the various Georges available in the late sixteenth century clarifies Spenser's uses of and departures from them. The most influential version of the George legend, in Voragine's *Legenda Aurea*, has several recurring themes: George's iconoclasm, his military prowess, the many conversions he inspires, and his final, bloody martyrdom.[11] In Caxton's translation of Voragine's text, the dragon George fights is the typical one of legend: his venomous breath poisons a city which to appease the dragon first offers a sacrifice of sheep and then of a young person chosen by lot. When George comes upon the next victim, the king's daughter, he makes the sign of the cross, throws the dragon to the ground, ties the maiden's girdle around the dragon's neck, leads him into the city, and offers to kill him if the citizens will be baptized. Not surprisingly they agree, and George baptizes over 1,500; in response, a magical fountain with the power to cure those the dragon sickened springs from the ground. George's struggle with the dragon is brief, sure, and a spectacular way to convert the town's citizens. His martial victory over the dragon both prompts and figures his parallel conquest of pagan souls.[12] Alongside this emphasis on mass conversion, this version insists upon George's control over his flesh: "George is sayd of Geos whiche is as moche to say as erthe and orge / that is tylyeng / so george is to say as tylyenge therthe that is his flesshe."[13] That control is figured most graphically in the tortures preceding George's martyrdom.[14] George's torturers are repaid in one of two ways: either they convert or the torture they inflict results in spectacular iconoclasm. After inspiring several conversions and triumphing over numerous tortures, George is finally beheaded, and the emperor and his household are consumed in flames of divine retribution.

Other English analogs also emphasize George's conversions, iconoclasm, and sufferings. John Lydgate emphasizes George's "martirdome, and his passyon."[15] Mantuan's version, which Spenser almost certainly knew, claims that as a young man George worshipped idols but converted to Christianity upon hearing the news of Christ. Alexander Barclay's translation of Mantuan stresses the "errour" in which George lived before his conversion and his subsequent iconoclastic fervor.[16] After killing the dragon, Barclay's George preaches a sermon to the citizens that links their "idollys" to his former erroneous worship. In response, they convert, destroy their idols, and replace them with a new image, a painting of the dragon killing. Brought before the emperor, George again suffers torments, converts witnesses, and destroys pagan idols; at the end of his life an angel hails him as the "ydollys conquerour."[17] All three versions emphasize George's triumph through his physical prowess and divinely aided endurance.

George was also associated with military victory in another sense: the conquest of the so-called infidel. According to Muriel C. McClendon, George's popularity in Europe grew from the time of the Crusades: "He was said to have appeared to the Christian army during the difficult siege of Antioch in 1098 during the First Crusade and so heartened the crusaders that they were able to turn the tide of that battle and take the city from its Muslim defenders. Saint George made a similar appearance during the battle for Jerusalem in the following year and was again credited with aiding the crusaders."[18] Redcrosse will, of course, discover himself and his true name outside the walls of the New Jerusalem; in a sense, George reappears outside the holy city, correcting the distortions Spenser finds in echoes of the crusading past. Redcrosse also echoes George's association with the Templars, the crusading military order that, together with the Hospitallers, combined military training and monasticism, representing the ideals of the Crusades; as Gregory Wilkin notes, the red cross Spenser's knight wears was the Templars' distinctive mark.[19]

The celebration of St. George's military prowess persisted in several forms in sixteenth-century England. As part of coronation processions and progresses, elaborate royal pageants emphasized St. George's association with the Order of the Garter and his status as England's patron saint.[20] This association was not always an easy one. King discusses Edwardian plans to change Garter jewels by deleting the dragon: "The Edwardian proposals would have supplanted the medieval dragon-slayer with a figure wielding allegorical armor appropriate not only to St. George, but to any member of the sainthood of the elect."[21] Despite this iconoclastic unease, the representation of the dragon fight persisted on the Order of the Garter's badges known as the greater and lesser Georges. This chivalric image of the saint fighting the dragon was occasionally invoked as a symbol of international Protestant military alliances – alliances that often fell short, however, of their idealistic goals. In matters of international politics especially, "St. George . . . did not always slay the dragon."[22]

In contrast to the chivalric, aristocratic associations of the Order of the Garter, the more rural mummers' plays sacrifice St. George's stature to ritual demands. In these plays, a character named George fights a "Turkey" or Turkish knight or a similar character called "Slasher"; one knight, more often the foreign one, dies. The players then call for a doctor, a comic quack who resurrects the fallen knight.[23] The play's concern is not to praise one or the other contestant but to present the ritual resurrection; George's heroic slaying of the foe is usually undone by the demands of the ritual itself. This emphasis upon ritual meaning over a moralized martial triumph is perhaps disdainfully alluded to in the Elizabethan "Homily of the worthy receiving . . . of the Sacrament." The homily chastises those who come to the Lord's table to practice "grosse Idolatry": "What hath beene the cause of this mummish Massing, but the ignorance hereof?"[24] The word "mumming" or "mummish" can refer to unthinking ritualistic behavior, the mummers' plays, or both (*OED*). As Spenser's Redcrosse is a "clownish" man, rural and unsophisticated, who encounters and is deceived by various Catholic figures and whose military conquests are, at least early on, incomplete, the mummers' plays and popular St. George legends constitute a burden of cultural memory and meaning which must be reformed if Redcrosse is to be celebrated as the Protestant champion of holiness.

Indeed, sterner Protestants viewed George's dragon fight with suspicion or ridicule; the iconoclast of the George legend becomes the victim of iconoclasts. The dour Edward Dering characterized saints and other traditional heroes as "sprytuall enchauntmentes . . . which Sathan had made [and] hell had prynted."[25] In Barnabe Googe's *Shippe of Safegarde*, Googe's sailors pass the rock of idolatry on which lounges a portrait of none other than St. George killing the dragon. In another venue, Googe renders George and his dragon-killing not spiritually dangerous but merely ridiculous. In his translation of *The Popish Kingdome, or Reigne of Antichrist*, Googe mocks pageants associated with the traditional liturgical calendar and saints' days: "Christs passion here derided is, with sundrie maskes and playes . . . And valiant George with speare thou killest the dreadfull dragon here."[26] Divested of its heroism, the dragon-killing episode is reduced to buffoonery. Representations of George in civic pageants turned George's fighting prowess into cartoonish fun. In late sixteenth- and early seventeenth-century Norwich, traditional pageants celebrating George and the dragon were revised into a simple parade of

George's dragon without the dragon killer, a dragon townspeople affectionately nicknamed "Snap."[27]

Rather than ridiculing the legend as Dering and Googe did, Spenser recasts the major emphases of late medieval George legends: his iconoclasm, his martial prowess, the conversions he inspires, and his martyrdom. For Spenser, George's iconoclasm turns inward to some degree, since his own image needs reforming. Spenser's narrative encodes George's traditional iconoclasm in more limited forms that turn back on themselves, troped in the narrative's recursive tendencies to revisit the various threats to its hero in order to make them more visible and, ultimately, more conquerable.[28] The martial victories traditional Georges enjoyed, victories either subordinated to ritual (in mummers' plays) or readily interpretable as spiritual victories (as in Voragine), become much more complex. George's military prowess is qualified, as inward battles become more important (often figural through psychomachia). Indeed, martial victory in Book I's early cantos does not signal total spiritual conquest. This disjunction between physical and spiritual conquest becomes evident only upon rereading: only *after* Redcrosse has defeated Error and still proceeds to err or wander does it become clear that his victory was incomplete. The poem's insistence that the reader revise earlier conclusions means that the conversions the saint traditionally effects are relocated to the growth in readers' interpretive habits.[29] Finally, George's martyrdom, instead of being rendered in all its traditional, gory detail, is reworked into hints of suffering found at key moments of Redcrosse's education and redemption. As hints of suffering gradually become more explicit (in the book's latter half) and begin to effect redemption, Spenser works to separate the many traces of traditional, competing George legends from the paradigm he attempts to forge of a Reformed saint.

### FOXE, SPENSER, AND RECURSIVE ERRANTRY

The closest Spenserian echo of George's traditional tortures is in Redcrosse's stomach-churning subjection to penitential torment in the House of Holiness:

> And bitter *Penaunce* with an yron whip,
> Was wont him once to disple every day:
> And sharpe *Remorse* his hart did prick and nip,
> That drops of blood thence like a well did play;
> And sad *Repentance* used to embay,
> His blamefull body in salt water sore,

> The filthy blottes of sin to wash away.
> So in short space they did to health restore
> The man that would not live, but erst lay at deathes dore.
> In which his torment often was so great,
> That like a Lyon he would cry and rore,
> And rend his flesh, and his owne synewes eat.[30]     (x.27, 28.1–3)

The closing image of auto-cannibalism is particularly striking. Anthony Low is certainly right that this "whole theatrical spectacle of torture and healing is – as it must be – an interior drama."[31] Even so, it alludes to the lesser-known half of George's legend, specifically the tortures preceding his martyrdom. Spenser's cannibalistic image of turning back on the self in order to make spiritual progress is symptomatic of the broad, insistent recursiveness of Book I, a recursiveness that has spawned numerous interpretive problems. For instance, Redcrosse relapses into a form of despair in the House of Holiness (x.21) after escaping (albeit narrowly) Despair in canto ix; he has little problem with the House of Pride, it seems, but then falls victim to Orgoglio whose name alludes to the Italian word for pride or disdain; and dragon-like adversaries keep cropping up: the dragon he finally defeats in canto xii is at least the fourth dragon-like creature to appear in Book I.[32] These episodes are not slavish repetitions, of course. Still, through presenting Redcrosse with challenges that ring changes on earlier ones, Book I insists on revisiting its own hero's recent narrative past alongside his legendary ones.

The project of revisiting the past, of rereading in order to get history right, is also central to Protestant historians like Foxe. In Foxe's work the martyrs and their historian examine their experiences, reinterpreting the details of individual lives and deaths in the broader framework of apocalyptic suffering and confrontation with the Antichrist. Despite Foxe's rejection of Catholic hagiographies like *The Golden Legend*, some of hagiography's allegorical residue remains: each martyr's life is to resemble the larger struggles of the true faith across time.[33] Foxe's early church martyrs thus both ground his historical narrative and gesture beyond historical specificity. As the different names which Foxe gave his great work indicate, the chronicling of martyrs yields both "ecclesiastical history" (1570 edition) and a "story" (1583 edition) that transcends time. Sometimes, however, the struggles of certain martyrs need rewriting in order to figure transhistorical themes. As he surveys the early church martyrs, Foxe revises problematic aspects of their legends so they may fit into his overarching narrative of the struggle between true and false churches. This project of historical cleansing and reclamation includes St. George's legend. Foxe mentions George in a list of Diocletian martyrs and closely links the torture he suffered with his iconoclasm:

Georgius, a younge man of Capadocia . . . stoutly inveighing against the impyous idolatry of the Emperours, was apprehended and cast into prison; then torn with hooked irons, burnt with hoate lyme, stretched with cordes; after that, his hands and feete with other members of his body being cut of, at last with a sword he had his head cut of.[34]

Torments like those Redcrosse suffers in the House of Holiness are rendered not as penance but as a martyr's sacrifice, and, by Foxean standards at least, in a matter-of-fact way. Foxe omits the tradition of George's mass conversions and the dragon fight deserves no mention whatsoever; only his sufferings, brought on by his iconoclasm, merit attention.

To Foxe's portrayal of the martyr suffering at Diocletian's hands, Spenser restores the dragon-killing; he adds hints of a martyr's suffering to a legend that had seemed to sterner Protestants alternately cartoonish and threatening. Echoes of both halves of George's traditional legend – the dragon fight *and* his spectacular martyrdom – resurface throughout Book I as Spenser balances George as military-chivalric hero with George as suffering Christian. In working through different possible Georges, Spenser admits, more than does Foxe, the difficulty of identifying a valid saintly model amid Reformation-era controversies over locating Christ's true bride. This is most poignantly realized in Una, who wanders because the true church is no longer, as in conventional medieval figuration, a comforting mother but a lover one must seek, and continue to seek, through time.[35]

Una's and Redcrosse's initial wandering psychomachically invokes Error herself. The expectation for George's traditional dragon fight has been established from stanza 3: "And ever as he rode, his hart did earne / To prove his puissance in battell brave . . . Upon his foe, a Dragon horrible and stearne" (6–7, 9). In his marginalia, John Dixon identifies this "Dragon" as "error," the first foe Redcrosse encounters.[36] Indeed, in Caxton, Lydgate, Barclay, and other traditional versions of the legend, the dragon fight is George's first adventure and produces a decisive victory. Though most obviously indebted to Hesiod's *Theogony*, Spenser's Error also resembles the dragon of legend; she is an incomplete copy or oblique rendering of the beast Redcrosse has set out to fight.[37] Like the dragon Redcrosse finally encounters in canto xi, the end of her tail harbors a "mortall sting" (15.4). The dragon of legend has horribly bad breath, due to its nasty habit of consuming live flesh; Error shares the habit and the foul breath it engenders. Error's vomit clarifies her resemblance both to the legendary dragon (who spits out bits of flesh) and to Revelation 16's beast (who spews frogs):

> . . . she spewd out of her filthie maw
> A floud of poyson horrible and blacke,
> Full of great lumps of flesh and gobbets raw,
> Which stunck so vildly, that it forst him slacke
> His grasping hold, and from her turne him backe:
> Her vomit full of bookes and papers was,
> With loathly frogs and toades, which eyes did lacke,
> And creeping sought way in the weedy gras:
> Her filthie parbreake all the place defiled has.          (i.20.1–9)

Error's vomit contains text, "bookes and papers" frequently glossed as controversial books and pamphlets, or erroneous Catholic doctrine, or, more broadly, the massive textual promulgation printing made possible.[38] The presence of text amid echoes of both the traditional legend's dragon ("great lumpes of flesh and gobbets raw") and Revelation's beast ("loathly frogs and toades") also implies that what is at stake here is an ideal saintly paradigm, to be assembled from the fragments of various stories of sainthood. The problems of competing textual accounts thus inaugurate Spenser's attempt to synchronize the George of legend with Protestant apocalyptics.

In this battle, Spenser departs from the *Legenda Aurea,* for Voragine's George has no difficulty defeating his dragon; its noxious breath does not trouble him as Redcrosse is troubled here. Indeed, the manner in which Redcrosse defeats this dragon-like monster has incurred much comment. Redcrosse famously responds to Una's warning about the danger of Error's den with chivalric bravado: "Vertue gives her selfe light, through darkenesse for to wade" (12.9). Entering Error's cave, Redcrosse learns that he is only partially right: his armor provides "a litle glooming light" that nevertheless allows him to see "the ugly monster plaine" (14.5, 6). After the fight is joined and Redcrosse is tightly wrapped in Error's snaky train, Una cries "Add faith unto your force, and be not faint" (19.3). Yet Redcrosse seems to add anger, not faith:

> That when he heard, in great perplexitie,
> His gall did grate for griefe and high disdaine,
> And knitting all his force got one hand free,
> Wherewith he grypt her gorge with so great paine,
> That soone to loose her wicked bands did her constraine.          (19.5–9)

Nevertheless, the exertion of "gall" is enough to bring about Error's down-fall, at least in the most literal sense. Still, the chivalric militarism to which Redcrosse adheres – he is "fearefull more of shame, / Then of the certaine perill he stood in" (24.1–2) – is sufficient for only an incomplete victory, for of course he and Una proceed to wander separately for the next six cantos. The consequences of this first fight have often been explained in terms of the knight's own moral or ontological shortcomings. King, for instance, argues that the "knight's unregenerate condition rendered him incapable of defeating his monstrous opponent"; because Redcrosse relies not upon faith but on "brute force" he "does conquer Error, but he has first erred."[39] Yet the "error" here may also be read as a temporal one, that is, as an initial mistaking that is perhaps inevitable or even necessary to Spenser's reimagining of this saint figure whose roots lie in the Catholic past.

This sort of error is figured in John Bale's commentary on Revelation, *The Image of Both Churches*. Revelation, whose imagery Spenser interweaves with that of the George legend, is notoriously difficult to interpret, not least because of its own recursiveness. As Claire McEachern observes, "it is unclear at points whether additional episodes and agents are being introduced, or whether they are merely recapitulations of earlier moments." She argues that Bale's process of reading Revelation has a "profoundly historical character": in Bale's infamous words on the difficulty of spying the Whore of Babylon, "a whore at *first* blush seemeth only a woman." As McEachern notes, what is interesting about this remark is that Bale's sentence, glossing Revelation 17, introduces an ambiguity where, uncharacteristically for this text, there is none:

the confusion that the first blush limns is an inaugural one, the result of a temporal problem of priority. The blush describes a necessary convergence, but not a permanent one: between types of churches, their symbolic effects, and the women that figure them. In other words, having once blushed, or misread, the outward sign, is a precondition of reading it rightly, in an interior manner. A chaste reading is only possible in the context of an earlier unchaste one.[40]

Book I's historical character – in the sense not just of its historical allegory and allusions but its insistent questioning about what the histories of England's patron saint mean for contemporary sainthood – invites a similar approach.

What is true for Bale, then, is even more true of Spenser's "dark conceit": many of Redcrosse's apparently moral errors are in some sense temporal ones, initial mistakes that help distinguish between a useable proto-Protestant past and other distorted, Catholic, or legendary ones. The "Legend of Holiness" demands that its reader look more closely, beyond surface similarities in different versions of the George legends, so that she may penetrate to a level of significant difference and formulate a holy distinction. In Spenser's poem, temporal and temporary errors stem from a past which is a site of error but also has redeemable elements, elements which are uncovered by marking the George legend's points of similarity and difference with the ideals of the Protestant present. For historians like Foxe, that present is nothing more nor less than the recovery of Christianity's early purity; the future is in important ways a return to a purer past. What Spenser adds to this vision of history is a fuller sense of the confusion that multiple claims to Christianity's past engendered. If Spenser in some ways extends Foxe's project by recuperating "*Saint George* of mery England" (x.61.9), he does it with a fuller representation of competing saintly models, shadowed in the incarnations of many of Redcrosse's foes, and with a greater sense of the slow, painstaking historiographical process required to assimilate a legendary martyr's past to a Protestant future. Rather than wrestling Spenser's repetitions into a linear trajectory of a particular character's development, I argue that they may be read instead as instances of the poem's reiterative search for a complete allegory of Protestant sainthood, gradually assembled from the vocabulary of the past – an early church martyr's legend – and of Revelation's apocalyptic future. What is at stake for Spenser is not necessarily or only the linear progression of a particular character, "Redcrosse," and the consequences of his particular moral choices but the reform of the hagiographic paradigm itself. This reformation is achieved not through Foxe's insistence on all-encompassing historiographical paradigms and, it must be said, editorial bullying, but through a prolonged, painful confrontation with the past figured as battles in which the hero confronts aspects of his own, temporally divided self.

For the Error episode, then, the question is not so much what mistake Redcrosse made to bring about an only partial victory, but why this oblique incarnation of the George legend's initial conflict is off-center and incomplete – or, in terms of the penance scenario in the House of Holiness, what needs consuming, purging, interiorizing, or restoring in order to make the reclamation of the early church martyr-hero work. In the Error episode, Redcrosse trusts in chivalric norms, which is not unwarranted: virtue does give enough light to see the monster by; Redcrosse does kill Error and win the praise of the woman he most desires to please. The issue is not the incorrectness of trust in chivalric norms but the incompleteness of that trust. There is an implicit commentary on the easy glossing of military victory as spiritual conquest in other George legends as such interpretation

is associated with Archimago, who tells of the dragon's conquests in ways
that reduce Redcrosse "to a mere chivalric knight":[41] "For to all knighthood
it is foule disgrace, / That such a cursed creature lives so long a space"
(i.31.8–9). Frustrating straightforward martial allegory, Book I insistently
revisits earlier moments in the martyr-saint's history in order to respond to
Una's invitation to Redcrosse: "shew what ye bee" (i.19.2). Increasingly,
Redcrosse's quest will turn inward, as he and we with him reread his past in
order to purge it and reshape it into a model of holiness that is not static but
gains its force precisely through the *process* of constant reinterpretation.

### DUPLICATION AND DISTINCTION

The poem's agonistic rereading of competing George legends is most
obvious in the numerous erroneous duplications of Redcrosse himself.
The doubling so intrinsic to Spenser's poetics helps to invoke – so that it
might, through chastening suffering, expel – the danger of too closely
echoing or replicating the Georges of the past. The doubling Archimago
effects through creating the false Una (designed to divide Redcrosse and
Una into "double parts") continues to haunt the allegory as Redcrosse
confronts specters from his own legendary past. These include the links
between St. George and the crusading Knights Templar as well as the ritual
reenactments of George's battles in mumming plays. In Spenser's hands,
both moments from George's past reveal a saint who too much resembles
his ostensible enemy. Contemporary martyrologists also wrestled with the
problem of effecting distinction amid uncomfortable similarities. As
Reformation martyrologists were well aware, in cases of potentially misleading resemblance the burden of distinction falls on the reader. Questing
through a world that mimics the epistemological difficulties Reformation
controversy spawned, Redcrosse errs so that Spenser's reader may learn
how to navigate an increasingly complicated religious landscape.

　　Though Wilkin notes several echoes of the Templars and their crusades
in *The Faerie Queene*, he does not discuss Redcrosse's battles with the
Saracen brothers. Yet these battles contain the most straightforward references to George's crusading past, a past whose heroism Spenser heavily
qualifies. The very fact that Redcrosse appears in an allegory challenges the
crusading ideal's sharp division between Christian knight and Muslim
infidel, for the logic of allegory usually dictates that the foes one fights
are in a sense versions of oneself. The initial confrontation between
Redcrosse and Sansfoy leaves them both "Astonied with the stroke of
their owne hand" so that both "Do backe rebutte and ech to other yealdeth

land" (ii.15.8–9). The singular form of "hand" is (pardon the pun) striking: the poetry folds each knight's heroic agency (his hand) into that of the other one, and the episode's ending effects only a partial separation. The simile of the two rams whose confrontation renders both "Astonied" is suggested by "rebutte" and enforces a moment of stillness in which an uncomfortable exchange of qualities takes place:

> As when two rams stird with ambitious pride,
> Fight for the rule of the rich fleeced flocke,
> Their horned fronts so fierce on either side
> Doe meete, that with the terror of the shocke
> Astonied both, stand sencelesse as a blocke,
> Forgetfull of the hanging victory:
> So stood these twaine, unmoved as a rocke,
> Both staring fierce, and holding idely
> The broken reliques of their former cruelty. (ii.16)

The double meaning of the word "twaine" (twinned, or separated) distills the problem of this episode: the knights are alike, by the terms of the allegory in which the foes one confronts are versions of one's own psychological turmoil, and distinct, by the terms of the chivalric confrontation between Redcrosse and a Saracen.[42]

Foxe explicitly argues that the Crusaders themselves suffered from infidelity. He describes the Crusaders' grumblings against God after a series of setbacks:

Such murmuring wordes of an unstable faith, many there began to cast out, as taking displeasure for their sufferings, but not considering on the other side what Idolaters they were, what pride and discorde was amongst them, what crueltie and murther they had shewed at home in persecuting the poore Albingenses, what superstition they first brought out wyth them, with what idolatry they proceded, putting their trust in masses, in the popes indulgences, in worshipping of images, and praying to saintes. And what helpe then coulde they looke for at Gods hand, which had Images in their temples, to fight against them which had none? Or what marvell, if the Lord of hostes went not with their armie, committing such idolatrie every day in their pavilions to their Sacramentall bread and wine as they did, and fighting with the strength of their owne merits, and not only by the power of their faith in Christ, which is only the victory that overcommeth the worlde?[43]

Though Spenser's poem shares the sense that the crusaders were much like infidels themselves, his allegory preserves more of the crusader's triumph: Redcrosse's shield of faith protects him from Sansfoy's furious blows. The problem is not that the saint and his foe are interchangeable (only Archimago conflates Redcrosse wholly with "Paynims", in vi.38.5) but that the insufficient distinction between Redcrosse and his foe will yield an incomplete victory. Redcrosse, cut free from Una, preserves vestiges of Christian heroism but on the whole resembles his foe too closely in this struggle for him to figure the holiness for which Spenser quests.

Redcrosse continues, of course, to run into difficult Saracens. In the encounter with Sansjoy, the poem both demands that readers distinguish Redcrosse from Sansjoy and frustrates such a distinction, a conflict represented in the discrepancy between the argument to canto 5 and the simile describing the two combatants as they fight. The argument differentiates Redcrosse and Sansjoy clearly: "The faithfull knight in equall field / subdewes his faithlesse foe." Yet the argument's simplistic gloss is challenged by the infamously problematic simile of the griffon and dragon, a simile comparing Redcrosse to a beast – the griffon – whose moral associations are not entirely clear.[44] The episode presents another oblique rendering of George's traditional battle, a rendering whose obscurity and incompleteness is linked to incorrect reading. When Sansjoy and Redcrosse come to blows, a specter of the dragon George should fight appears in the simile Spenser uses:

> So th' one for wrong, the other strives for right:
> As when a Gryfon seized of his pray,
> A Dragon fiers encountreth in his flight,
> Through widest ayre making his ydle way,
> That would his rightfull ravine rend away:
> With hideous horrour both together smight,
> And souce so sore, that they the heavens affray:
> The wise Southsayer seeing so sad sight,
> Th'amazed vulgar telles of warres and mortall fight. (v.8)

The simile glances towards the apocalyptic battle Redcrosse will fight at the end of the book but cedes interpretation to the soothsayer who seems unable to do much to enlighten the "amazed vulgar" on the meaning of this event[45] – or if he can, it is only to tell what seems obvious: that the upset of the heavens indicates wars and fights. Comically, the fight ends on misinterpretation, as Redcrosse hears Duessa's cry to Sansjoy, "Thine the shield, and I, and all," and understands it as an encouraging call of support similar to Una's in the Error episode. Though the narrator gives us a proper distinction of truth from falsehood, Spenser reenacts the problems of making such distinctions through Redcrosse's erroneous response to Duessa. In Redcrosse's encounters with specters from his own legendary past, Spenser figures the problem of incomplete differentiations, of foes and heroes who too much resemble each other, a problem that resonates with the processes of distinction between false and true martyrs with which his contemporaries struggled.

SUFFERING, PURGATION, AND RESTORATION

The problem of insistent doubling in the Saracen fights moves towards resolution only when suffering is used to separate problematic from reformed martyr-saints; suffering is both the punishment and cure for erroneous duplication. The allegory's proliferation of competing George figures, from Archimago's disguise as St. George to the echoes of the crusading saint in the Saracen battles, reaches its apex in the Orgoglio episode. Orgoglio is linked to the traditional etymology of George's name as given by Caxton – "earthe and orge" – through his name as well as his description and genealogy, both of which emphasize his earthy, fleshly monstrosity. When Spenser's "man of earth" encounters Orgoglio, that "monstrous masse of earthly slime" (vii.9.8), Redcross confronts not only his own immediate spiritual and sexual trespasses but also an earlier, unholy version of himself. Appearing after Redcrosse's liaison with Duessa, Orgoglio becomes associated with St. George's own Romish past.[46]

It is at this point that Spenser's inversion of the George legend – so that suffering is a prerequisite for victory – becomes clear. In the "Legend of Holiness," suffering does not provide narrative closure, as one might reasonably expect if the hero suffers like a martyr; instead, it often functions meta-fictionally. For Spenser suffering both punishes and redeems the temporal errors discussed above; suffering also effects the distinction between reformed saint and his less-than-holy past for which the poem has struggled and, as a corollary, makes the evil Redcrosse fights show itself more clearly so that it might be defeated. Hints of martyr-like suffering are insistent and pervasive in Book I's second half. In vii.17.9, a dragon-like beast appears which is explicitly associated with the blood of persecution ("all embrewd in blood"). In canto viii the beast is likened again both to the fire-breathing dragon of folklore and to Revelation's "woman drunken with the blood of the Martyrs of Jesus" (Geneva gloss, Revelation 17:6).[47] Arthur discovers within Orgoglio's dungeon an altar "on which trew Christians blood was often spilt, / And holy Martyres often doen to dye" (viii.36.3–4); the dungeon's interior is "filthy" "With blood of guiltlesse babes, and innocents trew, / Which there were slaine, as sheepe out of the fold, / Defiled was, that dreadfull was to vew, / And sacred ashes over it was strowed new"(35.5–9). The new-strewn ashes invoke the Marian persecution, crucial to Foxe's historical scheme because it showed most clearly the true church's persecution under the reign of Antichrist; the burning of Marian martyrs illuminated the persistence of *the* true, suffering church. This power of distinction is also at work in Spenser's poem to the extent that suffering permits Redcrosse's separation from his legendary counterparts; after a painful nine-month imprisonment, Redcrosse is reborn into grace. The rebirth is the most productive response yet to Una's wish that Redcrosse should "shew what ye bee" as Duessa is at last stripped of her scarlet robe and its attendant persecutory power. Indeed, in Spenser's rendition faith itself is founded in triumphing over persecution. Fidelia's cup holds a serpent, suggesting a link to St. John of Patmos: the Emperor Domitian gave him poison to drink and it "miraculously condensed into a serpent and left the cup."[48]

Yet Redcrosse continues to suffer, as in the penance episode discussed above. In Foxe's 1583 edition of the *Actes and Monuments*, the last published during his lifetime, Foxe attempts to consolidate his English readership behind the advances the English Reformation had made and to guard against intra-Protestant divisions. Spenser is more interested in the ongoing interpretive work of reclaiming the past than he is in establishing the monumental results of that reclamation. The process of revisiting the past thus is central to Spenser's House of Holiness, in which Redcrosse reexperiences earlier moments in his quest, this time in a salvific context: he experiences a form of despair (x.22), descends into a dungeon (to be rid of "proud humors," 26.2), and is again associated with new birth (x.29).[49] Even after Contemplation's revelation that Redcrosse is not of "base Elfin brood" but from "ancient race / Of *Saxon* kings" (65.8, 1–2) – he is, in other words, the true St. George, not the changeling imposter whom a fairy trick let loose on the world – Spenser continues to reassemble a new legend for Redcrosse from the vocabulary of his own past and to insist, in his most pointed departure from Redcrosse's legendary prototype, that his saint must suffer *before* defeating the dragon. The dragon fight is the culmination of Spenser's quest to assemble a new saint's legend from the remnants of the old; the fight revisits Redcrosse's earlier battles and places suffering before triumph. Importantly, Redcrosse's earlier moments of weakness are recuperated to become part of the final victory. The dragon's wings, likened to "hollow wynd" (xi.10.2), maintain something of Orgoglio's blustery hollowness; his tail (or "traine," in 37.5) and the "blood and gobbets raw" (13.3) that drip from his mouth resemble and intensify aspects of Error. Redcrosse again endures severe pain. On the battle's first day he suffers "scorching flame" which sears his body despite his armor: he is "Faynt, wearie, sore, emboyled, grieved, brent / With heat, toyle, wounds, armes, smart, and inward fire" (26.6, 28.1–2).[50] After this moment of suffering, the knight again longs to die (28.4). The aid the knight receives from the well of life and the tree of life restore him for the fight; importantly, the baptismal well of legend here renews only the knight himself, in contrast to the legendary font which springs up after George's victory for use in baptizing those he has saved.[51] The knight's struggle with his traditional foe centers and intensifies episodes from his narrative past. His eventual triumph recuperates and reassembles earlier moments of failure, misreading, and suffering into the legendary victory for which this would-be St. George has long sought, a paradigmatic moment of saintly suffering and redemptive conquest.

Still, by deferring Redcrosse's apocalyptic marriage and entry into the New Jerusalem the allegory suggests that the post-Reformation world demands ongoing interpretational work. Redcrosse's struggles with specters of George's legendary pasts mean that the knight functions as a scapegoat for holy interpretation and reformed hagiography, one whose struggles both train others to read well and reshape legendary materials into something approximating a Protestant legend of holiness. Martyrs' epistemological function in the post-Reformation world was to provide, through acts of suffering and witness, instances of clarity in an otherwise confusing landscape. Yet in Spenser's poem that clarity is not as easily or widely established as martyrologists might have hoped. Redcrosse's ability to defeat his enemies shifts dramatically with the level of his own spiritual development. But that development is not automatically extended to other figures in the poem. The specter of Error recurs as the townspeople, noticeably unconverted next to the citizens of legend, still fear "some hidden nest / Of many Dragonettes" (xii.10.5–6); dreading the dragon's replication and revival, they misread the battle's significance. The continued threat of dangerous similarities is suggested when Archimago escapes; although Redcross and Una can now recognize his deceptions, no other figures in the poem can. The poem's struggle to free Redcrosse from his own cultural history results in a saint whose struggles must be imitated by others; as Guyon's Palmer tells Redcrosse, "wretched we, where ye have left your marke, / Must now anew begin, like race to ronne" (II.i.32.6–7). Rewriting St. George's history, the poem gestures towards a model hagiography in Redcrosse's conquering of the dragon. Simultaneously, however, that model requires of the saints who would follow it the continual struggle its hero undergoes. Spenser's poem insists that the problems of distinguishing among seemingly similar hagiographic paradigms are solvable only through ongoing errancy and interpretive work.

Protestant historians' revisions of early church history valorized martyrdom by reinterpreting early church martyrs as witnesses for their cause. Yet if there is a Foxe-like purgation of legendary excesses in Book I (a cleansing of false images, as some scholars have found in Spenser), there is also a marked investment of spiritual significance in the dragon fight. If every saint has a past, for Spenser it is a usable past, not to be turned from in horror but to be recovered through reiteration and reinterpretation. Spenser shares with Foxe a basic approach to the pre-Reformation past, but the ambiguities of quest allegory create a Reformation poetics with more emphasis on process and development, on the evolutionary, even errant nature of true church and true Christian hero.

### TREASON AND TRANSCENDENCE: A CATHOLIC READS *THE FAERIE QUEENE*

Spenser's revision of George's legend did not go unnoticed by English Catholics. Published at roughly the same time that John Dixon was writing his commentary, Anthony Copley's *A Fig for Fortune* (1596) revises cantos ix–xii of Book I to challenge Spenser's use of suffering, questing, and martyrdom to induce and authenticate Protestant holiness.[52] In an earlier (1595) miscellany entitled *Wits Fittes and Fancies*, Copley had tried to catch Spenser's eye. In his dedication "To the Gentlemen Readers" Copley asked "M. Daniel, M. Spencer, & other the Prime Poets of our time, to pardon [this book] with as easie a frowne as they please, for that I give them to understand, that an Universitie Muse never pend it, though umbly devoted thereunto." If *Wits Fittes and Fancies* was meant to win Spenser's approval, perhaps *A Fig for Fortune* was meant to win his soul. *A Fig for Fortune* both recycles some of Spenser's praise for his Queen and revises Spenser's allegory into an argument for Roman Catholicism as the only true religion. Copley's poem is valuable both for its complex response to Spenser's combination of Revelation with reformed hagiography and for what it reveals about the possibilities and limitations of moderate Catholic thought amid Elizabethan persecutions.

Most obviously, Copley's poem highlights the aspects of Spenser's poem that a contemporary Catholic found religiously offensive. Copley's poem teaches us, for instance, that Spenser's relative moderation still posed many problems for Catholic readers. For Copley, Spenser's syncretism threatened to overtake Revelation's symbolic vocabulary and to enclose contemporary religious struggles within a Protestant eschatological frame. In turn, Copley has been seen as a relatively moderate Catholic. Scholars have usually read *A Fig for Fortune* as a fervently loyalist text, a "barely-concealed plea for Catholic toleration, couched in terms of hyperbolic praise."[53] Yet if *A Fig for Fortune* sometimes reads like a plea for toleration amid hymns to Eliza, it is simultaneously an argument for a single truth upheld by Catholic martyrdom and available only in the liturgy of the Catholic Church. The assumptions that supported religious persecution in sixteenth-century England – that religious truth is singular and knowable, that dissenters must be silenced and believers willing to suffer for the truth – also undergird, sometimes problematically, Copley's attempt to write a poem that contains lines of nationalistic praise and is faithful to his Catholicism. Copley's moments of comparative moderation co-exist uneasily alongside his insistence that Catholicism is superior to the threats and inconstancies of "Fortune," by which Copley usually means "Protestantism."[54] Copley's qualified praise for Elizabeth, his passionate recuperation of Revelation for Catholic allegory, and his belief in future rewards for suffering Catholics suggest his clear understanding of martyrological contestations over interpreting Revelation as a means of understanding contemporary persecutions.

Copley's poem maintains a crucial feature of Spenser's allegory: the shaping of allegorical conflicts to figure the challenges of a post-Reformation world. Copley addresses two common Protestant claims about martyrdom: that Protestant martyrs are the true descendants of early church martyrs and that Catholic martyrs die as miserable traitors. The dedications to numerous Catholic martyrologies make explicit the link between early Christian martyrs and contemporary English Catholic ones, arguing for the continuity of their church and of its martyrs' testimony.[55] Perhaps following these cues, Copley responds to Spenser's attempt to unite the cleansed past of England's patron saint with contemporary Protestant ideals; he argues for a different, superior form of transhistorical continuity made possible only through the liturgy of the Mass. Copley is well aware of the competitive nature of martyrdom in the early modern period and works to distinguish false (Protestant) martyrdom, supported by bad interpretations of Revelation, from true, Catholic martyrdom and its simultaneous properties of historical continuity and timelessness. For Catholics, of course, the primary threat to these claims for a historical continuity of witnesses was the treason charges under which English Catholic martyrs were executed. The problem facing Copley, then, is that his knight must demonstrate loyalty to two conflicting authorities: his nation and his faith.

What little we know about Copley's life reveals a man who struggled with the conflicting claims of religion and nation. Copley was born in 1567. His parents fled England in 1569; at age fifteen Copley went abroad to join them. He returned to England illegally in 1590 and was immediately arrested.[56] In a statement taken on 6 January 1590, Copley admits that he spent time in Rome at the English College there, held a pension from the pope, and, most damning in the government's eyes, fought for Spain in Flanders, for which he "humbly crave(s) pardon of her majesty and my country."[57] After providing information on English Catholics living abroad, Copley was released. Nevertheless, the government continued to watch him carefully. Richard Topcliffe, the most notorious of the Elizabethan spies known as "priest-catchers," characterized Copley in June 1592 as "the most desperate youth that liveth... There liveth not the like, I think, in England for sudden attempts."[58] Copley's unwillingness to make certain "sudden attempts," however, also apparently caused him problems. In a later pamphlet written in support of the Appellant priests against the Jesuits, Copley says that *A Fig for Fortune* was meant to be an

attestation to the world of my Catholike soule to God and his Church, and of my resolution against the Jesuitical obloquie which heretofore attached me for no other fault in the world then refusing to concurre with a Jesuitical instrument in firing the Queenes Navie throughout the South and West of England ... I give in that Poeme her Majestie some praise and honour as for temporall state, which a Jesuit cannot endure in the behalf of the house of Austrich.[59]

*A Fig for Fortune* was to proclaim his Catholicism, despite his apparent reluctance to commit violent treason. Copley did resist in nonviolent ways; he appears on recusant rolls for one month's recusancy in January 1596, the very month that *A Fig for Fortune* was entered in the Stationer's Register. He was indicted twice more for one month's recusancy (in June 1602 and January 1603), and "on 31 January 1600/1 he and his wife Elizabeth were excommunicated for persistent recusancy."[60] Copley's poem addresses the hardships of those who, like he himself, weighed the options available to recusant Catholics in the 1590s: flight into exile, violent resistance, or patient, martyr-like suffering.

That Copley's poem endorses the third option, patient suffering, is clear in its dedicatory verse. Addressed to Anthony Browne, second Viscount Montague, the dedication claims that disaster in worldly fortunes leads to "Sionrie," the perfect worship and glory of the New Jerusalem.[61] *A Fig for Fortune* elevates Catholicism's claim to a heavenly future and reassesses worldly fortune: "Daigne in your grace the spirit of a man / Disastred for vertue; if at least it be / Disaster to be winnowed out Fortunes Fan / Into the Fan of Grace and Sionrie / Wherein repurify'd to Gods eternall glorie / The Devill rues in man old Adams injurie."[62] The worldly disasters facing staunch Catholics are evident in Montague's biography. In 1602 John Ellis, a former Catholic turned informer, said that "the Catholics depended more on the 2nd. Viscount Montague than on any other person in England."[63] Yet Montague did not escape religious persecution. In early 1594, he was examined by the Archbishop of Canterbury and the Lord Keeper "for personally baptizing his son" (that is, refusing to give his son a baptism in the Church of England) and in June of 1594, "the house of the Dowager Lady Montague was searched on the orders of the Privy Council, and his grandfather's priests were interrogated."[64] In his dedication, Copley devalues worldly fortune so as to celebrate the future rewards awaiting those who, like Montague, suffer worldly setbacks. Copley uses the common sentiment that suffering purifies the Christian to redeem English Catholics' situation; "Disaster" is the means, painful though it may be, to attain grace and the New Zion. The dedication's encouragement to passive suffering both implies that Catholics will not respond violently to persecution and suggests that their loyalty will always be tempered by a radical devaluation of worldly things.

In its three main sections, Copley's poem develops this somewhat uneasy hybrid of patient suffering and anticipated apocalyptic triumphalism. These sections take on the aspects of Spenser's poem which Copley found most partisan – the Despair episode, the House of Holiness and Contemplation, the vision of the New Jerusalem, and the final apocalyptic battle – and transform them into a Catholic pattern of quest, suffering, and redemption. First, Copley revises Redcrosse's struggles with the hellish Despair into a twinned temptation to suicide or homicidal revenge. The temptation to despair and to desperate acts does not stem from an imperfect belief in God's grace and mercy (as in Spenser) but from persecution. The potential for spiritual health within Catholicism remains intact while the responsibility for the appearance of despair in the allegorical landscape is shifted onto "fortune," a thinly veiled way of adducing English Catholics' temporal sufferings at the hands of a Protestant government. Copley shows clearly that both suicidal despair and homicidal revenge have their lineage in hell and night.

Yet despite the poem's rejection of violent action in response to persecution, the temptations remain powerful and vaguely threatening, and the state's persecution of Catholics does not go uncriticized. Copley's knight first encounters Cato's ghost who urges him towards suicide as the only response to his misfortune. Cato refers transparently to the situation of Elizabethan Catholics: "Whilom I was a man of *Romes* rejoyce / Whiles happy Fortune my estate uppropped: / But once when *Caesar* over-topped all, / Then (loe) this mid-night shape did me befall" (p. 8). Caesar's overthrow of traditional Roman authority (an easy allusion to the authority of the Roman church) engenders despair; suicide's dangerous appeal comes from the sense of powerlessness and dishonor Cato feels at this overthrow. The second temptation, to Revenge, is the more seductive: Revenge claims that she advocates a "Masculine" course, which gives the frustrated Catholic the opportunity to die a tragic hero (p. 18). The hellish Revenge vanishes at sunrise and Copley's knight journeys on; instead of tragedy, the poem chooses the vagaries of allegorical quest narrative. Perhaps allegory's double-speak is more resonant with the position of the would-be Catholic loyalist. Yet that double-speak also allows some subtle criticism of the Elizabethan government's anti-Catholic legislation, for "Caesar's" rule is partly blamed for pushing young men towards revenge. Though the speaker rejects Revenge, "Yet for her speech was consonant to Nature, / I wisht sh'had been an Oracle of truth; / So credulous is *Angers* moodie vigure / When once it is in-Caesared in youth" (p. 25). The odd verbalization here – anger is "in-Caesared" – suggests that the ruler shares some blame for the frustration that tempts young Catholics to violence. The rejection of this temptation maintains some political bite.

In his poem's second section, Copley rewrites the House of Holiness and responds to Spenser's tendency to link his hero's progress in cantos vii, viii, x, and xi to suffering. Copley attempts to reclaim martyrdom's redemptive value for Catholicism; he elevates heavenly rewards over worldly things, inward peace over physical suffering. This elevation qualifies, however, praise bestowed on his Queen. The difficulty of simultaneously praising an eternal realm open only to Catholics and a queen who rules over an officially Protestant earthly one is made clear in Copley's version of the House of Holiness. After overcoming the temptations to despair and revenge, the speaker's old horse, Melancholy, disappears and a new one, Good Desire, takes him to the House of Devotion where he meets Catechrysius.[65] Kneeling before a crucifix, Catechrysius uses "needle-pointed Discipline" to correct his "Fleshes frailtie" and smears his cell with "penall bloud, and blubbering" (p. 28). Catechrysius with his painful "Crucifixe-contemplation" is clearly meant to supercede Spenser's merely malnourished mystic. Catechrysius shares the teaching burden of his Spenserian forerunner. In lengthy direct instruction, Catechrysius expounds the "Theame" of Devotion: *Happie they all that suffer for our*

*Lord, / For he to such his heaven will afoord*" (p. 57). Suffering wins one admission to Sion, or the New Jerusalem; the things of this world are to be despised in light of suffering's reward. This denigration of worldly fortune turns the poem's moments of praise for Elizabeth into somewhat back-handed compliments. Like Spenser's Caelia who remarks "Straunge thing it is an errant knight to see / Here in this place" (x.10.1–2), Catechrysius exclaims: "Rare, yea all too rare are now adayes / *Elizas* subjects seen to passe this wayes" (p. 31). Catechrysius assumes that Eliza's subjects do not seek the House of Devotion because they are so happy and fortunate. But in the poem's terms, to avoid Devotion's painful crucifix-contemplation is to avoid redemption. Catechrysius's praise of Elizabeth's subjects as "a Paradized" and "blessed people" (p. 31) sits uneasily alongside a reassessment of good and bad fortune in light of suffering's benefits.

Most radically, Copley challenges Spenser's use of Revelation in Redcrosse's vision of the New Jerusalem and in his final battle with the dragon. In *The Faerie Queene*, those two moments resonate across different temporal registers. Redcrosse finds his true past, present, and future in the revelations Contemplation grants him, and his battle with the dragon is prismatic: in ever-shifting associations, it seems to shadow the culmination of St. George's quest, the battle of the individual Christian with sinfulness, and, dimly at least, Christ's victory over sin and the future, final triumph of good over evil. Scholars have noted the fleeting nature of Redcrosse's vision of the New Jerusalem; he cannot enter eternal stasis till he has discharged his duty to the Faerie Queene, and after Redcrosse's and Una's betrothal Spenser endlessly defers what promises to be a divine consummation. In his poem's third section, Copley asserts the profound connections between the liturgy of the Mass and Revelation. Indeed, he argues that the temporal resonance Spenser's allegory seeks but does not ever grasp for long is present always and only in the Catholic Mass.

The third section of *A Fig for Fortune* conflates the liturgy of the Mass with a struggle between Protestantism (the wily Doblessa) and Catholicism that is both apocalyptic and resonant with the persecution contemporary English Catholics suffered. The second half of Spenser's Book I undergoes "a change in symbolic reference . . . a turn from projection to apocalypse, from enemies of flesh and blood to spiritual wickedness in high places";[66] Copley's poem attempts the same turn. Before being escorted to the Temple, the speaker undergoes a brief transfiguration into a "Figure of zeale" (p. 59). With this, the poem begins to shift from temporal to spiritual struggles. Only now does the speaker get his knightly armor (p. 60); revenge's seductive call to action is displaced onto spiritual warfare.

Called into the "Temple" of the New Jerusalem by a "sacring" bell (p. 63), the knight is being transported into the Mass and simultaneously into a set of loyalties to be preferred over worldly ones. Indeed, the supremacy of spiritual loyalties is so stark that the Temple's porter has been instructed not to admit any "Elizian" (p. 70); only Catechrysius's insistence that the speaker is a Catholic "Catechumen" wins his admission. The barring of Elizians from the poem's pinnacle vision raises the question of whether transfigured zeal can exist in an abstract spiritual realm without somehow affecting political behavior. The relationship between Catholic zeal and the decision whether to attend Church of England services (which Elizabethan officials deemed a political choice) is soon made clear.Copley shares the stern arguments of those like William Cardinal Allen who encouraged Catholics to endure suffering rather than conform to the Church of England. Doblessa, identified in the argument to the poem simply as "Fortune," here clearly represents the Church of England. She enters the Temple looking like a Catholic; she and her followers pretend to honor the rituals presented at the Mass. This Catholic look-alike offers a visual trick twinned with the worst temptation of all: to conform to the Church of England under the mistaken assumption that it too preserves the authentic rituals of the one true church. Doblessa seeks to seduce Catholics from suffering persecution into an easy church-papistry because she knows the benefits of persecution: "[well she wist that] Sion was as a bell / And Persecution but as a clapper / That made her silver-sound more far to scatter" (p. 77). What the Church of England desires, then, is conformity. Copley claims that true Catholics choose suffering, with its clear proclamation of difference and its eternal rewards. As in Spenser, the problem of deceptively similar women and, implicitly, churches rears its head; for Copley, as for Spenser, only suffering, or the willingness to suffer, allows distinction.

Copley's insistence on Catholicism's truth culminates in the implication that Spenser's vision of the New Jerusalem, with its temporariness and deferrals, is far inferior to the experience of Catholics at the Mass. Shell argues that Copley's Sion "begs comparison with Spenser's Cleopolis, or London."[67] Yet it seems rather to respond directly to Redcrosse's partial, fleeting glimpse of the New Jerusalem. Copley explicitly rewrites the moment when Contemplation corrects Redcrosse's criticism of Cleopolis, the Faerie Queene's city. Redcrosse denigrates Cleopolis as a "towre of glass," and Contemplation replies that Cleopolis is "for earthly frame / The fairest peece, that eie beholden can" (x.58.9, 59.2–3). The value of the two cities derives from their proper place in (or out of) time.[68]

Copley's Catechrysius insists that "faire Eliyzium" and its queen are worthy
of praise: "Our coasts is full of great *Elizabeth*, / Yea, all the world is fertill
of the same." Yet despite Catechrysius's two stanzas of praise for Elizabeth,
the proper hierarchy of loyalties is crystal clear: "But such her glories are
but eare-delightes / And lip-sweets only to our far awayes, / For we are no
*Elizium*-bred wightes / Nor have we any such like merrie dayes; / Wee have
our joyes in another kind / Ghostly innated in our soule and mind" (p. 65).
Earthly delights are demoted more firmly than in Spenser's poem; the
Catholic vision of the New Jerusalem, with its spiritual rewards, joys, and
triumphs, clearly supercedes any earthly Cleopolis.

This celebration of the New Jerusalem culminates in the Sionites'
experience at Mass. Reclaiming the language of Revelation as his catechumen walks along jeweled streets to the high Temple, Copley argues that the
worldly and the eternal touch in the liturgy of the Mass. Protestant
polemicists' uses of Revelation are now familiar:

the view that Revelation predicts the return to true faith during the Reformation
was well known during the Elizabethan age . . . Spenser was presumably familiar
with this polemical context, if only through the antipapal commentary for the
*Theatre for Worldlings* into which Jan van der Noot incorporated views derived
from Bale and Bullinger.[69]

Faced with Protestant interpretations of Revelation that linked Roman
Catholicism to the Whore of Babylon, Catholic writers reasserted a view
Catholic theologians had long held:[70] that Revelation is best understood in
the context of the Mass, a view evident in the Rheims New Testament of
1582. The translation's commentaries on Revelation insist that through the
Mass Catholics participate in the patterns and community of eternal wor-
ship. For instance, the "Sanctus" sung at Mass is taken from Revelation 4:8.
The Rheims New Testament glosses this verse:

This word is thrise repeated here, and Esa. 6: and to the imitation therof, in the
service of the holy Church, at Te Deum and at Masse, specially in the Preface next
before the great mysteries, for the honour of the three persons in the B. Trinitie,
and that the Church militant may joyne with the triumphant, and with al the
orders of Angels, who also are present at the consecration, and doe service there to
our common Lord and Master.[71]

Like the Douai translators, Copley insists on the unity between the rites of
heaven and earth: "Heer (loe) the amitie of men and Angels / In uniforme
adore of one true God, / Heer Peace and Pietie togither dwels, / Heer
Scisme, and Discords cloven-foot nere trod, / Heer sacred Ceremonies are
in ure / As wedlocke-rightes twixt Faith and Soules insure" (p. 66). In this

confluence, and not in Spenser's Arthur, is the supreme virtue of "high magnificence" (p. 70).

This confluence also complicates the allegory of the battle between Doblessa and the Sionites. Taking place as the Mass proceeds, this apocalyptic struggle displaces the sort of battle that cannot be fought by Catholics in a literal way if they are to succeed in winning any sort of toleration. At the same time, however, Copley's vision of the Mass as mediating between heaven and earth sets up correspondences between heavenly priorities and earthly actions that trouble slightly his earlier arguments that Catholics should not take action so that they might be tolerated. For instance, his assertion that in the Mass the Church Militant touches the Church Triumphant complicates his earlier distancing of his hero from worldly battles. In a stanza responding to Spenser's Una, Copley writes that as his knight approaches the Temple, he sees an inscription above the door that reads "*Una, Militans.*" This is the Church Militant, the church on earth; Copley glosses the inscription as meaning "Unitie, and Warre" (p. 70). The Church Militant does not necessarily imply, of course, a fighting church, merely one embroiled in the struggles of this world. Yet Copley's gloss almost demands a more literally militaristic reading. A correction he makes to the stanza describing "*Una, Militans*" underscores the point. Copley's corrections, printed at the front of his volume, note that the line describing the movement of Una Militans – which states that the Church's followers "peacefullie advance" – should read "pace-fullie advance" (p. 6). The correction does not make as much sense as the original; nevertheless, Copley has gone out of his way to make sure these devotees do not move "peacefullie."

Further, though the Sionites fight a spiritual war, Copley links this war to actions of nonobedience that Catholics take in England, actions defined by law as treasonous. For instance, Doblessa comes to capture priests during the sacrifice of the Mass (p. 76), a favorite technique of Elizabethan priest-catchers. Significantly, Copley's stanza on Catholic martyrs rewrites treason: "Subject they were to dreadfull persecution / By publick edict, and false brethrens treason" (p. 82). Turning in a priest is treason not to the state but to religion itself. The battle's end reveals that Copley desires a vigorous spiritual warfare in which Catholics achieve spiritual victory so that the question of tolerance becomes moot. The victory over evil that Copley's knight seeks is folded into the victory of the Mass over its detractors, so that Copley's battle incorporates triumph into the very body of the Catholic liturgy. The overlap of different allegorical registers, so much a feature of Spenser's dragon fight, is also present: Catholics' ultimate spiritual victory threatens to spill over into a triumph in mundane time as well. The need to render distinctions between seemingly similar saint-figures and legends of holiness is obviated by the Sionites' victory. This is not an argument that Elizabethan officials would have been likely to recognize as loyalist.

Although this poem contains moments of praise for Elizabeth and implicit pleas for toleration, the ways it argues for Catholicism's superiority renders problematic its attempts to articulate loyalty in the face of persecution. In fact, the poem shares with Protestant persecutors the assumption that only a common religious vision can bring lasting peace. This is most marked at the poem's close. After the victory the Sionites celebrate and a virgin appears in majesty, showering red and white roses on everyone. The Elizian knight promptly thinks of the Tudor rose and assumes the virgin is his Queen. The poem's argument explains that Copley's knight "thought it was his soveraigne Ladie Eliza, and those Roses hers, [and] was suddenly in joy thereof rapt home againe to Elizium" (p. 6).[72] The text of the poem itself, however, reads quite differently. Despite his tears of reverence for Elizabeth I, Catechrysius explains that this virgin is an "Esterne [Eastern] dame" (p. 90). That is, she is the Woman Clothed with the Sun, traditionally interpreted as a figure for Holy Mother Church and for the Virgin Mary.[73] The speaker's desire to praise Elizabeth and give thanks to her succumbs to the greater praise and honor he owes to his Church and Mary. The displacement of the world's virgin by an eternal one is an apt metaphor for the poem's often contradictory articulation of would-be loyalism alongside an argument for Catholic supremacy.

On 23 January 1596, *A Fig for Fortune* was entered in the Stationers' Register. Later that same year, Copley found himself in jail.[74] For the second time in six years, he was threatened with treason charges because he had fought for Spain in Flanders during the 1580s. The revival of old charges so close to *A Fig for Fortune*'s publication may indicate that Copley's articulation of loyalty to the Virgin Mary got him into trouble with the officials of the Virgin Queen. At the very least, 1596 was a year of especially heated conflict in the prolonged struggles between England and Spain, and *A Fig for Fortune*'s moderate protestations of loyalty were not enough to persuade officials of Copley's fealty to England given his problematic past. Indeed, Copley himself states in a later pamphlet that his poem had been "called in by the Protestants."[75] In 1596, as earlier in 1590, Copley evaded prosecution by giving authorities information about Catholic Englishmen residing in Flanders, all the while insisting that he thought those Englishmen would be loyal if only Elizabeth would let them return. His assertion of his patriotism reveals his mixed feelings about the information he provides: "I know my heart guilty of all love and duty to my country."[76] Later, in two pamphlets supporting the Appellant priests against the Jesuits, Copley implied that Catholics could and would be loyal to England.[77] Yet he seems to have soon succumbed to the seductions of Revenge: in 1603 he was convicted of treason and sentenced to death for his part in the Bye Plot against James I, "a conspiracy by catholic priests and laymen to kidnap James, and to hold him hostage against a guarantee of religious toleration and the wholesale removal of unsympathetic councillors."[78] Worrying aloud to his sister and to a priest about whether he could endorse violence against the monarch, Copley nervously uncovered the plot; both his sister and the priest raced to tell authorities of the conspiracy.[79] Copley was quickly arrested and information he provided on his co-conspirators led to his eventual pardon, after which he seems to have disappeared into Rome, his own personal New Jerusalem.[80] In his life, as in his poetry, Copley apparently found it exceedingly difficult to reconcile a moderate's supposed loyalty to the English government with a fervent commitment to Una Militans.

In reclaiming Revelation's symbolic vocabulary for the Catholic cause, Copley indicates how deeply religious controversy, persecution, and martyrdom informed even somewhat critical commentaries on Spenser's poem. The fact that Copley used Spenser's allegory to make an argument about the value of Catholic suffering also implies the pervasive literary impact of competing articulations of martyrdom, for Spenser's Redcrosse is clearly the hero against whom Copley's knight must assert his own quest for holiness. For both poets the struggle between true and false churches is realized on a narrative level as a struggle between true and false paradigms for martyr-saints. Copley's and Spenser's allegorical quest narratives invoke, prolong, and attempt to resolve, at least provisionally, the epistemological and hermeneutical problems that conflicting testimonies spawned. As characters in these two allegorical fictions struggle with the specters and memories of other, competing martyr-figures in order to emerge into a space of apocalyptic clarity, Copley's and Spenser's questing, suffering knights and their readers must confront and learn to see through deceptive alternatives. For Spenser, the cost of the apocalyptic clarity that his allegory briefly achieves is paid in repeated episodes of suffering, suffering that is the only means of making Redcrosse's foes visible and defeatable. The reshaping of the legendary past of England's patron saint cannot be accomplished without pain. For Copley, the cost of clarity is paid in his uneasy compromise between spiritualized apocalyptic struggle and the suffering passivity loyal English Catholics had to endure in the political world.

NOTES

1 Graham Hough, ed., *The First Commentary on The Faerie Queene* (privately published, 1964), 5.
2 Exceptions include John N. King, *Spenser's Poetry and the Reformation Tradition* (Princeton: Princeton University Press, 1990), 97–9, 190–2; and Kathryn Walls, "Spenser's Kirkrapine and John Foxe's Attack on Rome," *Notes and Queries* 220 (1984), 173–5.
3 James Nohrnberg, *Analogy of The Faerie Queene* (Princeton: Princeton University Press, 1976), 103; *AM* (1583), 98.
4 The Catholic Alfonso de Villegas's *Flos Sanctorum*, trans. Edward Kinesman (Douai, 1609) devotes one line to George's dragon fight and fifteen pages to his martyrdom; Foxe only discusses George's martyrdom. Other Protestant writers strip the story of spiritual significance to emphasize chivalric romance or nationalistic celebration; see Richard Johnson's popular *The most famous history of the seaven champions of Christendome* (first published, London, 1596); Gerrard de Malynes, *Saint George for England, Allegorically Described* (London, 1601); and "St. George for England," reprinted in *The Roxburghe Ballads*, ed. William Chappell (London, 1847), vol. 1, 379–88.
5 On the self-reflexiveness of Spenser's allegory, see Maureen Quilligan, *The Language of Allegory: Defining the Genre* (Ithaca: Cornell University Press, 1979); Carol Kaske, *Spenser and Biblical Poetics* (Ithaca: Cornell University Press, 1999); Gordon Teskey, "Allegory," in *The Spenser Encyclopedia*, ed. A. C. Hamilton (Toronto: University of Toronto Press, 1990), 16–22.
6 E.g. Ernest Gilman, *Iconoclasm and Poetry in the English Reformation: "Down Went Dagon"* (Chicago: University of Chicago Press, 1986). Other influential statements on Spenser and iconoclasm include Stephen Greenblatt, *Renaissance Self-Fashioning* (Chicago: University of Chicago Press, 1980), and Kenneth Gross, *Spenserian Poetics: Idolatry, Iconoclasm, and Magic* (Ithaca: Cornell University Press, 1985). John N. King (*Spenser's Poetry*, esp. 91 and 233–8), Carol Kaske (*Spenser and Biblical Poetics*), and Anne Lake Prescott ("Spenser's Chivalric Restoration: From Bateman's *Travayled Pylgrime* to the Redcrosse Knight," *Studies in Philology* 86 [1989], 166–97) argue for Spenser's moderation on this issue.
7 Paul Alpers, "How to Read *The Faerie Queene*," in *Essential Articles for the Study of Edmund Spenser*, ed. A. C. Hamilton (Hamden, CT: Archon Books, 1972), 334–46; Susanne Wofford, *The Choice of Achilles: the Ideology of Figure in the Epic* (Stanford: Stanford University Press, 1992); Harry Berger, Jr., *Revisionary Play: Studies in the Spenserian Dynamics* (Berkeley: University of California Press, 1988).
8 Richard Mallette, *Spenser and the Discourses of Reformation England* (Omaha: University of Nebraska Press, 1997), 35; King, *Spenser's Poetry*, 213.

9 On the reader's double position, see Wofford, *The Choice of Achilles*, 234–62.

10 I adapt Berger: "the hero is our scapegoat: he errs, sins, suffers, is alienated from the world of common day *so that* we may interpret" (*Revisionary Play*, 61).

11 The variorum editors believe Spenser probably knew Caxton's translation, *The Golden Legend*, which was reprinted eleven times between 1483 and 1527 (*The Works of Edmund Spenser: a Variorum Edition*, ed. Edwin Greenlaw, Charles G. Osgood, and Frederick M. Padelford, Baltimore: Johns Hopkins University Press, 1932–49), vol. I, 385.

12 *The Golden Legend*, trans. William Caxton (London, 1483), Clviii.

13 *Ibid.*, Clvii (the etymology is speculative).

14 Eamon Duffy notes that the most popular saints' legends in the late fifteenth and early sixteenth centuries featured suffering and torture (*The Stripping of the Altars: Traditional Religion in England 1400–1580*, New Haven: Yale University Press, 1992, 170).

15 Reprinted in *The Works of Edmund Spenser: a Variorum Edition*, vol. I, 386–8; Spenser knew this or some very similar version.

16 *The Life of St. George*, ed. William Nelson, with parallel text of Mantuan (London: Oxford University Press, 1955), lines 19, 236.

17 *Ibid.*, line 2554; Margaret Aston notes that "long after the Reformation, fossilized references to St. George's prowess against idols remained embedded in the chivalric ferrago of his chapbook fame"; *Faith and Fire: Popular and Unpopular Religion 1350–1600* (London: Hambledon Press, 1993), 274.

18 McClendon, "A Moveable Feast: Saint George's Day Celebrations and Religious Change in Early Modern England," *Journal of British Studies* 38 (1999), 4; see also Jonathon Bengston, "Saint George and the Formation of English Nationalism," *Journal of Medieval and Early Modern Studies* 27 (1997), 317–40.

19 Wilkin, "Spenser's Rehabilitation of the Templars," *Spenser Studies* 11 (1994), 89–100.

20 The variorum editors record two pageants in honor of Edward IV; a similar pageant was included in Edward VI's coronation procession (389–90).

21 King, *Spenser's Poetry*, 193.

22 Paul Voss, "*The Faerie Queene* 1590–1596: the Case of Saint George," *Ben Jonson Journal* 3 (1996), 70; cf. Michael Leslie, *Spenser's "Fierce Warres and Faithfull Loves": Martial and Chivalric Symbolism in The Faerie Queene* (Totona, NJ: D. S. Brewer, 1983), 186–95.

23 E. K. Chambers, *The English Folk-Play* (New York: Russell & Russell, 1964), 6–9; Reginald Tiddy, *The Mummer's Play* (Folcroft: The Folcroft Press, Inc., 1969). Most print sources date from the eighteenth century; on mummers' plays, Peter Burke, *Popular Culture in Early Modern Europe* (New York: Harper & Row, 1978), 85, argues for a regressive scholarly method drawing upon existing sources and contemporary survivals.

24 *Certain Sermons or Homilies Appointed to be Read in Churches, in the time of Queen Elizabeth I, 1547–1571* (Gainesville: Scholars' Facsimilies and Reprints, 1968), 199.

25 *A Short Catechisme for Householders* (London, 1581), introduction.

26 Googe, *A new Booke called the Shippe of safegarde* (London, 1569), D5v; Thomas Naogeorgus, *The Popish Kingdome*, trans. B. Googe (London, 1570), 53v.

27 Burke, *Popular Culture*, 216; McClendon, "A Moveable Feast," 23.

28 Berger, *Revisionary Play*, 81.

29 On recursive reading in the *Faerie Queene*, see Evelyn Tribble, "The Open Text: a Protestant Poetics of Reading and Teaching Book I," in *Approaches to Teaching Spenser's Faerie Queene*, ed. David Lee Miller and Alexander Dunlop (New York: MLA, 1994), 58, and Darryl Gless, *Interpretation and Theology in Spenser* (Cambridge: Cambridge University Press, 1994), esp. chapter 2.

30 *The Faerie Queene*, ed. A. C. Hamilton, Hiroshi Yamashita, and Toshiyuki Suzuki (London: Longman, 2001).

31 Low, "Sin, Penance, and Privatization in the Renaissance: Redcrosse and the True Church," *Ben Jonson Journal* 5 (1998), 18.

32 These include Error, the dragon beneath Lucifera's feet, and the dragon-like beast Duessa rides in canto vii.

33 On Foxe's efforts to reconcile individual narratives with transhistorical structures, see D. R. Woolf, "The Rhetoric of Martyrdom: Generic Contradiction and Narrative Strategy in John Foxe's *Acts and Monuments*," in *The Rhetoric of Life-Writing in Early Modern Europe*, ed. Woolf and Thomas F. Mayer (Ann Arbor: University of Michigan Press, 1995), 243–82, and Thomas Betteridge, "Truth and History in Foxe's *Actes and Monuments*," in *John Foxe and His World*, ed. Christopher Highley and John N. King (Aldershot: Ashgate, 2002), 145–59.

34 *AM* (1583), 92. George is also included in Foxe's controversial "Kalendar."

35 Low, "Sin, Penance, and Privatization," 27.

36 *The First Commentary on The Faerie Queene*, 2.

37 Cf. Nohrnberg: "the episode of Error contains, *in ovo*, the whole theme of the emergence of a dragon-slayer" (*Analogy of The Faerie Queene*, 136).

38 Anthea Hume, *Edmund Spenser: Protestant Poet* (Cambridge: Cambridge University Press, 1984), 78; Lawrence F. Rhu, "Romancing the Word: Pre-Texts and Contexts for the Errour Episode," *Spenser Studies* 11 (1994), 101–9.

39 King, *Spenser's Poetry*, 199, 197. King notes that Redcrosse's strangling of Error is a "striking departure" from usual representations of St. George (190).

40 McEachern, " 'A whore at the first blush seemeth only a woman': John Bale's *Image of Both Churches* and the Terms of Religious Difference in the Early English Reformation," *Journal of Medieval and Renaissance Studies* 25 (1995), 250, 268.

41 See Hamilton's note on I.i.31 (*The Faerie Queene*, ed. Hamilton, *et al.*).

42 Compare Wofford, *The Choice of Achilles*, 284.

43 *AM* (1583), 294.

44 Cf. Cheney, "From Plowman to Knight: the Hero's Dual Identity," in *Spenser: a Collection of Critical Essays*, ed. Harry Berger, Jr. (Englewood Cliffs: Prentice-Hall, 1968), 85; Hamilton notes that Dante uses the griffon as a

symbol for Christ, but that it is also associated with guarding gold and thus with covetousness (note to I.v.8, *The Faerie Queene*, ed. Hamilton, *et al.*).

45 Wofford, *The Choice of Achilles*, 245.

46 On links between libidinal trespass and idolatry in this episode, see S. K. Heninger, *Touches of Sweet Harmony: Pythagorean Cosmology and Renaissance Poetics* (San Marino: San Marino Press, 1974) and Linda Gregerson, "Protestant Erotics: Idolatry and Interpretation in Spenser's *Faerie Queene*," *English Literary History*, 58 (1991), 1–34.

47 Cf. Nohrnberg, *Analogy of The Faerie Queene*, 225.

48 Berger, *Revisionary Play*, 52; Kaske (*Spenser and Biblical Poetics*, 44–8) discusses good and bad cups in Spenser's allegory, though she does not arrive at Berger's conclusion.

49 Hamilton suggests that Redcrosse is in some sense the child born to Charissa and identifies a reference to the baptismal service in x.34.7–9 (notes on x.34, *The Faerie Queene*, ed. Hamilton, *et al.*).

50 The allegory of Redcrosse's sufferings could also allude to the Marian persecution; this is how John Dixon read the episode (*First Commentary on The Faerie Queene*, 8–9).

51 For Kaske, the dragon fight's three-day structure reenacts a struggle for deliverance in "three states of human nature"; Redcrosse does not backslide but fulfills an allegory larger than any one character ("The Dragon's Spark and Sting and the Structure of Red Cross's Dragon-fight: *The Faerie Queene*, I.xi–xii," in *Essential Articles*, 446).

52 Scholarship on this poem includes Paul Voss, "The Catholic Presence in English Renaissance Literature," *The Ben Jonson Journal* 7 (2000), 1–26; Alison Shell, *Catholicism, Controversy, and the English Literary Imagination, 1558–1660* (Cambridge: Cambridge University Press, 1999), 133–7; and Jeffrey Knapp, *An Empire Nowhere: England, America, and Literature from "Utopia" to "The Tempest"* (Berkeley: University of California Press, 1992), 85–6.

53 Corser, *Collectanea Anglo-Poetica* (London: printed for the Chetham Society, 1869), 460; cf. Shell, *Catholicism*, 134. Though I quibble here, I have learned much from Shell's intelligent book. The editor of "Spenser Allusions" concludes that Copley's praise for Eliza is "purely a blind"; see "Spenser Allusions in the Sixteenth and Seventeenth Centuries," ed. William Wells, compiled by Ray Heffner, Dorothy E. Mason, and Frederick M. Padelford, *Studies in Philology* 68 (1971), 47.

54 See C. S. Lewis: "Doblessa, though equated in the 'Argument' with Fortune, obviously symbolizes the Protestant religion" (*English Literature in the Sixteenth Century, Excluding Drama*, Oxford: Clarendon, 1954, 464).

55 Compare Anne Dillon, *The Construction of Martyrdom in the English Catholic Community, 1535–1603* (Aldershot: Ashgate, 2002), chapter 2.

56 Christopher Devlin, *The Life of Robert Southwell, Poet and Martyr* (London: Longmans, 1956), 11, and Timothy J. McCann, " 'The Known Style of a Dedication is Flattery': Anthony Browne, 2nd. Viscount Montague of Cowdray and His Sussex Flatterers," *Recusant History* 19 (1989), 400.

Anthony Copley was Robert Southwell's first cousin and Robert Cecil's distant relative; Devlin hypothesizes that Southwell may have lived with the Copleys till they left the country (5, 11–13).

57 Strype, *Annals of the Reformation* (reprinted New York: Burt Franklin, 1968), vol. 4, 13.

58 *Ibid.*, 186. This remark appears in a report about Robert Southwell's arrest; despite Topcliffe's possible hyperbole (in hope of a greater reward), the record supports his assessment of Copley as a trouble-maker.

59 *Another Letter of Mr A. C. to his Dis-Jesuited Kinsman, Concerning the Appeale* (London, 1602), 57–8.

60 McCann, " 'The Known Style,' " 400.

61 This Anthony Browne is the grandson of the first Viscount Montague, also named Anthony Browne, who had a reputation for loyalism and staunch Catholicism (*DNB*).

62 *A Fig for Fortune*, The Spenser Society No. 35 (originally published 1883, reprint New York: Burt Franklin, 1967), 3; I cite this edition's page numbers.

63 McCann, " 'The Known Style,' " 399.

64 *Ibid* ., 398. Montague later suffered more indignities: he was imprisoned in 1604, 1605, and 1611 for various offenses, including suspected involvement in the Gunpowder Plot and refusal to take James's Oath of Allegiance (*Ibid.*, 398).

65 See Voss on the theological distinction Copley formulates here ("The Catholic Presence," 9).

66 Berger, *Revisionary Play*, 79.

67 Shell, *Catholicism*, 136.

68 Tamara Goeglein, "Utterances of the Protestant Soul in *The Faerie Queene*: the Allegory of Holiness and the Humanist Discourse of Reason," *Criticism* 36 (1994), 13.

69 King, *Spenser's Poetry*, 72.

70 See, e.g., O. Piper, "The Apocalypse of John and the Liturgy of the Ancient Church," *Church History* 20 (1951), 10–22.

71 See also glosses on Revelation 3–4 (the priest praying at the altar "is a figure" for the angel with incense) and on "Alleluia" in Revelation 19 (the Mass incorporates this word "to joyne with the Church triumphant, consisting of Angels and Saincts, who . . . laude and praise God . . . by this word Alleluia").

72 Voss ("The Catholic Presence") notes that Copley's argument is often misleading.

73 The Rheims gloss explains that "This is properly & principally spoken of the Church: and by allusion, of our B. Lady also" (commentary on Revelation 12).

74 Strype reprints a statement taken from Copley in the Tower dated only 1596. Since Strype uses old-style dates, one may infer that this interrogation took place after 23 March 1596, and thus after the poem had been entered into the Stationers' Register. No records of this interrogation survive in the *Calendar of State Papers* or in the *Acts of the Privy Council* for the years 1596 or 1597.

75 *Another Letter of Mr A. C.*, 58.

76  Strype, *Annals*, 385.

77  *An Answere to a Letter of a Jesuited Gentleman, by his Cosin, Maister A. C. Concerning the Appeale* (London, 1601) and *Another Letter of Mr. A. C.*

78  Mark Nicholls, "Treason's Reward: the Punishment of Conspirators in the Bye Plot of 1603," *The Historical Journal* 38 (1995), 821.

79  This priest was George Blackwell, the "Archpriest" against whose cause Copley wrote his Appellant pamphlets (Nicholls, "Treason's Reward," 831). Proclamations for Copley's arrest were issued in London and in the Low Countries, where Copley's suspicious activities were still remembered (STC 8323 and 8323.5). The information Copley provided led to the swift arrests of his co-conspirators (Nicholls, "Treason's Reward," 831).

80  The last surviving records of Copley place him in the English College at Rome in 1607 and as a pilgrim in Jerusalem in 1609 (McCann, " 'The Known Style,' " 401).

# CHAPTER 5

# When the truth hurts:
# suffering and the question of religious confidence

In the early modern period, as numerous martyrs knew all too well, the truth could really hurt. Their consolation came from the belief that suffering for truth could confer deep spiritual confidence. Protestant and Catholic authors shared the conviction, rooted in biblical precepts, that suffering identifies the true Christian. Their arguments about how suffering confirms religious identity differ only slightly, though those differences are significant. As I suggested above, Protestant martyrologists used martyrs' suffering to help readers dismiss the anxiety predestinarian beliefs might provoke and embrace confident assurance. The preacher and martyr George Marsh writes that "if we can finde in our hartes paciently to suffer persecutions and tribulations, it is a sure token... that we are counted worthy of the kingdom of God."[1] Catholic writers condemned the notion that one could be absolutely certain about salvation (the so-called doctrine of assurance) as presumptuous and heretical, usually stressing instead the virtues of perseverance.[2] In his *Epistle of Comfort*, the Jesuit Robert Southwell makes an argument similar to Marsh's with one important nuance: those who suffer for the Catholic faith should be comforted because "it is a very great signe that they are delivered out of [the devill's] power, & by him accounted for sheepe of Gods flocke... otherwise he would never so heavilye pursue them."[3] Given Catholic rejection of the doctrine of assurance, Marsh's "sure token" becomes Southwell's "very great signe." Yet some sixteenth-century Catholics, and in particular many Jesuits, argued that martyrdom could confer a special sort of merit, cleansing the martyr from sin and allowing the martyr's soul to bypass purgatory.[4] In this view, martyrs endured final *agon* as secure as they could be in their eternal destinies.

The religious poetry and prose of Robert Southwell and John Donne engage the various connections martyrologists forged between martyrs' sufferings and their inward confidence. These writers are two of the period's most important religious lyricists. Less recognized are their contributions to the literature of martyrdom: Southwell's *Epistle of Comfort* (London, 1587–8) and Donne's *Pseudo-Martyr* (London, 1610) are arguably the two most important English-language tracts in ongoing controversies over whether English Catholics' suffering was meritorious. This chapter argues for close connections between their prose and poetic work and, implicitly, for close connections between martyrological writing and the development of the seventeenth-century religious lyric. In their prose both writers explore the relationships between salvational confidence, suffering, and the criteria for true martyrdom, while the dynamics of suffering and reward which animated contemporary discussions of martyrdom also shape their poetic explorations of spiritual pain and consolation. Yet each takes a dramatically different approach to martyrological arguments about suffering's rewards. Southwell makes some of the period's boldest claims for martyrdom's power, insisting that the willingness to suffer for one's faith is the only sure foundation upon which to construct a stable, integrated self. Donne's pre-ordination prose questions common martyrological assumptions, arguments, and rhetoric. His poetry explores the psychological effects of the notion that suffering could confer religious confidence, while his sermons postulate alternative, spiritualized forms of agonistic struggle that both honor intense spiritual quests and confer the benefits of religious confidence without the actual shedding of blood.

As its primary focus, Southwell's apostolate of letters articulates Catholic concepts of religious certainty in suffering and often challenges competing discourses of suffering. Southwell wrote in the service of the Catholic mission to which he devoted his life and for which he suffered martyrdom. Born in England in 1561, Southwell went abroad for schooling in 1576. He entered the Society of Jesus in 1578 and continued his training on the Continent until 1586. In July 1586, Southwell returned to England to serve in the English mission. After six years of work during which he was one of the most sought-after Catholic priests, Southwell was betrayed by an acquaintance's sister to Richard Topcliffe, the notorious Elizabethan priest-catcher, and was arrested on 25 June, 1592. He spent three years in prison, endured numerous tortures, and was martyred on 21 February, 1595.[5] He has since been canonized. During his incarceration, Southwell was denied access to paper and pen, a fact that suggests his literary talents were known and feared.[6] Southwell's English prose and poetry were written during the six years he worked in England. His prose has received much less attention than his poetry, while scholarship on his poetry has largely focused on the extent to which it develops Counter-Reformation, baroque and/or Jesuit poetics.[7] But Southwell was also acutely aware of the religious controversies that, he believed, threatened to undermine religion itself: "the varietye of religions, hath abolished almost all religion, and the uncertaintye which emongest so many is truest, hath made the greatest parte of our contrey to believe none at all."[8] Southwell wrote primarily to strengthen the Catholic community's devotion and to encourage Catholics to risk persecution rather than conform. Remarkably consistent in its themes, Southwell's writing argues that the willingness to endure suffering and martyrdom may increase salvational confidence, yield a stable sense of self, and, in a corollary important to Southwell, inspire sound poetic practice.

In contrast, as Helen C. White famously remarked, John Donne was born with the chance to be a Catholic martyr and rejected it.[9] Donne's treatment of martyrdom in his poetry and prose seeks to justify and compensate for that rejected chance. His early prose tracts, including *Biathanatos, Pseudo-Martyr*, and *Ignatius His Conclave*, undermine the arguments for Catholic martyrdom that Jesuits like Southwell propagated and cast doubt upon claims that martyrdom for Catholic recusancy could confer salvational confidence.[10] In his religious lyrics and sermons, Donne continues questioning Catholic formulations of martyrdom. But rather than simply celebrating Protestant and/or Foxean versions of martyrdom instead, as many contemporaries did, Donne often posits alternative forms of interior, spiritualized suffering and argues that those forms of suffering may confer all of martyrdom's benefits, including religious confidence. In a compensatory but also deeply compassionate substitution, Donne imagines how those who reject the dubious opportunity to be a martyr must work through agonizing spiritual struggles. For Donne, these struggles are intensified by his complications of the stark oppositions between confident assurance, on the one hand, and indecisiveness, confusion, or outright hypocrisy on the other – the oppositions into which martyrs and martyrologists divided their worlds. Donne's persistent engagements with martyrdom undergird his reconciliation of his conformity to the Church of England with his family's sufferings for Catholicism. Southwell's and Donne's shared focus on the links martyrologists forged between suffering and religious confidence reveals how deeply controversies over martyrdom influenced those who would dramatize the throes of an often painful love relationship with the divine.

## "THAT SACRIFICE TO CHRISTE I MAY RETORNE": SOUTHWELL AND THE POETICS OF SUFFERING

Much current scholarship depicts Southwell as a relatively non-controversial Jesuit and stresses the pastoral aspects of his writing.[11] His plea for

Catholic toleration, *A Humble Supplication* (1591), and its publishing history support this depiction, as do his lyrics' evident concern for the spiritual health of those to whom he ministered.[12] Yet what Southwell considers pastoral is encouraging his flock to embrace the real possibility of suffering. This in turn inevitably leads him into controversial territory.[13] Further, Southwell contributed to Catholic propaganda about the English persecution. While at the English College in Rome, Southwell wrote letters, brochures, and newsletters reporting the behavior and final words of English Catholic martyrs; he continued writing such dispatches once in England.[14] In his English-language prose and poetry, Southwell extends this work on behalf of Catholic martyrdom, challenges Protestant martyrologies (sometimes overtly and sometimes subtly), and tackles theological discrepancies between the Calvinist-influenced Church of England and the Church of Rome on the issue of assurance as he seeks to reunite common rhetorics of martyrdom with Catholic doctrines and practices.

Applying his training to the dire English situation, Southwell's earliest published piece is an encouragement to martyrdom. Addressed to both priests and laity, *An Epistle of Comfort* (London, 1587–8) continues the training priests received for the English mission and extends that preparation for suffering and martyrdom to lay people.[15] Southwell thus imported not only the Jesuit poetics and tears-literature with which he is readily credited but also the arguments on behalf of martyrdom central to continental seminary training.[16] The tract is both consolatory, as its title suggests, and controversial. Consolation and controversy are not mutually exclusive in the period but instead often reinforce each other, for what many considered consoling was the belief that one adheres to and is willing to suffer for a righteous cause. The tract mounts four principal arguments about suffering: suffering provides assurance of Christian identity; suffering is an imitation of Christ; martyrdom provides passage to security in heaven; and martyrdom confers a supreme sort of merit. These arguments seem designed both to comfort Southwell's readers and to respond to competing forms of consolation and comfort offered in Foxe's *Actes and Monuments*. Southwell's reiteration of encouragements to suffering and martyrdom across his canon suggests that the complex English religious situation, including the ongoing Catholic persecution and the competing set of martyrs Foxe celebrated, influenced his thinking and poetics as deeply as continental aesthetic theories.[17]

The assumption that suffering confirms Christian identity recurs throughout his work. In his *Exercitia Devotiones*, a private journal kept during his studies, Southwell wrote: "I am to think it an especial mark of

God's favour to me if I am burdened with perpetual afflictions and wearied with constant difficulties, especially as in this manner alone may I become like unto Christ."[18] In *An Epistle of Comfort*, Southwell advances the common martyrological (and, ultimately, biblical) precept that suffering yields Christian self-identification: "the Devill [is] permitted to tempt thee . . . for thy benefite, that thou mayest be exercised, proved, and come to knowledge of thy selfe that knewest not thy selfe before."[19] While Catholics may not presume upon their election as Protestants do, suffering's benefit lies in this self-knowledge. In his treatise on ordering lay Catholics' domestic lives, *Short Rule for a Good Life*, Southwell reiterates this leitmotif: "For whom [God] loveth, he chastiseth, and prooveth like golde in the fornace."[20] Southwell reclaims what one scholar has identified as a recurrent metaphor in Foxe's *Actes and Monuments*; despite its ubiquity in Foxe's text, the image of refining metal is not particularly Protestant, any more than is the process of coming to know oneself through the crucible.[21] Advertising this principle of suffering as self-identification, the *Epistle*'s title page cites Matthew 11:12: "Regnum coelorum vim patitur, et violenti rapiunt illud; the kingdom of God suffereth violence, and the violent bear it awaye." Southwell always glosses this violence "in a favorable allegorizing sense," stressing the construction of the self *in* and through suffering, not the unmaking of the self amid excruciating pain, as Elaine Scarry has theorized.[22] Using rhetoric common in martyrological writing and prominent in Catholic poems on suffering, Southwell condenses martyrdom and militarism to argue that violence confirms one's Christian identity: "we are Christians, whose captayne is a crucifixe, whose standard the Crosse, whose armoure patience, whose battayle persecution, whose victorye death, whose triumphe martirdome."[23]

The sufferer becomes a *militans Christi* and also enacts a powerful *imitatio Christi*. The question of agency is crucial. One chooses to imitate Christ; suffering is the essence of that imitation. Significantly for Southwell's poetics, the imitation of Christ through suffering is characterized in anti-representational terms:

so muche therefore as immitation in deede, is better then representation in the figure, and desyre in the thoughte: So muche doth the baptisme of blood, surpasse those of water and spirite . . . how perfectly therfore doth Martyrs resemble theyr Captayne, seeinge these figures and types, that foreshewed him, maye also be aptly applyed unto them?[24]

The martyrs' literal suffering, their "imitation in deed," surpasses "representation in the figure"; suffering assimilates martyr-soldiers to their captain so fully that they become typological fulfillments alongside him, enacting, in flesh and blood, sacramental figurations. Characterizing a willingness to suffer as the appropriate response to Christ's sacrifice, Southwell's tract is designed to move its reader through self-identification to action and imitation "in deed." Yet Southwell also asserts that suffering results from inadequate responses, a paradox he characterizes in the language of love lyric. Southwell sensuously describes Christ's passion:

like a most faythfull paramour of our soule, hanging in moste rufull maner naked, wounded, and redye to dye upon the Crosse, he hath often sent us embassyes of love, sayinge *Dicite dilecto meo, quia amore langueo.* Tell my beloved, that I languishe for love.[25]

Like the stereotypical sonneteer Christ suffers from unrequited love, his disdainful mistress the unresponsive Christian. Indifference to his suffering produces ours: "seing that he can not move us with so manye griefes susteyned in our behalfe, he obscureth the sonne of our comfortes, he sendeth earthquakes of tribulations, he maketh the graves open, and setteth death before our eyes, to wynne in a maner by force, sith by love he coulde not."[26] Christ has, it seems, resources unavailable to scorned poets. The consolation for this violent wooing is further imitation of Christ: "As we are fellowes of his passions, so shall we be of his comforte, and if with him we dye, with him shall we live, and if we suffer his Crosse, we shall be partners of his Crowne."[27]

The importance of imitation "in deed" means that church-papists' appearance of conformity tempts damnation. In caustic direct address, Southwell attacks the reasoning of conforming Catholics: "to saye that goinge to churche at suche tymes as theyre service and sacramentes are mynistred, theyre doctrine preached, or the rites of theyre secte practised, is not a spiritual, but a civile action, is against all sense and reason . . . it is the verye principall signe of spirituall dutye, to be presente at suche thinges, wherby religion is chiefelye professed."[28] Even Protestants like Calvin, Melancthon, and Peter Martyr – heretics, in Southwell's view – castigate outward, hypocritical conformity and link the proclamation of Christian truth to suffering; those who conform to avoid violence risk condemnation by Catholics and heretics alike. Attending Protestant services is a "scandal," for it weakens others' faith: "the pastors, yea al Catholikes of this time [are] bound to endure the pinchinge and freesinge colde of what adversitye soever, yea and the hazardes of cruel persecutors . . . rather then to suffer . . . Christes flocke ether to be scandalized by our example, or destitute of our necessarye endevours."[29] Southwell's long poem "St. Peter's

Complaint" dilates on scandalous conformity: after denying Christ, Peter describes himself not as *petra*, the rock upon which the church is founded (in Matthew 16:18), but "the rock of scandal" (708) whose resolution was destroyed by "fear of woman's breath" (316), a line in which Brown finds a glance at Elizabeth I. "St. Peter's Complaint" turns Peter from "the rock of scandal" to a model of contrition and reconciliation to the true church (thus enacting what the *Epistle* is designed to do) so as to avoid the "scandal" of misleading and endangering souls through apparent conformity to a heretical church.[30]

Southwell also worries that the searing clarity the imitation of Christ, even to death, should provide could be clouded by competing martyrs and witnesses. The Genevan exiles who fled Marian England haunt Southwell's *Humble Supplication*, for instance, as he repeatedly likens the situation of Catholics abroad to that of those Protestant exiles but distinguishes Catholics' willingness to suffer from their flight to live in relative comfort.[31] In the *Epistle of Comfort*, Southwell states that he will discuss twelve sources of comfort in tribulation in each of twelve chapters but must add to this neat plan three chapters dealing with schismatics, persecutors, and those who died for heresy. Southwell clearly knew Foxe's *Actes and Monuments*; he alludes to John Bradford's and John Hullier's letters and insists that "though it hath bene the propertye of heretickes, to vaunte of suche as dyed for theyr religion, and to terme them martyrs . . . Yet . . . it hathe always appeared, that as theyr doctrine was heresye, so theyre death desperation."[32] His rhetoric suggests that he has Foxean martyrs in mind: those who "walke in the fruitlesse fielde of heresye" mistakenly glean from "the heate of their just persecution and thirst of comforte in theyre punishmentes . . . a vayne presumption of future joyes: yett in trueth all their hope is like a paynted fountayne, that rather increseth, then diminisheth their payne."[33] The punishments' "heate" alludes to heretics' burnings, as does Southwell's amplification of I Corinthians 13:3: "though I deliver my bodye to be burned, and have no charitye and union with God, and his true church: it avayleth me no thinge."[34] Southwell's expansion of the verse – "and union with God, and his true church" – shows the necessity of arguing that martyrdom's glory should be linked only with the Catholic Church:

Nether can any say that it is not our Church, but theirs that was thus persecuted. For there is no tirannical persecution, but hath always bene most violentlye bent, against the sea of *Rome*, and agaynst the *Pope* and his followers . . . if we reede all antiquitye, we shall not fynde one, that hath suffered for anye parte of our adversaryes religion, but onlye such, as are by all auncient authors registred for damnable heretickes.[35]

Competing martyr-accounts mean that Southwell's portrayal of suffering's rewards is, of necessity, agonistic.

That agonistic edge is further sharpened as Southwell articulates the advantages Catholic martyrdom could confer against the similar claims others advanced for Protestant martyrdom. Specifically, Southwell attacks predestination and its corollaries: that the human will is not free and that the elect enjoy assurance. Indeed, predestination and assurance are the only theological issues discussed at any length in the *Epistle*, which implies that the links between Foxe's martyrs and these doctrines, for which I argued in chapter 1, were recognized by contemporary Catholic writers. As Southwell is well aware, the doctrine of assurance is the main form of comfort with which he must compete:

> he that beleeveth the commaundements of God to be impossible for man to keepe, and withall that howsoever he breake them, it nether can nor ought to make him doubt of his election, which dependeth only upon gods predestination, why should he not thincke it follye to endevoure to observe Gods lawe being an impossibillitye: yea and uppon certaintye of his salvation, become carelesse to breake anye commandement.[36]

In contrast to a "certaintye" derived from predestined election, Southwell proclaims martyrdom as the only means of attaining certainty:

> [The] soule... is not only exiled from her native countrye, like a caytive, fettered in a most filthye dungeon, like a forlorne & left widow deprived of her spouses felowshipp, & in most lamentable sort debarred from her kingdome: but is so perilouslye besett... that it standeth in continuall hazarde, to encrease her presente miserye, with an eternall losse... O harde and heavye daunger, that receyveth no security, whose easiest and only remedy, is the severinge of soule and bodye asunder. Thryse happye are the Martirs, whose bloodye agonyes, purchase assurance of happines, and acquite them from all perill of ensewing tormentes.[37]

In a figure resonant with the pains English Catholics endured – imprisonment, exile, hazardous temptations towards conformity – Southwell emphasizes that while the soul remains imprisoned in the body, so does the possibility for sin. In the chapter in which this passage appears, Southwell dwells on life's miseries; the sentence on martyrs' joy is the sole hopeful note. Only martyrs "purchase assurance of happiness"; martyrdom is "a sure waye to an unspeakable glorye."[38] The contrast between life's uncertainty and martyrdom's rewards also figures prominently in *Triumphs over Death* (London, 1595), and in his *Humble Supplication* Southwell extols martyrdom's benefits even as he pleads for toleration: "We come to shedd our owne, not to seeke the effusion of others bloud... we rather hope to make our owne Martyrdomes our steppes to

a glorious eternity, then others deaths our purchase of eternall dishonour."[39] This insistence that martyrdom ushers in a glorious eternity
explains Southwell's elevation of martyrdom over baptism in certain
respects. In the *Epistle* he elaborates Augustine's assertion that "In the
Martyr all his sinnes are quite extinguished":

> though baptisme perfectlye clense the soule, and release not onlye the offence, but
> also the temporal punishment due unto the same: Yet sticketh the roote of sinn in
> the flesh, & the partye baptysed retayneth in him, the badge and cognizance . . . of
> a sinner. But Martirdomes vertue is such, that it not onlye worketh the same
> effecte of baptisme, but purchaseth also to the soule, forth with a perfect riddance
> of all concupiscence and inclynation to sinne, and maketh it not only without
> offence, but unable to offende anye more.[40]

Martyrdom releases the soul from the world, rewards the martyr's perseverance, and cleanses the soul of sinfulness. For Southwell, it is the
Catholic's best, indeed his/her only, secure repose.

Southwell's prose encouragement to suffering profoundly shapes his
poetics: in his poetry, Southwell uses arguments first published in *Epistle of
Comfort* to advocate a didactic poetics of suffering that promotes religious
over secular lyric. Southwell stresses repeatedly the world's uncertainty and
instability; only a devotion which embraces the possibility of suffering can
provide the stable self-integration his speakers seek. For Southwell, an undue
attachment to worldly things produces the shifting instability of the stereotypical Petrarchan speaker. Representation in deed is preferred to representation in the figure: Southwell's poetry strives to inspire the former by
disparaging mere figures of suffering in contemporary secular verse, so that
his lyrics often push figurative suffering towards the literal. To the extent that
Southwell's poetics proved influential for the subsequent vogue in religious
poetry, martyrdom and its confirming function are also foundational for the
early modern religious lyric. By the 1590s, Southwell was not the only
advocate of religious verse: in *La Muse Chretienne* du Bartas argued for
poetry inspired by a Christian muse, and the sonnets of Anne Lock (1560)
and Henry Lock (1593) showcase religious poetry's possibilities. Shell has
demonstrated, however, that du Bartas's London publications, at least
initially, grew alongside Southwell's.[41] The Locks' sonnets may point to a
Protestant genealogy for religious poetry. But Southwell outsold them:
judging by the number of editions published, Southwell's connection of
suffering to poetic reform clearly caught English readers' attention, a connection made powerful and infamous by his own martyrdom. Janel Mueller
has recently argued that the role suffering plays in identity formation in the
*Actes and Monuments* shaped Herbert's and Donne's religious poetry. Yet

Southwell is a crucial intermediate step: while Donne and Herbert may draw on Foxean discursive formations, it is Southwell who connects a willingness to suffer with poetic reform and whose work demanded a poetic response, sometimes complementary and sometimes agonistic, from later writers.[42]

Southwell's sacred parodies of love lyric have attracted attention as exemplars of Jesuit literary theories about adapting classical and secular forms to religious ends.[43] In his prose dedication "The Author to his loving Cosen" Southwell accuses poets of "abusing their talent, and making the follies and fayninges of love, the customary subject of their base endevours." Religious adaptations of love lyric can remedy the situation: "because the best course to let them see the errour of their workes, is to weave a new webbe in their owne loome; I have here layd a few course threds together, to invite some skillfuller wits to goe forward in the same . . . wherein it may be seene, how well verse and vertue sute together."[44] What has not been sufficiently recognized is that Southwell's sacred parody owes something to religious controversy as well as Jesuit literary theory. By extending Jesuit theory to the current suffering wars, Southwell contributes to and extends the practice of Catholic martyrologists who conflated Catholicism's enemies with hyperbolic, misleading literary efforts. In his *A Briefe Historie* William Allen refers to Campion's execution as a tragedy badly staged by the English government, while a prefatory poem to *The Life and Death of Mr. Edmund Geninges* contrasts the true matter in that book with feigned poetic matter like "King Leire."[45] Similarly, in *An Epistle of Comfort* Southwell contrasts literary sign-making with Catholic truth: "the articles of your fayth are no fables: the wordes and contentes of the Scripture, no Poets fictions."[46] Southwell's lyric voices sharply distinguish those willing to suffer for truth from feigning, lying poets by developing connections between truth and martyrdom drawn in martyrological writing. Significantly for the later vogue in religious poetry, Southwell uses martyrdom's authority to challenge contemporary poetic practice and, by implication, all false forms of suffering. Protestant attempts at justifying religious verse prior to the first publication of Southwell's work (probably in March 1595, just after his execution) do not take this approach, which must have been all the more sensational after Southwell's own martyrdom. If so, then debates about whether native or continental influences were most important for the development of English devotional poetry need to be reconsidered in light of the influence of martyrological controversies.[47] As Southwell's case demonstrates, those controversies both marshal continental imaginative resources and gain most pointed relevance in their English context.

The appeal of suffering as a way to ascertain Christian identity, imitate Christ, attain religious confidence and certainty, and, not coincidentally, rejuvenate hackneyed figures of suffering was significant: Southwell's poetry gained a wide, cross-confessional audience. Southwell's lyrics circulated in manuscript and printed collections. The most authoritative manuscript collections preserve 52 lyrics in much the same order, suggesting that Southwell may have arranged his poems in that way. His earliest publishers do not follow the order preserved by the manuscript copyists, probably because those publishers worked from inferior manuscripts. In the manuscript collections, the sequence on Mary's life and Christ's childhood comes first, followed by poems on the Nativity and Passion, a poem on "Joseph's Amazement," a pair on the sacraments, a remorse group, and poems of moral instruction, the largest group in the collections.[48] While a lyric "I" appears only once in the sequence on Mary and Christ, the "I" recurs more insistently in the groups of poems that follow, so that those poems often model responses to Southwell's intensely imagined depictions of key moments from Christ's life. In the authoritative manuscripts, the poems after those on the sacraments move roughly from remorse for sin to a resolve to turn away from worldly pleasures, most notably earthly love, and to suffer pain for otherworldly rewards. This general progression suggests a didactic purpose similar to that of the *Epistle of Comfort*: Southwell encourages the reader towards repentance, firm recusancy (not scandalous conformity), and a willingness to suffer. Yet his work clearly also appealed beyond Catholic communities. Although the printed editions do not preserve the manuscript collections' order, they show a fascination with the last group of poems in those collections: in the first edition of *Saint Peters Complaint,* eight of its twelve short lyrics come from the end of the manuscript collection, as do all eight lyrics added to the second edition. In *Moeniae* – the second collection of Southwell's work to be published in 1595 – two of the remaining four poems from the end of the sequence were published (the exceptions are "Decease release" and "I dye without desert," both politically sensitive). Partly a result of the manuscripts from which the publishers were working, this publishing record also suggests a particular interest on the part of some copyists and the London book trade in those poems focusing on the misleading nature of devotion to love and the self-integration that a willingness to suffer for higher causes could induce.

The first poem in the manuscript collections' largest, last group of poems, "Marie Magdalens complaint at Christs death," establishes the themes of those to follow: love is properly focused beyond this world

("I live not where I love"). The second poem, "Decease release," concerns Mary Stuart and was not published in the early editions given its inflammatory political implications.[49] Nevertheless, the poem suggests the religio-political context in which this group on moral instruction could have been understood by manuscript collection readers. The printed editions lack this context, making subsequent encouragements to suffering more generic. In "Decease release," the speaker stresses the triumph her tormenters unwittingly granted her: "Alive a Queene, now dead I am a Sainte, / Once N: calld, my name nowe Martyr is, / From earthly raigne debarred by restraint, / In liew whereof I raigne in heavenly blisse" (13–16). Clearly, given the meter and alliteration with "Martyr," Mary is the name to be read for "N." Mary contrasts her reign as a saint triumphant in heaven with an earthly reign to which, the poem implies, she was nevertheless entitled. The poem bolsters this image of a rightful queen not only restored but infinitely glorified with reference to a theology of suffering under which Mary's death hastens and ensures her eternal reward. "My speedy death hath shortned longe annoye, / And losse of life an endles life assur'd" (19–20). The closing stanza triumphantly asserts her advancement through martyrdom: "By death from prisoner to a prince enhaunc'd, / From Crosse to Crowne, from thrall to throne againe, / My ruth my right, my trapp my stile advaunc'd, / From woe to weale, from hell to heavenly raigne" (33–6).

Southwell's lyrics also invoke martyrdom more subtly as they develop ideas taken from the *Epistle*. Many poems imagine self-identification agonistically, drawing contrasts between Petrarchan uncertainties and the certainty of heavenly repose, between suffering for earthly love and for eternal truth. The opening stanza of "What joy to live?", a poem based on Petrarch's *Rime* 134, invokes lyric commonplaces:

> I wage no warre yet peace I none enjoy,
> I hope, I feare, I frye, in freesing cold:
> I mount in mirth still prostrate in annoy,
> I all the world embrace yet nothing holde.
> All wealth is want where cheefest wishes faile,
> Yea life is loath'd, where love may not prevaile.   (1–6)

The second stanza declares its independence from poetic fads: "for that I love I long, but that I lacke…They loving where they live, long life require, / To live where best I love, death I desire" (7–8, 11–12). The poem contrasts martyrdom with the supposed deaths incurred by ladies' disdain: "O who would live so many deathes to trye?" (25). The ending moves to direct admonition: "pleasures upshot is to die accurst" (30). The poem extends to poetics a key argument of the *Epistle*: the claim that enjoying "all sortes of delighte" is "a token of a reprobate soule."[50] Conversely, other lyrics assert that suffering reveals that one is beloved of God. In "I dye without desert," unpublished in the early editions, the speaker suffers in a world where "The badd are blissd, god murdred in the good" (24). Later lines echo the *Epistle*'s assertion that suffering may be a sign of God's favor: "But let my fall though ruefull none offend. / God doth sometymes first cropp the sweetest floure, / And leaves the weede till tyme do it devoure" (34–6).

Several poems reframe the *Epistle*'s arguments about the imitation of Christ in intensely subjective ways. "Christs bloody sweat," first published in *Moeniae*, carefully works through the image of Christ's suffering in the Garden of Gethsemane to a self-sacrificing response. In doing so, it revisits imagery the *Epistle* used to explain suffering: "Let every one, that commeth to the service of God perswade him selfe, that he is come lyke a grape to the winepresse, he shal-be crushed, squeysed, and presed, not so much to procure his death, to the worlde, as his reservation in gods seller."[51] Southwell's poem uses similar imagery but portrays Christ's sweatdrops of blood as falling like an overripe harvest that releases its bounty without force: "Fat soile, full spring, sweete olive, grape of blisse, / That yeelds, that streams, that pours, that dost distil, / Untild, undrawne, unstampt, untoucht of presse" (1–3). Christ's *voluntary* shedding of sweatdrops of blood ("at will") is reciprocated by the speaker's willingness to sacrifice himself in return. In the poem's final stanzas the speaker invokes the fire Elijah called down to consume a sacrificial offering (in 1 Kings 18), a fire that consumed not only the offering but the wood and stones upon which it lay and the water Elijah poured on top of it. The speaker wishes to become the stone and wood Elijah's fire consumed so that he might repay Christ's sacrifice:

> O sacred Fire come shewe thy force on me
> That sacrifice to Christe I maye retorne,
> If withered wood for fuell fittest bee,
> If stones and dust, yf fleshe and blood will burne,
> I withered am and stonye to all good,
> A sacke of dust, a masse of fleshe and bloode.　　(19–24)

Southwell's poem dramatizes a paradox outlined in the *Epistle*: Christians repay Christ's pain through self-sacrifice ("That sacrifice to Christe I maye retorne") while also recognizing their suffering as just punishment ("stonye to all good").[52]

The idea of giving up life as repayment for Christ's love recurs in other poems; "Lifes death loves life," for instance, urges "Let us in life, yea with our life, / Requite his living love: / For best we live when least we live, / If love our life remove." As in "Lifes death loves life," Southwell's speakers typically locate stability only in the heavenly future that death could secure. Poems such as "Fortunes Falsehood," "Look home" and "At home in heaven" aim to reorganize readers' priorities along these lines. "I die alive" depicts the suffering of one who longs to die: "My feast is done, my soule would be at ease, / My grace is said, O death come take away" (3–4). The speaker closes with a dual vision of an otherworldly future and the worldly dangers which could soon usher in that future: "Not where I breath, but where I love I live, / Not where I love, but where I am I die: / The life I wish, must future glory give, / The deathes I feele, in present dangers lie" (13–16). The speaker has already relocated his true life to heaven, embracing, even daring to hope for, martyrdom's glory; "present dangers" would have resonated richly for Elizabethan Catholics.

At times the poetry's connections to the martyrological controversies become more direct. The title of "Life is but Losse" may allude to Henry Walpole's poem on Edmund Campion, "Why do I use my paper, inke, and pen," in which Campion's death proves "that life is but losse" (1. 171).[53] Southwell's "Life is but Losse" reaches a note of triumph at the end through turning to martyr-like resolve. Because life is full of uncertainty, the speaker longs for death: "Alas thou doest me wrong, / To let me live more anger to provoke: / Thy right is had, when thou hast stopt my breath, / Why shouldst thou stay, to worke my double death?" (21–4). Because the speaker seeks certainty, stasis, and freedom from sin, death is not something to be feared but a delaying tyrant. The fifth stanza briefly considers suicide but notes that it is unlawful and therefore not an appropriate way to circumvent death's tyrannous prolonging of life.[54] The poem then breaks suddenly to a final consolation:

> Avaunt O viper, I thy spight defie,
> There is a God that over-rules thy force,
> Who can thy weapons to his will apply,
> And shorten or prolong our brittle course:
> I on his mercie, not thy might relye,
> To him I live, for him I hope to dye.    (37–42)

God uses death but as a tool; divine mercy may, in its own time, turn a wished-for death into a means for God's glory. The reliance on mercy and the wish to die for God free the speaker from his fear of missteps before death, moving "Life is but Losse" out of its opening paradoxes towards bold confidence. The ways in which the poems from the final manuscript group encourage readers to embrace a paradoxically life-giving suffering resonate with arguments found in the *Epistle of Comfort*. The popularity of Southwell's poetry, which develops arguments found in his prose tracts encouraging Catholics to find comfort in suffering, suggests that the subsequent vogue for devotional poetry owes something to the emphases of martyrological writing.

In his final work, a letter penned to Cecil on the one occasion during his long imprisonment on which he was given writing materials, Southwell pleads for his life while reaffirming his belief in martyrdom as the "worthiest price of eternity."[55] Importantly, the issue of certainty was precisely the theological issue with which Southwell was confronted at his execution. Just before he ascended the scaffold, the Tower's chaplain taunted him with Catholicism's rejection of the doctrine of assurance: "You hould the decrees of the Council of Trent . . . Therein . . . is decreed that no man shall presume to beleeve that he is sure to be saved, but is to doubt. If you believe to be saved, you contradicte the councell; if you doubt (being to die) your case is hard; and you doubting, we must needs doubt." Southwell met this final test by returning to the only basis for certainty his writing ever proposed: "I humbly desire almightie God that it would please his goodnes, to take and excepte this my death, the laste farewell to this miserable and infortunate lyfe (althoughe in this moste happy and fortunate) in full satisfaction for all my sinnes and offences, and for the Comfort of many others; which [death] albeit that it seeme here disgracefull, yet I hope that in tyme to come it will be to my eternall glory."[56] Southwell's dying words reaffirm the argument his work and life articulated in the face of Protestant theological and martyrological challenges: his hope and trust in martyrdom's cleansing, comforting, redemptive power.

## "TO SOME / NOT TO BE MARTYRS, IS A MARTYRDOM": DONNE AND LIVING MARTYRDOM

Like Southwell's, Donne's engagement with the subject of martyrdom is prolonged, encompassing his early prose tracts, devotional poetry, and sermons. Donne's self-proclaimed religious moderation (or desire for it) almost demands that he modulate contemporary enthusiasms for martyrdom;[57] yet martyrdom still occupies a central place in his thought and writing. Donne's persistent engagements with the subject challenge conventional arguments about the various forms of certainty martyrdom could confer and instead formulate new ways to reap martyrdom's spiritual benefits without suffering literal, physical martyrdom. In his pre-ordination prose, Donne characterizes martyrdom in less exalted terms than those his contemporaries typically used. Donne fiercely attacks Jesuit ideas about martyrdom, exhibits subtle misgivings about Protestant constructions and uses of martyrdom, and claims that martyrdom draws as much on human weakness as divine inspiration. Donne consistently evinces some defensiveness on the topic, as might be expected. Brad Gregory argues that "conversion presupposed rejecting... the martyrological tradition... of one's present Christian community for the sake of a different one."[58] John Donne's eventual conformity to the Church of England seemingly rejects his own family's history of recusancy, suffering, and martyrdom. Still, his decision to avoid literal suffering need not be seen as that of an apostate or blasphemer, but rather of one who decided to survive the English persecution in other ways.[59] Nor should his reconceptualization of martyrdom be read simply as motivated by socio-political concerns, though they certainly come into play.[60] Instead, Donne's revisioning of martyrdom across time, genres, and various contexts represents a careful, intellectually rigorous attempt to formulate a moderate response to the powerful contemporary martyr-complex linking suffering with religious confidence.

In a trio of tracts written between 1607 and 1611 (*Biathanatos, Pseudo-Martyr,* and *Ignatius His Conclave*), Donne denounces Jesuit ideas about martyrdom, demystifies martyrdom somewhat, and distances honorable martyrdom from contemporary religious controversies. The first of these tracts, *Biathanatos,* purports to be a limited defense of suicide. Scholars have debated whether this provocative tract, which remained unpublished during Donne's lifetime, is in earnest. Slights, Hughes, and Webber privilege its satirical elements.[61] Indeed, it is hard to take straightforwardly a tract which likens the enlightenment it wishes to inspire to the fall: "as the Eyes of Eve were opened by the tast of the Apple, though it be sayd before that she saw the beauty of the tree, so the digesting of this, may, thoughe not present faire objects, yet bring them to see the nakednesse and deformity of theyr owne reasons, founded upon a rigorous suspicion."[62] Conversely, Brown and Sullivan read *Biathanatos* as a serious casuistical exercise in defense of suicide, and once published in 1647 it was taken seriously by several contemporaries.[63] *Biathanatos* argues overtly for a charitable approach to suicide, pleading that each case of suicide should be examined individually, not simply condemned out of hand. In this way the tract seems an instance of case divinity as Brown claims. But an additional ironic purpose becomes clear in its approach to martyrdom. Taking martyrdom as a primary instance of suicide, Donne naturalizes and demystifies martyrdom. Simultaneously, he limits acceptable suicide to cases in which "the Honor of God may be promov'd by that way, and no other."[64] The tract Donne twice terms a "paradox" argues that martyrdom is a form of suicide, and that suicide is only acceptable in cases of true martyrdom. This elaborate casuistical treatise implies that if martyrdom is suicide and if suicide ought to be strictly limited, then martyrdom cannot be widely encouraged. In this sense the tract performs crucial intellectual, even iconoclastic, work for Donne, setting up the more straightforward argument in *Pseudo-Martyr* that some Catholics construe and encourage martyrdom far too widely. The tract's treatment of martyrdom helps explain its odd combination of elaborate scholarly apparatus and seeming earnestness with sometimes questionable logic: the tract functions at least in part as an ironic rebuttal of Jesuit promotions of martyrdom, wrestling with the ghosts of those with whom Donne had his "first breeding... Men of a suppressd and afflicted Religion, accustomed to the despite of death, and hungry of an imagin'd Martyrdome."[65]

Donne uses martyrdom as the third major support for his argument that suicide is not against nature. Donne claims that Christianity collapsed earlier motivations for suicide into a desire for martyrdom and concludes that suicidal impulses stem from human nature, not divine inspiration.[66] The historical argument soon turns, however, towards limiting martyrdom's reach and thus the natural inclination towards suicide Donne claims to defend. Because early Christians showed great desire for death, heretics too sought martyrdom's power. Martyrdoms motivated variously by "the true spirit of God," "the spirit of contention," and "naturall infirmities" meant that the church gradually curbed this desire:

Thus when the true spirit of God drew many, the spirit of contention many, and other naturall infirmities more, to expose themselves easely to death... the Authors of these later ages have somewhat remitted the intensnes of Martyrdome, and mingled more allay, or rather more Mettall, and not made it of so great valew alone, as those earnest tymes did, for since S. Thomas sayd That though Martyrdome be a Worke of greatest perfection, yet it is not of it selfe, but as it is wrought by Charity, and... it is not, says he, a sacrifice, nor worke of Religion, but of fortitude, which is but a morall vertue. Therefore it is now taught That it is a mortall sinne, to provoke another to inflict Martyrdome. And a Martyr (though Martyrdome purge much) is bound to clense himselfe by every one of the degrees of penance; for sayth Carbo It is not *Sacramentum*, but *Opus privilegiatum*. So they seeme tender, and loth by addition of religious incitements, to cherish or further that desire of dying, to which, by reason of our Weaknesse, and this worlds encombrances, our Nature is too propense and inclined. Only the Jesuites boast of theyr hunting out of Martyrdome in the new worlds and of theyr rage till they finde it... so that if this desire of dying be not agreeable to the Nature of man, but against it, yet it seemes, that it is not against the Nature of a Jesuite.[67]

The discussion begins to turn upon itself, undermining Donne's purported contention that suicide may sometimes be defensible because martyrdom is an acceptable form of suicide. Instead Donne explicitly challenges the view, attributed to Jesuits, that martyrdom functions as a sacrament does, *ex opera operato*, and that martyrdom purges sins. The tract's irony emerges in his jab at Jesuits so eager for martyrdom that they are in fact too eager for suicide.

Similar ironies appear in Donne's citations of supposedly authoritative texts. Donne invokes, with seeming earnestness, Catholic sources celebrating extreme self-abnegation, the same sources that in *Pseudo-Martyr* he mocks mercilessly. In *Biathanatos* Donne cites an anecdote of extreme self-denial: "a holy old man, seeing his servant mistake poyson for hony, and put it into his broth, eat it neverthelesse, without chiding: and when the servant perceiv'd it, and exclaim'd, Sir I have killd you, answer'd, It is all one, for if God would have had me eat hony, he would have directed thy hand to hony."[68] In *Pseudo-Martyr*, however, Donne cites the same source to condemn the near self-murder of this "holy old man":

who would have consented to the Christian buriall of that Monke, which Dorotheus speakes of, if he had died of that Poison, which hee saw his Servant mistake for Honie, and put it into his Brothe, and never reprehended him, before nor after he had eaten the Soppes: But when his Servant apprehended it, and was much mooved, the master pacified him with this, If God would have had me eate Honie, either thou shouldest have taken the Honie, or hee would have changed the Poison into Honie.[69]

The recurrence of the anecdote in *Pseudo-Martyr* creates suspicion that its purpose in *Biathanatos* is less to uphold the extreme self-denial of this "holy old man" than to illustrate that some forms of supposedly holy death and self-resignation are too much like suicides.

Donne purports to defend suicide through limiting it to circumstances in which no other action may promote God's glory. Yet those circumstances seem stricter than those upheld by many of the Catholic authorities he cites. Indeed, several discussions of suicides canonized as martyrs undermine their canonization as much as defend their deaths. Donne questions authorities who justify the martyr Apollonia by attributing to divine inspiration her running into the fire stoked for her martyrdom: "but that another divine inspiration, which is true Charity, moved the beholders then to beleeve, and the Churche ever since to acknowledge, that she did therein a noble and Christian act, to the especiall glory of God, this act of hers, as well as any other, might have bene calumniated to have bene done, out of wearinesse of Life, or feare of relapse, or hast to heaven, or Ambition of Martyrdome."[70] The testimony both of the martyr's conscience and of the church's ruling are questioned:

because most will be grounded, either upon the Conscyence of the Doer, or upon the Churches Opinion of the fact when it is done, we will onely consider how far an erring Conscyence may justify any act; and then produce some examples, of persons guilty of this, and yet Canonizd by the Churche, by admission into the Martyrologe, and assigning them theyr feasts, and Offices, and Vigills, and like religious Celebrations.[71]

Cases like Apollonia's unsettle both the testimony of consciences and Roman canonizing processes. The tract questions the canonizing of martyrs who seem to be suicides and insists that the only true martyrs are those who die for core Christian beliefs, such as the belief in a triune deity – beliefs not at stake, Donne implies, in contemporary England.

The conclusion makes explicit Donne's doubts about contemporary enthusiasm for martyrdom. In his last paragraph, Donne likens the strict limitation of suicide for God's glory to the limitation of the so-called healing king's touch to actual kings:

to cure diseases by Touche, or by Charme . . . be forbidden by divers Laws, out of a just prejudice that vulgar owners of such a vertue would misemploy it, yet none Mislikes that the Kings of England and France should cure one sicknesse by such meanes . . . because Kings are justly presumed to use all theyr power to the glory of God, so is it fit that this privilege, of which we speake should be contracted and restraynd.[72]

Donne nearly implies that true martyrdom owes something to the king's permission.[73] The analogy between the restrictions on the king's touch and on acceptable suicide resonates with *Pseudo-Martyr*'s argument that to die for elevating papal supremacy over monarchical power in worldly things is to die a mere suicide.

Published in 1610, *Pseudo-Martyr* argues that Catholics who expose themselves to danger by refusing to swear James I's Oath of Allegiance are no martyrs. Provoked by the Gunpowder Plot of November 1605, the oath required subjects to swear that James was the lawful King of England and contained this troublesome statement: "I do from my heart abhor, detest and abjure as impious and heretical, this damnable doctrine and position, that princes which be excommunicated or deprived by the pope may be deposed or murdered by their subjects or any other whatsoever."[74] Many Catholics were hesitant to swear that this "doctrine and position," though heavily contested in Catholic circles, was "impious and heretical." The oath entangled members of Donne's family: Mrs. Donne's third husband, Richard Rainsford, was imprisoned between 1611 and 1613 for refusing to take it.[75] A lengthy print controversy ensued. In 1606, the pope issued a *breve* condemning the oath. George Blackwell, England's Archpriest, concealed the *breve*, urged Catholics to take the oath, and did so himself; English Jesuits opposed Blackwell's position. When the pope issued a second *breve*, Bellarmine condemned the oath as contrary to the Catholic faith. James wrote a supposedly anonymous reply, *Triplici Nodo Triplex Cuneus*, in February 1608; Bellarmine answered in his aptly titled *Responsio*. James then issued a revised version of his tract, the *Apology*, under his own name, and Bellarmine responded with his *Apologia* of 1609. James chose William Barlow, Lancelot Andrewes, and John Barclay to defend the oath further. In a 1609 letter to Henry Goodyer, Donne pronounces Barlow's book "full of falsifications in words and in sense, and of falsehoods in matter of fact and of unscholarlike arguings."[76] Donne then entered the lists himself.

*Pseudo-Martyr*, Donne's first prose publication and first public challenge to the faith of his youth, has been seen as a "remarkable act of submission to the system," or, in Oliver's phrase, part of Donne's "discourse of feigned devotion."[77] Donne apparently held more moderate views on the Oath controversy than *Pseudo-Martyr* indicates. To Goodyer, Donne writes that,

> both sides may be in justice and innocence . . . clearly, our state cannot be safe without the oath, since they profess that clergymen, though traitors, are no subjects, and that all the rest may be none tomorrow. And as clearly, the supremacy which the Roman Church pretends were diminished, if it were limited, and will as ill abide that, or disputation, as the prerogative of temporal kings, who, being the only judges of their prerogative, why may not Roman bishops (so enlightened as they are presumed by them) be good witnesses of their own supremacy, which is now so much impugned?[78]

In *Pseudo-Martyr* Donne suppresses the "justice" he saw on the Catholic side.[79] Yet the tract is not necessarily or merely a submission to power, for it also develops the challenges to contemporary thinking about martyrdom that Donne began in *Biathanatos*. Donne attacks Jesuits' arguments, exorbitant promises about martyrdom's rewards, and Roman canonizing processes; he even raises, briefly but significantly, doubts about the textual canonizing Protestant martyrs underwent in Foxe's editorial hands.

Donne's tract bitterly attacks Jesuit arguments about martyrdom's rewards. The tract's opening two chapters qualify martyrdom's glory even as they purport to defend it in limited circumstances. Echoing *Biathanatos*, Donne argues that martyrdom is a concession to our "corruption and Ambition of beeing Lord of our selves," a selfish desire that prompts suicide: "Almightie God himselfe, who disposes all things sweetely, hath beene so indulgent to our nature, and the frailty thereof, that he hath afforded us a meanes, how wee may give away our life, and make him, in a pious interpretation, beholden to us for it; which is by delivering our selves to Martyredome."[80] Martyrdom redeems our own sinful tendencies. Yet this gift of quasi-suicidal martyrdom should not be used too freely. Donne's second chapter proposes "That there may be an inordinate and corrupt affectation of Martyrdome." This brief, crucial chapter stresses that martyrdom is only legitimate when a major question of faith is at issue.[81] Donne doubts that contemporary martyrdoms are required to defend the faith: Christ now comes to us "in his word and Sacraments, and doth not so frequently call witnesses and Martyrs, as he did in the Primitive church, when he induced a new Religion, and saw that, that maner of confirmation was expedient for the credite and conveyance thereof."[82] He insists that we must be willing to sacrifice ourselves if called upon but distances martyrdom's "dignitie" from contemporary martyrdoms.

In a move increasingly important to his work, Donne diffuses the potency of literal, physical martyrdom by arguing that martyrdom's rewards may be reaped from more mundane (literally, worldly) forms of suffering: "So is the treasure and crowne of Martyredome seposed for them, who take up devoutly the crosses of this life, whether of poverty, or anguish'd consciences, or obedience of lawes which seeme burdenous, and distastefull to them; for all that time a man serves for his freedome, and God keeps his reckoning, from the inchoation of his Martyredome, which was from his first submission to these tribulations."[83] Counter to Southwell's advice, Donne tells Catholics that submitting one's conscience to laws that are hateful, suffering an "anguish'd" conscience, is itself a form of martyrdom. Further, Donne emphasizes that living out one's calling, acting in the world, may do more for God than suffering and dying. In his preface to the Jesuits, Donne insists that,

Wee are not sent into this world, to *Suffer*, but to *Doe*, and to performe the Office of societie, required by our severall callings. The way to triumph in secular Armies, was not to be slaine in the battell, but to have kept the station, and done all Militarie duties. And as it was in the Romane Armies, so it ought to be taught in the Romane Church, *Ius legionis facile: Non sequi, non fugere.* For we must neither pursue persecution so forwardly, that our naturall preservation be neglected, nor runne away from it so farre, that Gods cause be scandaliz'd, and his Honour diminshd.[84]

Donne valorizes laboring in a calling over too-readily dying in one, with the ironic result of advising Catholics how to be more effective proselytizers:

being overeager for martyrdom could hinder the work of conversion (often militarized in Catholic poetry about the English mission), just as an excessive number of soldiers' deaths can hinder military conquest.

Raspa has remarked on this tract's deafening silence about Robert Southwell.[85] Yet Donne attacks with bitter precision the theological points Southwell helped popularize (though he generally attributes them to Bellarmine and does not mention Southwell). Donne argues specifically that recusant Catholics' longing for martyrdom stems from faulty theology (on the points of merit and purgatory) and from the Jesuits who spread it: "the doctrine of merites, dooth misprovoke and inordinately put forward inconsiderate men, to this vitious affectation of Martyrdome."[86] He challenges the notions that martyrdom purges sin ("Martyrdome is in their Doctrine, that *Opus privilegiatum,* which takes away al sinnes)" and that martyrdom "doth save a man, *ex opere operato,*" functioning as a sacrament does. Because Jesuits cherish what Donne terms "false-Martyrdome," they come in for heated attacks, here and elsewhere.[87] In *Ignatius His Conclave,* a mockery of Bellarmine's attacks on the English oath, Donne heaps scorn on Jesuits for their exaltations of martyrdom. As in *Pseudo-Martyr,* Donne likens Jesuits to the Circumcellions who provoked and urged others to martyr them.[88] Most sharply, Donne calls Ignatius's English Legion "capistrata."[89] The verb *capistrare* means to fit with a halter or harness. Donne's sharp satire calls martyrs like Campion and Garnet, literally, not martyrs but harnessed things. In attacking some Catholics' arguments for refusing the oath, Donne challenges the connections writers like Bellarmine and Southwell drew between martyrdom for particular Catholic causes (the refusal of the Oath; strict recusancy) and salvational confidence.

Yet Donne does not wholeheartedly endorse all claims advanced on behalf of Protestant martyrs, either. Donne's title reveals his engagement with the martyrological controversies this book traces. Catholic writers including Caesar Baronius, Robert Persons, and Pedro Ribadeneira called Foxe's martyrs pseudo-martyrs; in *Pseudo-Martyr* Donne refers to their arguments.[90] Still, in a tract obviously turning that charge back onto Catholic martyrs, Donne invokes Protestant martyrdom in an odd fashion. He admits the possibility of errors in Protestant martyrologies but argues that they are not so dangerous as Catholic errors because Catholic doctrine elevates martyrs to such a high position: "if we have committed any such slip in storie and matter of fact, there is not that danger in our transgression, which is in you, because you, by giving them that title, assure the world of a certaine and infallible present salvation, by vertue of that suffering, and that they have title thereby to our Adoration, and are in present possession of the office of Advocation for us."[91] More broadly, Donne's *The Courtier's Library*, a *jeu d'esprit* likely written between 1603 and 1610, takes a satirical swipe at Foxe's inaccuracies. In that work Donne lists imaginary books that supposedly provide a courtier with all he needs to succeed. The third title is "The Art of copying out within the compass of a Penny all the truthful statements made to that end by John Foxe."[92] It would be a mistake to read this as evidence that Donne found Foxe unbelievable, but given *Pseudo-Martyr*'s more measured statement about Foxe's occasional slips we may reasonably infer that Donne harbored suspicions about Protestant martyrological excesses. Donne's tendency to dampen enthusiasm for and about martyrs here extends to the Protestant tradition of which he is, generally speaking, much more respectful. Donne's pre-ordination prose thus casts suspicion (though certainly with differing degrees of intensity) on the processes of authentication upon which the making of Roman Catholic and Foxean martyrs depended.

Donne continued to wrestle with martyrological links between suffering and religious confidence in his work in other genres. Donne's religious lyrics explore the notion of suffering as a sign of divine ownership in the context not of casuistry but psychological drama and spiritual struggle. Articulated at a time when suffering for one's faith was a real possibility, Donne's famous invocations of divine violence may be read as pleas for the clear testimony suffering was thought to offer. These pleas are prompted, ironically, by the poems' simultaneous desire to test the theological perspectives from which arguments connecting suffering and religious confidence emerged. In Donne's religious lyrics concerned with suffering and/or violence, the *variety* of theological perspectives is striking in comparison with a poet like Southwell.[93] While the pre-ordination prose tracts criticized arguments linking martyrdom with religious confidence, Donne's violent imaginings of divine action in his religious lyrics deal with the deeply subjective effects of both those arguments and criticisms of them. Several devotional lyrics test arguments common in Protestant and/or Catholic martyrological literature and either find them lacking or dramatize powerfully the sorts of spiritual angst that could fuel the desire for the searing certainty suffering was thought to confer.

In "Spit in my face, you Jewes," Donne's speaker probes an idea prominent in Catholic martyrological writing and especially in Southwell: that imitating Christ's suffering is a way to repay Christ's sacrifice. Martz argues that Ignatian meditation, which typically begins with a *compositio loci*, influences this sonnet.[94] Yet the pose struck in the opening four lines rapidly disintegrates. The poem develops instead a rejection of the conception of suffering as a *quid pro quo* repayment for Christ's sacrifice. In the opening quatrain the speaker tries to put himself in Christ's position, so he may pay for his continuing sinfulness: "Spit in my face, you Jewes, and pierce my side, / Buffet, and scoffe, scourge, and crucifie mee, / For I have sinn'd, and sinn'd, and onely hee, / Who could do no iniquitie, hath dyed." As Lewalski notes, Donne "imagines himself undertaking the role of the crucified Christ in a surprising reversal of the meditator's usual stance before the crucified one."[95] Arguments found in Catholic writing help explain this surprise. As in Southwell's "Christs bloody sweat," the speaker here tries to imitate Christ through imaginatively subjecting himself to suffer in like fashion.[96] The speaker's sense of ongoing, pervasive sinfulness – "For I have sinn'd, and sinn'd" – is parallel to that of Southwell's speaker who calls himself "stonye to all good"; the speaker desires to imitate Christ in repayment for sinfulness, believing that, as argued in Southwell's *Epistle*, suffering is both deserved and a way to respond to Christ's sacrifice.

Yet the moment at which "Christs bloody sweat" ends – the attempt to repay Christ through weak imitation – is unattainable for Donne's speaker: "But by my death can not be satisfied / My sinnes, which passe the Jewes impiety: / They kill'd once an inglorious man, but I / Crucifie him daily, being now glorified" (5–8). The enjambed "I" traps the speaker between the sins of those supposedly responsible for the historical crucifixion and the worse, perpetual crucifixion effected by his ongoing sin. Southwell's speaker cast himself simultaneously as type, fulfillment, and duly-punished sinner; here that stance becomes unavailable as even the resurrected Christ gets caught in the speaker's temporal, sinful frame. The sestet does not resolve the problem of continual sin through "faith in Christ's infinite mercy" but continues to explore the *quid pro quo* logic implicit in the notion that one's own suffering could somehow begin to repay Christ.[97] The speaker is struck with the lack of reciprocity in divine love for the human:

> Oh let mee then, his strange love still admire:
> Kings pardon, but he bore our punishment.
> And *Jacob* came cloth'd in vile harsh attire
> But to supplant, and with gainfull intent:
> God cloth'd himselfe in vile mans flesh, that so
> Hee might be weake enough to suffer woe.          (9–14)

Still exploring what might be gained through suffering, the speaker indicates that what is "strange" about God's love is that it does not engage in the *quid pro quo* sacrificial economy with which the first two quatrains wrestled. The two examples with which Christ is compared are odd ones to choose if the purpose is to stress mercy or redemption. Kings may take action to pardon offenders, a generous act perhaps, but Christ goes further in bearing another's suffering. Similarly, Jacob's descent into "vile harsh attire" for gainful purposes is an instance of the sort of *quid pro quo* in which God does not participate. The closing couplet reiterates the sense of "strange love" for which I have been arguing. God is superior to the compensatory stance invoked and rejected in the first two quatrains, for what God gains through a willingness to suffer seems to be simply more suffering. Donne probes the speaker's initial hyperbolic desire to suffer in Christ's stead in order to test the ramifications of suffering under Southwellian logic and, ultimately, to reject them. Donne's poem deflates an understanding of suffering as repayment, a deflation which leaves the speaker in wonder before the divine, strange love of one who is willing to suffer with no motivation for gain, certainly no motivation articulated explicitly in this sonnet.

While Donne rejects the notion that one should respond to Christ's suffering with one's own, the idea that persecution and suffering reveal that one belongs to God remains compelling for him and shapes the pleas for divine violence found in a number of his religious lyrics. "Batter my heart" probes Protestant associations between suffering and certainty: specifically, the belief (as in much English Protestant martyrological literature) that suffering helps confirm election. The martyr Thomas Whittle identifies God's people by their suffering, an identification especially meaningful given that Whittle submitted to authorities before finally resolving for martyrdom: "This is Gods will & ordinaunce, that his people shall here both be punished in the fleshe, and tried in theyr fayth . . . Many are the troubles of the righteous, but the Lord delivereth them out of all . . . strive ye to go to heaven by the path which is strait to flesh and blood."[98] In Foxe's text, Protestants frequently console each other with the idea that suffering confirms election. In "Batter my heart," divine violence is invoked precisely because the speaker lacks assurance, due in part to theological confusions about how exactly salvation comes about.[99]

The poem may be read as a threefold meditation on the overlapping discourses of predestination, assurance, and martyrdom. It is a psychological explication of the instability theological indecision could provoke, a dramatization of the difficulties predestinarian thought could cause for the less-than-confident, and a characterization of the desire for suffering as proceeding from confused desperation. Southwell's poetry achieves its desired reform of poetics by pushing common figures of suffering towards the literal. Donne's "Batter my heart" invokes figures of divine violence according to the logic of certainty usually reserved for literal suffering; he, like Southwell, treats poetic figures of suffering as if they were subject to martyrological argumentation but with rather the opposite outcome. The poem first probes a psychological state in which a nominally Protestant understanding of grace does not yield comfort but instead regresses into a profound uncertainty about how exactly saving grace works. In response to his own confusion and the demonic violence from whose effects he feels quite sure he suffers, the speaker begs for divine action whose dramatic violence would be, unlike his theological quandries, unmistakeably clear. The poem exhibits not a consistently Protestant request for sanctification, as Lewalski suggests, but rather a nagging inconsistency about the exact relationship between self-effort and salvation, as implied by its many hesitations and qualifications: "yet" (2), "but" (6), "But" and "or" (8), "Yet" (9), "But" (10), "or" (11), "except" and "Except" (13, 14). Donne's speaker begins with a plea for divine violence whose rough rhythm seeks to shake up the smooth but insufficiently convincing relationship he has enjoyed with the divine: "Batter my heart, three-person'd God; for, you / As yet but knocke, breathe, shine, and seeke to mend; / That I may rise, and stand, o'erthrow mee, and bend / Your force to breake, blowe, burn and make me new" (1–4). A speaker who characterizes grace as irresistible characterizes his God as operating entirely differently, through mending and gentle reform. In subsequent lines, theological inconsistency persists. The speaker deems his efforts ineffective, as any good Calvinist would assert: "I, like an usurpt towne, to another due, / Labour to admit you, but, Oh, to no end"(5–6). Still, he feels none of the comfort that should, according to mainline Protestant thought, accompany reliance on God alone: "Yet dearely I love you, and would be loved faine, / But am betroth'd unto your enemie"(9–10).[100] Convinced that God does not love him, the speaker begs for dramatic divine action.

Donne's famous pleas for sexual violence emerge from the speaker's recurrent sense that he does not belong to God: "Yet dearely I love you, and would be loved faine." Donne's closing line ("Nor ever chaste, unless you ravish me") bears traces of the tradition linking martyrdom to ravishment in its wish for a violent, desired, divine consummation to overcome the devilish betrothal in which the speaker is ensnared.[101] In "The Litanie," Donne invokes that tradition as he calls the would-be executioners of virgin confessors "Ravishers" (4); the virgins' willingness to suffer martyrdom is termed a betrothal and martyrdom itself a marriage. Not yet assured of salvation but quite sure that salvation requires God's dramatic action, the speaker seeks certainty through pain, desired as proof of divine love. This is metaphorical pain to be sure, but it is imagined in terms that owe some of their power to common martyrological assumptions about the value of suffering. Pleas for violent confirmation of divine ownership are a spiritual last resort for a speaker urgently seeking an assurance his conflicted, imperfect Calvinist theology has been unable to confer.

Similarly, in "Good Friday 1613, Riding Westward," Donne's speaker asks for divine violence, requesting that his corruptions be burned away before he turns to face his God. Repeatedly placing Christ almost beyond sight and then returning him to the agony of his crucifixion, the speaker suggests that he has been looking towards Christ all along: "Though these things, as I ride, be from mine eye, / They are present yet unto my memory, For that looks towards them; and thou look'st towards mee" (33–5). As he imagines this reciprocal gazing, the speaker suddenly and dramatically collapses in humility, reinterpreting his westward ride as a wish for suffering like that Christ undergoes but for a different purpose, as a means of certifying that he belongs to Christ:

> O Saviour, as thou hang'st upon the tree;
> I turne my backe to thee, but to receive
> Corrections, till thy mercies bid thee leave.
> O thinke mee worth thine anger, punish mee,
> Burne off my rusts, and my deformity,
> Restore thine Image, so much, by thy grace,
> That thou may'st know mee, and I'll turne my face.     (36–42)

The speaker, who has been busy crafting apologies for riding the wrong way on Good Friday, worries whether anyone upstairs has noticed his wayward excursion ("thinke mee worth thine anger"); the language of "worth" resonates powerfully with martyrological claims that those who suffered could be sure they belonged to God.[102] Theresa Dipasquale argues that the speaker still seeks to control his own "turne" at the end of this poem and cannot bring himself to sacrifice his own poetic agency.[103] If so, the speaker's clinging to poetic agency reads like a urgent attempt to strike a bargain in order to bring about punitive attention. The closing lines suggest not necessarily the speaker's identification with Christ and assumption of his suffering but rather a desire for that sort of identification ("Restore thine Image");[104] the moment of reciprocal gaze imagined in the final line is projected into the future, after divine anger has proven the speaker worthy.

In "I am a little world made cunningly" the speaker requests suffering, punishment, and redemption, imagined as dependent on each other. Foxe frequently links suffering, punishment, and redemption, on occasion implying that sin may be purged by suffering. Regarding Cranmer's martyrdom, Foxe writes: "So good was the Lord . . . to the man with this crosse of tribulation, to purge his offences in this world."[105] Similarly, Southwell's *Epistle* suggests that suffering is just punishment for sinfulness. Donne's speaker seeks a parallel but markedly internalized route to redemption. He first attempts to exploit his Renaissance conceit of the self as a little world so that he might use newly discovered seas to weep efficaciously: "You which beyond that heaven which was most high / Have found new sphears, and of new lands can write, / Powre new seas in mine eyes, that so I might / Drowne my world with my weeping earnestly" (5–8). This suggestion of efficacious weeping (perhaps a subtle response to Catholic tears-poetry, in which weeping effusively is associated with effective repentance) is checked by post-Noah limitations on flooding: "Or wash it if it must be drown'd no more" (9). Yet washing is not enough: "But oh it must be burnt! alas the fire / Of lust and envie have burnt it heretofore, / And made it fouler" (10–12). The poem's close draws upon Psalm 69:9 to find a way of destroying the speaker's little world with flames that will not simply make it fouler. Lewalski has argued that "there is still a way to suffer burning which would be restorative and (almost paraphrasing Psalm 69:9) he prays for that."[106] The final lines do suggest restorative burning: "Let their flames retire, / And burne me o Lord, with a fiery zeale / Of thee and thy house, which doth in eating heale" (12–14). There is a significant distinction, however, between the psalmist's and Donne's characterizations of healing flame. In the first movement of Psalm 69, the psalmist mourns because his religious devotion makes him the target of persecution: "For the zeal of thine house hath eaten me up; and the reproaches of them that reproached thee are fallen upon me" (verses 8–9, KJV). The psalmist suffers at the hands of others because of the zeal by which he has already been consumed. Donne's speaker however, imagines this zealous burning as something which will be internal, and which he has not yet experienced. Donne collapses zeal and suffering into the image of a "fiery zeale" which both destroys and heals, for he wishes to suffer for his own sins; Donne substitutes divine fire's healing power for the persecutory suffering in Psalm 69 so that his little world may undergo a redemptive suffering that is ultimately a mark of divine favor.

These lyrics take the martyrological commonplace that suffering is the mark of the true Christian as the psychological basis for their meditations; they imagine confirmation of divine ownership through violent metaphors. In other poems Donne explicitly rewrites paradigms of martyrdom into spiritualized conflicts so as to make martyrdom's supposed benefits of assurance, confirmation, and confidence more widely accessible. As Valbuena states in her discussion of *Pseudo-Martyr*, for Donne "Authentic martyrdom begins and ends in this life."[107] The displacement of martyrdom onto internal spiritual struggles controls the enthusiasms spawned by links between martyrdom and certainty but also preserves something of martyrdom's dramatic rituals of suffering and confirmation. This displacement is marked in "The Litanie," written during the winter of 1608–9. The litany is a traditional liturgical form, usually penitential, comprising a series of petitions voiced by a clergyman to which the congregation offers a set response. Donne's litany works suffering into a penitential framework and makes it part of the regular rhythms of Christian life. The poem's opening, following liturgical tradition, addresses each member of the trinity.[108] Yet Donne's poem links each address with a petition for cleansing through suffering: the "Father" is to "purge away / All vicious tinctures"; the "Sonne" is asked to apply his "paine" to the speaker so he may be "slaine" in Christ's "passion." Donne's address to the "Holy Ghost" may echo the imagery of the final stanza of Southwell's "Christs bloody sweat," in which the speaker longed to become like the stone altar, wood, and sacrificed animal consumed by the fire Elijah invoked. Like Southwell's speaker, Donne's is "stony to all good," a "sacke of dust": though he is supposed to be the Holy Spirit's temple, his "mudde walls, and condensed dust" are "sacrilegiously / Halfe wasted with youths fires, of pride and lust" (20–1). Donne does not include Southwell's emphasis on suffering as repayment but does transform pentecostal flames into fires of purgation that consume the speaker's sinful self, imagined as encompassing all sacrificial components: "Double in my heart thy flame / Which let devout sad teares intend; and let / (Though this glasse lanthorne, flesh, do suffer maime) / Fire, Sacrifice, Priest, Altar be the same" (24–8). As in the Elijah story, water ("teares") intensifies ("intend") consuming flames. Donne's opening stanzas differ markedly from the English litanies' requests that God protect or deliver petitioners from difficulties; here, the desired regeneration is articulated through images of suffering and is turned inward, into the self who is sacrificing priest, means of sacrifice, and sacrificed offering.

Similarly, in several stanzas dedicated to those who suffer or are willing to suffer, Donne uses martyrdom to figure struggles with temptation in this life. "The Confessors" suggests that although confessors were not actually martyred, they understood suffering: "They know, and pray, that wee may know, / In every Christian / Hourly tempestuous persecutions grow; / Tentations martyr us alive; A man / Is to himselfe a Dioclesian" (95–9).

Persecutors are internalized as temptations; martyrdom becomes a paradigm for individual struggles with sin. Poignantly, in the stanza on "The Martyrs" Donne articulates both human and divine longing for martyrdom and posits an alternative in which martyrdom is the consequence for *not* suffering martyrdom:

> And since thou so desirously
> Didst long to die, that long before thou couldst,
>     And long since thou no more couldst die,
> Thou in thy scattered mystic body wouldst
>         In Abel die, and ever since
>         In thine, let their blood come
> To beg for us, a discreet patience
> Of death, or of worse life; for oh, to some
> Not to be martyrs, is a martyrdom.          (82–90)

Equivocating on the question of invocation, Donne asks God to let the martyrs beg patience for "us" to endure the suffering "of death, or of worse life." A deep but frustrated longing for martyrdom is shared with the divine and results in a kind of spiritual pain that is its own cross.

Donne's casuistical questioning of martyrological pieties (in *Biathanatos* and *Pseudo-Martyr*) and psychologizing of martyrdom's relationship to certainty and assurance (in several religious lyrics) prepare the way for his treatment of martyrdom in the sermons he preached as a Church of England minister. Many sermons praise martyrs while carefully accommodating martyrdom's spiritual value to more everyday scenarios. The preacher's job is, of course, to apply religious precepts to listeners' struggles. But Donne exceeds the preacher's regular duties by arguing that biblical verses typically interpreted as about literal, physical martyrdom ought to be read more broadly. Those unorthodox readings are often linked to Donne's encouragement of all believers away from a narrowly limited predestinarianism towards general confidence and assurance in election:[109] as he offers internalized, spiritualized versions of martyrdom, the rewards it was thought to confer become more widely available and literal, physical martyrdom begins to recede. His sermons' handling of martyrdom is thus a logical extension of arguments about martyrdom that Donne had been formulating for a long time, across many genres.

In the early modern period, one did not have to die to appear in a martyrology; Foxe celebrates Luther, for, inter alia, his willingness to brave persecution. But Donne's understanding of martyrdom is broader yet. In a sermon preached at Easter 1627 just after his daughter Lucy's death, Donne's explication of the phrase "better resurrection" (from

Hebrews 11:35) indicates respect for martyrdom as it is usually construed. Yet he also makes martyrdom's rewards available, potentially, to everyone:

There is a *Better Resurrection*. A *Better Resurrection* reserved for them, and appropriated to them *That fulfill the sufferings of Christ, in their flesh*, by Martyrdome, and so become witnesses to that Conveyance which he hath sealed with his blood, by shedding their blood; and glorifie him upon earth (as far as it is possible for man) by the same way that he hath glorified them in heaven; and are admitted to such a conformity with Christ, as that (if we may have leave to expresse it so) they have dyed for one another. Neither is this *Martyrdome*, and so this *Better Resurrection*, appropriated to a reall, and actuall, and absolute dying for Christ; but every suffering of ours, by which suffering, he may be glorified, is a degree of Martyrdome, and so a degree of improving and bettering our Resurrection. For as S. *Jerome* sayes, *That chastity is a perpetuall martyrdome*, So every war maintained by us, against our own desires, is a Martyrdome too.[110]

Every man is to himself a Diocletian: the martyr's "*Better Resurrection*" is available to those who struggle against temptations. Similarly, in a sermon on the proto-martyr St. Stephen Donne locates martyrdom in the world, not only as an exit out of it. While Donne insists that suffering for God is "the highest point of mans exaltation," he also expands "the extent, and latitude, and compass of Martyrdome," for "All Martyrdome is not a *Smithfeild* Martyrdome, to burn for religion" (Smithfield was the London site of numerous Marian burnings).[111]

Most remarkably, Donne's sermons on biblical passages often interpreted as referring to martyrs retreat from discussing literal, physical martyrdom. Of course, even Foxe, drawing on biblical precepts, formulates a mundane *imitatio martyriorum*, recommending that readers daily mortify sinful desires. Yet Donne tends to dissociate the struggle with sin from the imitation of recent martyrs; martyrdom becomes more of a figure, less of a monument. It is striking that when the opportunity arises to address contemporary martyrdom, Donne usually turns to alternative readings that internalize suffering and provide forms of comfort and assurance. For instance, while many of Foxe's martyrs interpreted the narrow path and straight gate referred to in Matthew 7:13 as a statement about the suffering one must endure in order to enter heaven, in a 1624 sermon on Revelation 7:9 Donne suggests that the path to heaven is narrow because it is suited to the narrowest, simplest person and that the way is "strait" "because a man must strippe himselfe of all inordinate affections, of all desires of ill getting, and of all possessions that are ill gotten. In a word, it is not strait to a mans selfe, but if a man will carry his sinfull company, his sinfull affections with him, and his sinfull possessions, it is strait."[112] Similarly, in a sermon preached at Lincoln's Inn Donne reinterprets the verse Southwell uses so often, Matthew 11:12: "the kingdom of heaven suffereth violence, and the violent take it by force" (KJV). For Southwell, this violence was literal persecution and the violent were persecutors; extolling the benefits of suffering such violence was the focal point of his life's work. Donne also reads this violence in a positive sense but radically reinterprets it as the violence of the church struggling to lay hold of religious truths: "whereas from the time of *John Baptist*, the *kingdome of heaven suffers violence* [Matt. 11:12], and every *violent* Man, that is, every earnest, and zealous, and spiritually valiant Man, may take hold of it, we may be much more sure of doing so, in the Congregation . . . when in the whole body, we Muster our forces, and *besiege* God."[113] The church batters heaven; the congregation anticipates the reward of the perfect "tranquillity" of those "at peace with God," a reward bestowed not for suffering but for persistent besieging.[114]

Importantly, Donne often makes martyrdom's reward as Foxe understood it – the assurance it could confer – available to those who endure internalized suffering. Donne's insistence that martyrdom's rewards are available through worldly, everyday scenarios is evident in his reinterpretations of Revelation 7. In each of three sermons on this chapter, Donne acknowledges that it is often understood to refer to the triumph of martyrs and the faithful in heaven, but repeatedly insists that the triumph he is most interested in is a spiritual one occurring in this world.[115] In a sermon on Revelation 7:2–3, probably preached on All Saints' Day, 1623, Donne refers the passage to the triumph and celebration available to the Church Militant: "God seales us in the heart, that we might love him, and in the fore-head, that we might professe it, and in the hand, that we might declare and practise it; and then the whole purpose of this blessed Angel in our Text, is perfected in us, and we our selves are made partakers of the solemnity of this day, which we celebrate, for we our selves enter in the Communion of Saints, by these three seales, Of Beliefe, Of Profession, Of Works and Practise."[116] In a christening sermon preached on Revelation 7:17, Donne seeks to make the comfort which martyrs expect accessible to those who suffer in more mundane forms. The wiping of tears to which this verse refers belongs to this world, not the next:

as he hath promised inestimable blessings to them, that are *sealed*, and *washed* in him, so he hath given you security, that these blessings belong to you: for, if you find, that he hath *governed* you, (bred you in his visible Church) and *led you to his fountain of the water of life* in *baptisme*, you may be sure, that he will in his due time, *wipe all teares from your eyes*, establish the kingdom of heaven upon you, *in this life*, in a holy, and modest *infallibility*.[117]

The promise that martyrs will be comforted is extended to listeners who may enjoy "security" in God's blessings "in this life."

In the 1624 sermon on Revelation 7:9, Donne makes the martyr's traditional iconography – the palm and white robe – available to all persistent Christians. This verse was not always read so: Foxe's title page provides a series of illustrations linking the verse's iconography to the martyrs he celebrates. But the conclusion to Donne's sermon refuses to limit the struggles of martyrdom to a Foxean pyre. Donne remarks that the Antichrist is as much in us as in the "Turk" or the pope: Antichrist is "that opposition to the kingdom of Christ, which is in our selves."[118] Donne consequently extends the martyrs' triumph over Antichrist to all believers:

This part of the book of the *Revelation*, is literally, and primarily, the glorious victory of them, who, in the later end of the world, having stood out the persecutions of the *Antichrist*, enter into the triumph of heaven: And it extends it self to all, by way of fair accommodation, who after a battel with their own *Antichrists*, and victory over their owne enemies, are also made partakers of those triumphs, those joyes, those glories.[119]

This triumph of the fairly accommodated mundane martyr over inner temptation is linked to the assurance martyrs were thought to feel. Stressing that salvation is open to many and encouraging listeners to embrace a hopeful assurance, Donne urges that "nothing hinders our own salvation more, then to deny salvation, to all but our selves."[120] Because the martyr's assurance is made widely available, the martyr's iconography is assimilated to confidence that one will enter heaven. Donne reads martyrs' robes as the Lamb's fleece which will cover all sin; their white color indicates our innocence once covered. The palms become signs of comfort and confidence, "infinite seales, infinite testimonies, infinite extensions, infinite durations of infinite glory."[121] The sermon's powerful close, building on this broadened interpretation of martyrdom and of the assurance it was thought to confer, urges auditors to contemplate heaven with confidence.

Across different genres and circumstances, Donne reconceptualizes common arguments about martyrdom and religious certainty. His pre-ordination prose attacks Catholic arguments linking martyrdom and certainty and casts a lightly skeptical eye on their Protestant counterparts; his religious lyrics take notions of suffering as deserved punishment, sign of divine favor, and mark of eventual redemption and apply them to various psycho-spiritual struggles; and his sermons broaden the rewards of martyrdom as martyrologists understood them and as outlined in biblical texts to all who struggle for holiness. Donne attempts to displace the drama of martyrdom into bloodless contexts and ultimately, in the sermons, to render martyrdom's rewards of confidence and spiritual serenity widely available in this world. For Southwell, of course, no such dissipation of literal martyrdom's power was necessary or desirable: he challenged Protestant claims about martyrdom and assurance head-on, attacking Protestant pseudo-martyrdom and proclaiming the value of Catholic martyrdom. The more moderate and, it must be said, more ambivalent Donne avoids both the Scylla of painful literalism and the Charybdis of radical skepticism by searching for ways to reap a martyr's rewards without suffering actual martyrdom. Southwell's and Donne's works represent two distinct ways of responding to the ongoing English Catholic persecution. The first seeks to find grace in pain, redeeming suffering through arguing for the spiritual rewards it brings; the second seeks to redefine suffering and its concomitant rewards so as to make actual martyrdom unnecessary (and to enable a sort of truce with temporal power). Both writers' persistent, prolonged engagements with the intersections between martyrdom and salvational confidence across prose and poetic genres suggest the central role martyrological discourse played in shaping the early modern dynamics of spiritual pain and consolation, the poles between which contemporary religious lyric ranged and from which it took its spiritual bearings.

NOTES

1 *Actes and Monuments* (1583), 1568.
2 The Council of Trent anathematized the proposition "That a man reborn and justified is bound by faith to believe that he is assuredly in the number of the predestinate"; reprinted in *Documents of the Christian Church*, ed. Henry Bettenson (Oxford: Oxford University Press, 1963), 263. Of course, Protestants were divided about the degree to which one must feel assurance; see Peter Lake, "Calvinism and the English Church, 1570–1635," *Past and Present* 114 (1987), 32–76.
3 *Epistle of Comfort* (London, 1587?–8), 4r.
4 Pierre Janelle writes that for Southwell, "death in martyrdom is the gate that leads one straight into the heavenly home"; *Robert Southwell the Writer: a Study in Religious Inspiration* (London: Sheed and Ward, 1935), 30.
5 Biographical studies include Christopher Devlin, *The Life of Robert Southwell: Poet and Martyr* (London: Longman, 1956), Janelle (*Robert Southwell the Writer*), and Nancy Pollard Brown's introduction to *The Poems of Robert Southwell, S.J.* (ed. James McDonald and Brown, Oxford: Clarendon Press, 1967).
6 Brown, *The Poems of Robert Southwell*, xxix.
7 Anthony Raspa, *The Emotive Image: Jesuit Poetics in the English Renaissance* (Fort Worth: Texas Christian University Press, 1983); Anthony D. Cousins, *The*

*Catholic Religious Poets from Southwell to Crashaw* (London: Sheed & Ward, 1991); Louis Martz, *The Poetry of Meditation: a Study in English Religious Literature of the Seventeenth Century*, 2nd ed. (New Haven: Yale University Press, 1962); Helen C. White, *The Metaphysical Poets: a Study in Religious Experience* (New York: Macmillan, 1936); Scott Pilarz, " 'To Help Souls': Recovering the Purpose of Southwell's Poetry and Prose," in *Discovering and (Re)Covering the Seventeenth Century Religious Lyric*, ed. Eugene R. Cunnar and Jeffrey Johnson (Pittsburgh: Duquesne University Press, 2001), 41–61; John and Lorraine Roberts, " 'To weave a new webbe in their owne loome': Robert Southwell and Counter-Reformation Poetics," in *Sacred and Profane: Secular and Devotional Interplay in Early Modern British Literature*, ed. Helen Wilcox, Richard Todd, and Alasdair MacDonald (Amsterdam: VU University Press, 1996), 63–77.

8  *Epistle of Comfort*, 85r.
9  White, *The Metaphysical Poets*, 96. Her view is distinct from John Carey's argument that apostasy shaped Donne's "life and art" ( *John Donne, Life, Mind, and Art*, London: Faber and Faber, 1981); the rejection of the grim opportunity to be a martyr need not be judged so harshly.
10  Given Southwell's popularity it is unlikely Donne did not know of him. R. C. Bald and Ceri Sullivan note possible connections; see *John Donne: a Life* (New York: Oxford University Press, 1970), 63–6; "Donne's Sifted Soul," *Notes and Queries* 42 (240)(1995), 345–6.
11  See Pilarz, " 'To Help Souls,' " who follows Janelle's lead.
12  The tract was printed in 1600, in the context of the Jesuit/Appellant controversies; given its occasional praise for Elizabeth, the tract may have been published to embarrass the Jesuit order.
13  His temperate approach is itself, as Geoffrey Hill remarks, a controversialist position ( *The Lords of Limit: Essays on Literature and Ideas*, New York: Oxford University Press, 1984, chapter 2).
14  Devlin, *Life of Robert Southwell*, 51–7, 172–5, 213; Brown, *The Poems of Robert Southwell*, xxv, xxviii.
15  The tract was printed by a secret press in England between 1587 and 1588 (Brown, *The Poems of Robert Southwell*, xxiii); an undated copy bears a Paris printer's mark but was printed on English paper.
16  See Richard Williams, " 'Libels and payntinges': Elizabethan Catholics and the International Campaign of Visual Propaganda", in *John Foxe and His World*, ed. Christopher Highley and John N. King, (Aldershot: Ashgate, 2002), 198–215, on the purpose of frescoes of martyrs at the English College in Rome; Alison Shell on the auto-didacticism of literature about Catholic martyrs ( *Catholicism, Controversy, and the English Literary Imagination*, Cambridge: Cambridge University Press, 1999), and Devlin ( *Life of Robert Southwell*) on the training for persecution that priests received.
17  On the debate over whether native or continental influences are strongest in Southwell's poetry; see Janelle ( *Robert Southwell the Writer*), Martz ( *Poetry of*

*Meditation*), Pilarz ("'To Help Souls'"), and Roberts ("'To weave a new webbe'").

18 Cited in Brown, ed., *Two Letters and Short Rules of a Good Life*, published for the Folger Shakespeare Library (Charlottesville, VA: The University of Virginia Press, 1973), xxxi.

19 *Epistle of Comfort*, 24r–v.

20 *A Short Rule of Good Life* (London(?) 1598(?)), 104; cf. the *Epistle of Comfort*: "Whome God loveth, he chastiseth" (11v).

21 Janel Mueller, "Pain, Persecution, and the Construction of Selfhood in Foxe's *Actes and Monuments*," in *Religion and Culture in Renaissance England*, ed. Claire McEachern and Debora Shuger (Cambridge: Cambridge University Press, 1997), 161–87.

22 Hill, *The Lords of Limit*, 28–9; Scarry, *The Body in Pain: the Making and Unmaking of the World* (Oxford: Oxford University Press, 1987).

23 *Epistle of Comfort*, 41r. Compare Southwell's "New Heaven, New Warre" and Walpole's "Why do I use my paper, inke, and pen?".

24 *Epistle of Comfort*, 140v, 161r.

25 *Ibid.*, 18r.

26 *Ibid.*, 18v–19r.

27 *Ibid.*, 22r.

28 *Ibid.*, 171r.

29 *Ibid.*, 171v, 98v.

30 For the best account of this poem to date, see Brian Cummings, *The Literary Culture of the Reformation: Grammar and Grace* (Oxford: Oxford University Press, 2002), pp. 355–64.

31 *Humble Supplication* (London, 1591), 4–5.

32 *Epistle of comfort*, 172v–173r, 182r–v.

33 *Ibid.*, 186v–187r.

34 *Ibid.*, 187r.

35 *Ibid.*, 79v. The Douai NT translation (1582) comments similarly: "no Heretike and Schismatike that uniteth not him self to the Catholic Church again, how great almes so ever he give, yea or shede his bloud for Christes name, can possibly be saved."

36 *Epistle of comfort*, 89v.

37 *Ibid.*, 46r–v.

38 *Ibid.*, 99r.

39 *Humble Supplication*, 32.

40 *Epistle of comfort*, 139r.

41 Shell, *Catholicism*, 65–6.

42 For instance, Herbert's "My God, where is that ancient heat" combines martyrdom (Mueller's focus in her discussion of the sonnet, "Pain, Persecution, and the Construction of Selfhood") with poetic reform in a way that both recalls Southwell and protestantizes his poetics with distinct allusions to Foxean martyrs' pyres.

43 See Janelle (*Robert Southwell the Writer*) and Roberts (" 'To weave a new webbe' ").

44 *The Poems of Robert Southwell, S.J.*, i.

45 Allen, *A Briefe Historie of XII Reverend Priests* (Rheims, 1582), e; John Geninges, *Life and Death of Mr. Edmund Geninges* (St. Omer, 1614), dedicatory poem, 4.

46 *Epistle of Comfort*, 176v.

47 This is a large, unresolved scholarly question: broadly, Louis Martz argued for continental influences (*The Poetry of Meditation*); Barbara Lewalski asserted that native Protestant influences were most dominant (*Protestant Poetics and the Seventeenth-Century Religious Lyric*, Princeton: Princeton University Press, 1979).

48 Brown, *The Poems of Robert Southwell*, xcii–xcviii.

49 This poem is identified in one of Bacon's papers, dated to 1596, as Southwell's (Brown, *The Poems of Robert Southwell*, lxxvii).

50 *Epistle of Comfort*, 14v.

51 *Ibid.*, 8v.

52 The last two stanzas of this poem are missing in the early published editions. The final stanza implies the possibility for a sinful, self-sacrificing subject to requite Christ's sacrifice in some degree, something Herbert does not allow in "The Reprisal"; even John Ford's *Christs Bloody Sweat*, a poem clearly imitating Southwell's, does not entertain the idea of returning a sacrifice in any physical sense (though this may be because Ford did not see the manuscript version of the poem).

53 Southwell knew about Sherwin's behavior at his death (Devlin, *Life of Robert Southwell*, 54); Walpole's poem was printed in Alfield's *A True Report of the Death and Martyrdome of M. Campion Jesuite and prieste* (London, 1582). Southwell's correspondence before and after his entry into England suggests his keen interest in the persecution. See the *Publications of the Catholic Record Society*, vol. 5, ed. John Hungerford Pollen, S.J. (London: J. Whitehead & Son, 1908), for Southwell's correspondence; see also Janelle (*Robert Southwell the Writer*).

54 Cf. Copley's similar resolution of despair in *A Fig for Fortune* (London, 1596), discussed above.

55 *Two Letters and Short Rules of a Good Life*, 83.

56 I cite Thomas Leake's report of his martyrdom, reprinted in *Publications of the Catholic Record Society*, vol. 5, 336.

57 As in a *c.* 1610 letter to Henry Goodyer: "I never fretted nor imprisoned the word Religion . . . nor immuring it in a *Rome*, or a *Wittemberg*, or a *Geneva*; they are all virtuall beams of one Sun"; *Letters to Severall Persons of Honour* (1651) (New York: George Olm Verlag, 1974), 29.

58 Brad Gregory, *Salvation at Stake: Christian Martyrdom in Early Modern Europe* (Cambridge, MA: Harvard University Press, 1999), 340.

59 Flynn, "Donne the Survivor," in *The Eagle and the Dove: Reassessing John Donne* (Columbia: University of Missouri Press, 1986), 15–24.

60 For the apostasy reading see Carey (*John Donne: Life, Mind, and Art*); Bald implies that Donne's careerism heavily influenced his writing (*John Donne: a*

*Life*). Flynn suggests both views' limitations ("Donne's Politics, 'Desperate Ambition,' and Meeting Paolo Sarpi in Venice," *Journal of English and Germanic Philology* 99:3 [2000], 334–55).

61 Camille Wells Slights, *The Casuistical Tradition in Shakespeare, Donne, Herbert, and Milton* (Princeton: Princeton University Press, 1981); Joan Webber, *Contrary Music* (Madison: University of Wisconsin Press, 1963), 11; Robert Hughes, *The Progress of the Soul: the Interior Career of John Donne* (New York: William Morrow and Co., 1968). Hughes notes that the tract commits each of Aristotle's ten logical fallacies (150).

62 *Biathanatos*, ed. Ernest W. Sullivan II (Newark: University of Delaware Press, 1984), 32.

63 Meg Lota Brown, *Donne and the Politics of Conscience in Early Modern England* (Leiden: Brill, 1995); Sullivan, *Biathanatos*, xxi–xxvi.

64 *Biathanatos*, 136.

65 *Ibid.*, 29.

66 *Ibid.*, 54–5.

67 *Ibid.*, 61–2.

68 *Ibid.*, 100.

69 Anthony Raspa, ed., *Pseudo-Martyr* (Montreal: McGill-Queen's University Press, 1993), 136–7. Compare also Donne's apparent approval of St. Brigid's apparitions in *Biathanatos* (129) with his claim in *Pseudo-Martyr* that Brigid's apparitions are "most weake and indeffensible" (93).

70 *Biathanatos*, 105.

71 *Ibid.*, 102.

72 *Ibid.*, 145–6.

73 On this tract's contradictory views of political institutions, see Adam Kitzes, "Paradoxical Donne: *Biathanatos* and the Problems with Political Assimilation," *Prose Studies* 24 (2001), 1–17.

74 G. W. Prothero, *Select Statutes and Other Constitutional Documents Illustrative of the Reigns of Elizabeth and James I*, 4th ed. (Oxford: Clarendon Press, 1954), 256.

75 Brown, *Donne and the Politics of Conscience*, 9.

76 Edmund W. Gosse, *The Life and Letters of John Donne* (London, 1899), vol. 1, 222–3. Thomas Healy notes the semi-official nature of Donne's entry into the controversy (*Ignatius His Conclave*, ed. Healy, Oxford: Clarendon Press, 1969, introduction).

77 Annabel Patterson, *Censorship and Interpretation: the Conditions of Writing and Reading in Early Modern England* (Madison: University of Wisconsin Press, 1984), 95; P. M. Oliver attributes the tract to Donne's desire for self-promotion (*Donne's Religious Writing: a Discourse of Feigned Devotion*, New York: Longman, 1997).

78 Gosse, *Life and Letters*, vol. 1, 221–2.

79 As Olga Valbuena and Raspa argue, Donne allows Catholics room to submit spiritually to the pope; he disputes only the papacy's claims to temporal power (Raspa, introduction to *Pseudo-Martyr*; Valbuena, "Casuistry, Martyrdom,

and the Allegiance Controversy in Donne's *Pseudo-Martyr*," *Religion and Literature* 32 [2000], 49–80). Donne's treatment of Venetian quarrels with the papacy speaks to this distinction; Flynn argues that Donne's Venetian trip *c.* 1605 may have been the final catalyst for his conversion, or at least may have led him to formulate the arguments about papal temporal power presented in *Pseudo-Martyr* ("Donne's Politics").

80 *Pseudo-Martyr*, 31.
81 *Ibid.*, 35.
82 *Ibid.*, 33.
83 *Ibid.*
84 *Ibid.*, 27.
85 Raspa, introduction to *Pseudo-Martyr*, xlv.
86 *Ibid.*, 92.
87 *Ibid.*, 105.
88 *Ignatius His Conclave*, ed. Timothy S. Heale (Oxford: Clarendon Press, 1969), 61.
89 *Ibid.*, 79.
90 Raspa, introduction to *Pseudo-Martyr*, xvi–xix.
91 *Pseudo-Martyr*, 162–3.
92 *The Courtier's Library*, ed. Evelyn Simpson, trans. Percy Simpson (London: Nonesuch Press, 1930), 30.
93 Strier convincingly argues that many sonnets do not exhibit a fully formed Protestant subjectivity given the marked absence of comfort or assurance: "John Donne Awry and Squint: the Holy Sonnets, 1608–1610," *Modern Philology* 86:4 (1989), 357–84.
94 Martz, *Poetry of Meditation*, 31. I cite Donne's poetry from John Donne, *Poetry and Prose*, ed. Frank J. Warnke (New York: Modern Library, 1967).
95 Lewalski, *Protestant Poetics*, 270; cf. Martz, *Poetry of Meditation*, 49–50.
96 Compare Smithin Wells's "To Christ Crucified": "Make me partaker of thy pain . . . if it be thy glorious will . . . I shall taste of this thy cup" (in Philip Caraman, ed., *The Other Face: Catholic Life Under Elizabeth I*, London: Longmans, 180).
97 Lewalski, *Protestant Poetics*, 271.
98 *AM* (1583), 1850.
99 Lewalski (*Protestant Poetics*) and Stachniewski (*The Persecutory Imagination: English Puritanism and the Literature of Religious Despair*, Oxford: Clarendon Press, 1991) see the poem as filtering Protestant regeneration or sanctification through an uncompromising Calvinism; Oliver (*Donne's Religious Writing*) argues that the poem asks brusquely for something a good Calvinist would believe was entirely at divine discretion (124); Strier ("John Donne Awry and Squint") stresses its marked lack of assurance.
100 Paul Sellin argues that the hope that the speaker would eventually feel assurance softens the poem's angst; I find little evidence for such hope in the text ("The Mimetic Poetry of Jack and John Donne: a Field Theory for the Amorous and the Divine," in *Sacred and Profane: Secular and Devotional*

*Interplay in Early Modern British Literature*, ed. Helen Wilcox, Richard Todd, and Alasdair MacDonald, Amsterdam: VU University Press, 1996, 163–73).

101 For a persuasive historicist reading of this image of competing suitors, see Arthur Lindley, "John Donne, 'Batter My Heart,' and English Rape Law," *John Donne Journal* 17 (1998), 75–88.

102 Joan Hartwig likens this moment to depictions of St. Paul's conversion; still, the speaker seems to need not conversion so much as confirmation ("Donne's Horse and Rider as Body and Soul," in *John Donne's Religious Imagination*, ed. Raymond-Jean Frontain and Frances Malpezzi, Conway, AR: University of Central Arkansas Press, 1995, 262–83).

103 *Literature and Sacrament: the Sacred and the Secular in John Donne* (Pittsburgh: Duquesne University Press, 1999), 125.

104 Contrast Frances Malpezzi, "'As I Ride': the Beast and His Burden in Donne's 'Goodfriday,'" *Religion and Literature* 24 (1992), 23–31; Paul W. Harland, "'A true Transubstantiation': Donne, Self-love, and the Passion," in *John Donne's Religious Imagination*, ed. Frontain and Malpezzi, 175.

105 *AM* (1583), 1888.

106 Lewalski, *Protestant Poetics*, 267–8.

107 58; cf. Oliver's discussion of "The Cross," in *John Donne's Religious Writing*, 75–8.

108 On the poem's relationship to liturgical tradition see Annabel Patterson, "A Man is to Himself a Diocletian: Donne's Rectified Litany," *John Donne Journal* 21 (2002), 35–49. About "The Litanie" Donne wrote: "'neither the Roman Church need call it defective, because it abhors not the particular mention of the blessed Triumphers in heaven; nor the Reformed can discreetly accuse it, of attributing more then a rectified devotion ought to doe'" (in Gosse, *Life and Letters*, vol. 1, 197).

109 For Donne's moderation on predestination and his tendency to embrace hypothetical universalism, see Jeanne Shami, "'Speaking Openly and Speaking First': John Donne, the Synod of Dort, and the Early Stuart Church," in *John Donne and the Protestant Reformation*, ed. Mary Arshagouni Papazian (Detroit: Wayne State University Press, 2003), 35–65; see also Lori Anne Ferrell, "Donne and His Master's Voice," *John Donne Journal* 11 (1992), 59–70.

110 *The Sermons of John Donne*, ed. Simpson and Potter, vol. 7 (Berkeley: University of California Press, 1954), 390–1.

111 *Sermons*, 8:185, 186.

112 *Sermons*, 6:164.

113 *Sermons*, 2:220.

114 *Ibid.*, 226.

115 Cf. *Sermons*, 10:7–8.

116 *Ibid.*, 64; on the date, see Simpson's introduction.

117 *Sermons*, 5:112.

118 *Sermons*, 6:151. Donne's broad-mindedness here should not blind us to forms of anti-Catholicism in his sermons. Noting two sorts of anti-Catholicism – theological and religiopolitical – in the sermons, Marotti argues that Donne defended a via media against "the extremes of Roman Catholicism and radical Protestantism" ("John Donne's Conflicted Anti-Catholicism," *JEGP* 101 [2002], 361). Gale Carrithers and James Hardy call Donne "an inclusivist of the middle way" ("Love, Power, Dust Royal, Gavelkind: Donne's Politics," *John Donne Journal* 14 [1992], 49).

119 *Sermons*, 6:151.

120 *Ibid.*, 163.

121 *Ibid.*, 167.

# CHAPTER 6

# The polemics of conscience in the history play

Martyrdom was powerful theatre: it was profoundly spectacular and it occasioned dramatic representation. But early modern drama could also question and even challenge some of the representational strategies martyrologists used to validate the spectacles of martyrs' deaths. The two plays discussed here, *The Book of Sir Thomas More* and *Henry VIII*, use martyrologies as sources, including Thomas Stapleton's *Tres Thomae* and Foxe's *Actes and Monuments*. Yet compared to much of the literature discussed above these plays respond more skeptically to martyrology's claim to represent truth embodied. Three factors account for this: the problems invited by performing the rhetoric of martyrdom on a public stage, the religious confusion inherent to Henry VIII's reign, and the rupture the plays open between individual martyrs' testimony and history itself. These plays demonstrate that some literary works in the period were capable of pushing competing testimonies to the point that those testimonies become mostly evidence of the martyr's own beliefs, with relatively unreliable reference to larger narratives of historical continuity and religious integration.

For these plays, the rhetoric of martyrdom enhances an act on a stage, a performance. Those performances both open up and collapse a gap in signification between a presumably authentic inwardness and observable outward behaviors. The possible gap between the realm of interior conscience through which truth was purportedly accessible and the external, witnessable act of martyrdom may be widened on stage, where any interiority or references to it are by definition performative. To enact interiority on stage is to risk an infinite regress, an endless series of performances. This regress is not inevitable, of course: some early modern plays handle martyrdom in quite orthodox ways.[1] Yet because *More* and *Henry VIII* are aware of both Protestant and Catholic martyrological discourses, they raise the possibility that martyrdoms may owe much of their power to convincing (though not necessarily insincere) performances drawn from a common set of expectations for a martyr's words and behavior. Although to different ends, both plays use that possibility to destabilize the relationship between common signs of martyrdom and the more evasive, other-worldly truths to which martyrdom, in numerous martyrological texts, was supposed to witness.

Both plays concern Henry VIII's reign, a period notorious for its religious instability.[2] Thanks to the unevenness of religious change under Henry, Protestants (such as Anne Askew) and Catholics (such as John Fisher and Thomas More) suffered martyrdom for different causes. These plays depict the history of that realm from the perspective of the late sixteenth and early seventeenth centuries, by which point a multitude of Protestant and Catholic texts had been written about those who suffered for their faiths from Henry forward. Focusing on Henry VIII's reign allows these plays to explore and exploit the potential confusion resulting from the period's array of texts celebrating martyrs for different faiths.

Finally, these plays put pressure on martyrologists' tendencies to construct a unified religious history from individual sufferers' testimonies. As I discussed in chapter 2, writers as diverse as John Foxe and Robert Persons strove to build a continuous religious narrative reaching from the days of the early church to the early modern period to demonstrate the truthfulness of their martyrs' confessions. That narrative is a tautological one, but no less powerful for its tautology: martyrs' testimonies reinforce the continuity of a given faith across time (and thus, implicitly, that faith's authenticity) while simultaneously the historical continuity in which a given martyr participates can validate that martyr's testimony. In both plays, this historiographical project is undermined, as they demonstrate the difficulty of staging a history of a religiously integrated England. Given problematic, persistent overlaps in martyrological rhetoric, martyrs are not so easily separated from traitors and heretics as Foxe and Persons might wish.

In both plays, common markers of martyrdom – specifically, the frequent assertion that a martyr dies to testify to his/her conscience and the insistence that a true, confident martyr will go to his/her death joyfully – are used not to reveal testimony that confirms particular beliefs but to uncover conflicting testimony (in *Henry VIII*) or to obscure a given individual's beliefs (in *Sir Thomas More*). Reading these plays against a martyrological backdrop clarifies long-standing controversies about the religious causes to which they most readily lend themselves. Despite literary scholars' best efforts, neither play can be made to fit neatly the agenda of any single religious faction since both plays question the historiographical foundations of propagandistic efforts to authorize a particular martyr-tradition.[3] Because both plays acknowledge that similar conventions were used to demonstrate the authenticity of martyrs for different causes, the plays question whether there is any unshakeable foundation upon which to construct histories of religious continuity. History and martyrdom do not confirm each other; martyrdom is rendered a powerful but religiously ambiguous performance.

### *THE BOOK OF SIR THOMAS MORE* AND THE LAUGHTER OF THE HEART

In *The Book of Sir Thomas More*, martyrdom is a moving but opaque performance, stripped of the testimony of conscience so common in martyrological writing. As the play reaches its climax, it maintains a curious silence about the reasons its lead character exits via the scaffold. Its silence about exactly why More is executed contrasts sharply with voluble displays of More's famous wry humor. Often referring to his "conscience" but never explaining why his conscience demands his self-sacrifice, the play's More hides behind his jokes. In contrast, contemporary Protestant and Catholic martyrologists, including those who wrote the play's sources, use joyfulness, wit, and gallows humor to reveal what is in the martyr's conscience, what motivates martyrs to endure suffering. The play's alterations to this convention shed light on one of its greatest surprises: its even-handed portrait of More.

The play was likely composed between 1592 and 1595,[4] in a climate of late Elizabethan anti-Catholicism. Anthony Munday, who worked for Richard Topcliffe as a spy discovering recusant Catholics,[5] wrote at least part of the original play and was its transcriber; additions are not in his hand. The extant manuscript, comprising the original play and six additions, bears the marks of seven hands. Four have been identified with near certainty: Anthony Munday, Henry Chettle, Thomas Dekker, and Edmund Tilney, Master of the Revels and the play's censor. Two others are tentative: Thomas Heywood and William Shakespeare; the seventh is likely a playhouse scribe's.[6] More might have been chosen as a subject because many Londoners still saw him as their special patron.[7] The play's authors had to negotiate, however, both their audience's affection for More and years of Protestant propaganda against one of England's most prominent Catholic martyrs. The play did encounter some trouble with the Master of the Revels. Edmund Tilney cut much of its opening sequence, depicting the riots of May Day 1517, and objected to the scene in which More and

Rochester refuse to subscribe to articles submitted to them;[8] we cannot be sure it was ever performed. Importantly, however, with the exception of the articles scene its portrait of More escaped censorship. In order to capitalize on More's continuing popularity, obscure his divisive religious commitments, and (potentially) earn Tilney's consent, the playwrights do not distance themselves from religious controversies over martyrs. Rather, they take advantage of and even extend the interpretational problems such controversies provoked.

Specifically, because both Protestant and Catholic martyrologies use joyfulness as a sign of a martyr's integrity, that sign had no necessary connection to particular beliefs. Writers had to delineate the faith motivating a joyful display, often by proclaiming a martyr's final verbal testimony as a true confession of his conscience. Unlike its martyrological sources, however, the play fails to link More's famous final jests to a declaration of his conscience. Instead, the play uses joyfulness to hide the inwardness of its protagonist and thus to conceal More's religiously controversial motivations. Even as their protagonist refuses to confess the reason for his joy, the playwrights strive to leave martyrdom's dramatic power intact. They succeed because they explore the connections between martyrdom and theatrical performance itself.

The Renaissance theatre with its limited representational capabilities demanded, in Katharine Eisaman Maus's words, "a deliberate, agreed-upon estrangement of fictional surface from truth": from within a nobleman's costume a plebeian actor plays England's most famous Lord Chancellor. Maus goes on to suggest that "the English Renaissance stage seems deliberately to foster theatergoers' capacity to use partial and limited presentations as a basis for conjecture about what is undisplayed or undisplayable." In *Sir Thomas More*, however, such conjecture is deliberately frustrated; the play extends what Maus calls theatrical "crises of authenticity" to martyrdom itself.[9] The playwrights were composing a play on one of the English Reformation's most controversial figures, for a London audience almost certainly comprising people with a range of religious opinions, from fervent Puritan to closeted Catholic. Attempting to appease a divided audience by portraying More as a joyful martyr who refuses to specify his inward convictions, the playwrights demonstrate that in a climate of religious controversy martyrdom may yield an estrangement of surface from reality akin to that which Renaissance theatrical practices invited.

The ways contemporary martyrologists handle the convention of joy suggest they worried over this potential estrangement of external appearance from inward conviction. John Knott has argued that joy is a key element in Foxe's depiction of Protestant martyrs.[10] For instance, Foxe's martyr Richard Woodman discovers inner joy while contemplating the prospect of martyrdom: "persuaded in my mynd to die... [I] had no regard of nothing in this worlde, but was as mery and glad and joyfull, I praise God, as ever I was... I feele no lothsomnes in my flesh to dye, but a joyfull conscience and a willing mynde thereto."[11] Woodman proclaims his joyful conscience to assert the truth of his faith, a faith he continually and clearly confesses. Yet such proclamations are by no means unique to Protestant martyrdom; Catholic martyrologists found a display of joy just as important. William Cardinal Allen records that the priest John Sherte, on the brink of his 1582 execution, thanked God for bringing him "to so glorious & happie a death for thy sake, although in the eies of worldlinges contumelious and reprochefull, yet to me most joyfull & glorious, and for the which I yeld the most hartie thankes"; in *Concertatio Ecclesiae Catholicae in Anglia* the priest George Haydock joyfully reacts to his sentencing and is later deeply dismayed at a rumor (proven false) that the Queen had decided to extend him mercy.[12] Because the convention of joyfulness is shared across confessional lines, the beliefs to which joy testifies must be spelled out. Thus in a final "warning and testimonie" Sherte proclaims the faith that inspires his joy: "'Whosoever dieth out of the Catholique Church he dieth in the state of damnation.'"[13]

Sherte's comments suggest divergent readings of his death: it is "contumelious and reprocheful" to worldlings (those who do not share his faith) while joyful and glorious to him. Those who witnessed a martyr's final words and actions could, and apparently sometimes did, interpret displays of joy in different ways. Martyrologists both acknowledge and attempt to resolve these interpretive discrepancies. In his life of the York martyr Margaret Clitherow (*d.* 1586), John Mush records debates about Clitherow's joyful appearance after her sentencing:

Some of the Councell sent to marke her countenance as she was carried forth of the halle; but she departed from thence, through the streets, with a joyfull countenance: whereat some said, I[t] must needes bee that shee received comfort from the holy Ghost, for all were astonished to see her of soe good cheare: Som said, it was not soe, but that she was possessed with a merrie Devill; and that shee sought her owne death.[14]

Mush records the debate over the source of Clitherow's joy (Holy Ghost or merry devil?), finding it necessary to delineate the possibilities before answering the question definitively. A later passage claims that public opinion finally settled on one interpretation: as Clitherow processed through York to her execution, everyone who saw her go "cheerfully to her marriage, as she called it" was greatly impressed: "They all marvelled to se her joyfull smiling countenance."[15] Significantly, Mush claims that Clitherow knows she must demonstrate joy in order to testify to her faith: "her mynde was alwaies on her end; Craving all good praiers for perseverance & Ghostly strength to overcome all Combate, and Joyfully to depart from this world, to Gods glorie and the advancement of his Catholick Church."[16] In her final public moments, a cheerful demeanor would testify to the rightness of her faith and soothe the doubts of those who suspected a merry possession.

Of course, a merry devil could inspire a disingenuous final performance: how might onlookers determine whether a happy demeanor testifies to a sincerely joyful inner state? Recent work on Renaissance inwardness has largely focused on those who equivocate, rather than confess, their faiths. The assumption is that stories of martyrs collapse the distance between an authentic yet incompletely accessible realm of inward knowledge and the rhetorics that make that realm readable. Yet martyrologists themselves were at pains to validate their martyrs' smiling countenances with references to their inwardly-held, and thus presumably genuine, faiths. In 1600 as he was led to his death, the Catholic layman John Rigbie was subjected to a final interrogation, as observers wondered at his joyful appearance and inquired about its authenticity. Rigbie's martyrologist Thomas Worthington writes that Rigbie was at peace, "as wel appeared by his swete Angelical con-tenaunce." Some onlookers, however, pressed to know what lay beneath the countenance they observed: "the standers by...asked him, if he laughed from his hart, he answered yes verily from my hart. And beare witnes with me, al good people, that I am now forthwith to give my life only for the Catholique cause."[17] The onlookers' question valorizes a presumably genuine inward state and also worries over potential discre-pancies between outward appearance and inward "hart." Rigbie carefully correlates outward appearance and inward joy; he then elaborates the cause for which he dies, the reason behind his laughter. Because observers do not simply assume that inward belief motivates outward appearance, Rigbie must argue that his joy is rooted in his religious confidence (and perhaps Worthington hoped that Rigbie's words would resolve similar doubts among his readers). In attempting to render this episode persuasive, Worthington's text must address the possibility that the appearance of joy might be misleading, that common martyrological conventions might not testify reliably or transparently to a martyr's religious convictions.

Given More's famous sense of humor, the need to demonstrate what lies behind a martyr's laughter shapes narratives of his martyrdom as well. *Sir Thomas More* draws upon Catholic and Protestant narratives about More without ever revealing, as those narratives do, either religious testimony or political transgression. The play's sources include Foxe's *Book of Martyrs*, Harpsfield's *The Life and Death of Sir Thomas Moore*, Stapleton's *Tres Thomae*, and Holinshed's *Chronicles*.[18] Four famous anecdotes about More's death appear in all four sources. The first recounts how More poked fun at his jailor. Upon entering the Tower of London, prisoners typically had to remove their outer jackets; when asked to remove his upper garment, however, More doffs his cap instead. The second jest is made to a poor woman. She asks More, as he is led to his execution, to entreat for the return of some important papers she had given him when he was in office. More remarks that Henry VIII has been so good as to free him from all administrative duties. The third joke is to an official at More's execution; More asks for help ascending the scaffold and quips that he will see to coming down himself. Finally, More jests to his executioner about his short neck and orders the executioner to make a clean cut or else he will have no future dealings with him. Each source assumes that these mirthful anecdotes are not self-explanatory but need careful interpretation to be read aright.

John Foxe relates the jests but disdains the man who ended his life "with a mocke." Concerning More and his fellow Catholic martyr John Fisher, Foxe remarks "There is no doubt but that the Popes holines hath halowed and dignified these two persons long since, for Catholicke martirs." For Foxe, the pope's hallowing of a mocking jester is to be abhorred. He condemns More's "blynd devotion" to the pope and stresses that true martyrdom is determined by the cause for which the martyr died: "if the end of martyrs is to be weyed by judgment, & not by affection: then . . . perhaps in the Popes kingdome they [More and Fisher] may go for martirs . . . but certes in Christes kingdome their cause wil not stand."[19] Foxe acknowledges the emotional response More still provoked from many ("affection") but stresses More's failure, given his mocks and misguided zeal, to measure up to martyrdom's standards.

The Catholic controversialist Nicholas Harpsfield stresses that More's conscience was his guide in all things and uses the familiar anecdotes to demonstrate More's steadiness of mind.[20] The historical Thomas More is notorious for his evasive statements before multiple interrogators; perhaps through his evasions, as More's most recent biographer suggests, he wished to demonstrate that he neither invited nor sought to avoid death.[21] Once his fate was sealed, however, More changed tactics. Richard Marius writes that after More's verdict was handed down, he spoke to "let his audience know unmistakably the reasons for his death."[22] Chambers records More's bold statement at his execution that he died the king's servant but God's first, a marked contrast to the more common, humble statements made by those such as Cromwell, who at his execution meekly asked forgiveness for offending his prince.[23] Harpsfield also carefully elucidates how More's behavior changed. After his conviction, More no longer maintains a cautious silence but fully explains his reasoning "in discharge of my conscience."[24] Harpsfield records More's displays of both his wit and his conscience's dictates at his execution. After joking as he ascends the scaffold, he makes a serious, earnest confession: "Then desired he all the people thereabout to praye for him, and to beare witnes with him that he should nowe [there] suffer death in and for the fayth of the holy Catholike Churche."[25] For Harpsfield, the death scene, combining witty anecdotes and a confession of conscience, reveals a calm, reasoned, glorious martyr.

Thomas Stapleton, author of another of the play's sources, devotes a chapter to explicating More's jests, carefully disclosing the joyful, devout conscience motivating More's laughter: "The never-broken serenity of his mind was doubtless due to the constant peace and joy of his conscience. The merriness of his speech and a clever wit were most helpful to More in most difficult circumstances, and were a sure protection to his innocence and his constancy."[26] Stapleton records both the death-scene anecdotes and the charges Protestants leveled against More:

His rivals and the heretics took offence at what they called his foolish levity in laughing and joking at so solemn a time. Edward Hall, the chronicler . . . calls More therefore a foolish sage or a wise fool. The insulting gibe of this trifler has been well answered by one of our writers . . . : 'To thee, fond Hall, seems More both fool and wise: / A fool to men may wise be in God's eyes.'[27]

Building on this Erasmian argument that what seems foolish to men is wisdom in God's eyes, Stapleton argues that More's final jests demonstrate a healthy state of mind: "He was in no way cast down or anxious in mind: he was . . . even cheerful and merry, according to his wont . . . But not for a moment did he put aside the fear of the Lord."[28] Since the "fear of the Lord" is, according to the Book of Proverbs, the beginning of wisdom, Stapleton balances More's wit with wisdom. Stapleton not only draws implicitly upon the *Praise of Folly* to demonstrate how More resolves the potential conflict between wit and wisdom; he also appends to his biography a letter purporting from Erasmus testifying to the quality of More's mind.[29] After recounting More's jests, Stapleton narrates More's final, solemn confession of the reasons for his death:

On the scaffold he wished to speak to the people, but was forbidden to do so . . . He contented himself, therefore, with saying: 'I call you to witness, brothers, that I die the faithful servant of God and the King, and in the faith of the Catholic Church.' Such were his words: and in truth no one in the kingdom could be matched with him for fidelity to the King: God he served with the greatest zeal and holiness of life: he died not only in the Catholic faith but on its behalf.[30]

In Stapleton's recounting, More's wit, wisdom, and confession of conscience together compose an authentic martyr.

In comparison to the clear stands taken by Protestant and Catholic martyrologists, the treatment of More in Holinshed's *Chronicles* is oddly mixed. This Protestant historical project struggles to account for the admiration More still evoked and for the problem of his Catholic religion.[31] Noting the cause for More's execution, the text gives a conflicted portrait: "This man was both learned and wise, and given much to a certeine pleasure in merie taunts and teasing in most of his communication, which maner he forgat not at the verie houre of his death." The slight disapproval of More's taunting and teasing is reinforced by Hall's remark that More's learning and wit were "mingled with taunting and mocking."[32] By separating temporal from spiritual graces, the work negotiates its criticism of More's mocking humor and its praise for his wisdom: "God had . . . pored his blessings upon this man, induing him with eloquence, wisedome and knowledge: but the grace of God withdrawne from him, he had the right use of none."[33] Perhaps best illustrating its lukewarm presentation of More, the text includes a 1584 sermon which claims More should be praised for his "zeale" ("to the rebuke of protestants," says the narrator) and yet is "to be abhorred" for "his religion."[34] The sermon frees zeal from its theological moorings, admiring zeal in itself, free of what it might or ought to signify. While Stapleton linked More's "zeal" to a "holiness of life," Holinshed's text achieves an uneasy ambiguity about More by separating a martyr's fervent devotion from the cause martyrdom might signify or support.

The play elaborates a similar ambiguity as its lead character increasingly refuses to disclose himself, hiding behind the familiar jests without revealing whether he is laughing from his heart. Like a jest that lacks a punchline, the play promises and then denies full disclosure, exploiting the potential discrepancy between a martyr's appearance and his inward state. Its ambiguous characterization of More seems to praise him for his wisdom and sense of humor while reserving judgment on whether More's refusal to submit to his king was admirable or foolish. Although some have argued that the play is constructed around the revelation of More's personality, the play in fact denies a full declaration of More's conscience.[35] It replaces those moments in the controversial sources where More is afforded such space with lines emphasizing continual withdrawal. Staging a martyr whose final performance is never probed for evidence of the religious convictions motivating it, the play invokes martyrological conventions while increasingly obfuscating what those conventions were supposed to reveal. In this play, the drama of martyrdom comes not from its confirmation of faith through recognizable outward behaviors but, paradoxically, from its refusal to perform hidden, divisive, and perhaps ultimately unknowable motivations. The power of the performance, it seems, is all.

The play's closing moments invoke two scripts simultaneously – that of the expected death scene of a convicted traitor, demonstrated by the rebel Lincoln's execution early in the play, and the death of a martyr, present in the play's Catholic sources. Nonetheless, the play resists the key moment in each script: the revelation of the dying man's conscience. Harpsfield, for instance, answers the pressing question of whether More's resistance was treasonous by claiming that More's behavior actually fulfilled the king's wishes. Harpsfield records the king's instructions to More upon More's first entering royal service:

in all his doinges and affaires touching the king, he should first respect and regarde God, and afterwarde the king his master. Which lesson and instruction never was there, I trowe, any Princes servaunt that more willingly heard, or more faithfully and effectually executed and accomplished, as ye shall hereafter better understand.[36]

When asked to give his opinion on the king's pending divorce, Harpsfield's More returns to this advice. More states that he will gladly serve the king in

any thing . . . whereby he could with his conscience safely serve his graces contentation; as that he alway bare in minde the most godly wordes that his highnes spake unto him at his first comming into his noble service, the most vertuous lesson that ever Prince taught his servaunt, willing him first to looke unto God, and after God unto him, as, in good fayth, he saide he did, or els might his grace well accompt him his most unworthy servaunt.[37]

For Harpsfield, More's principles stem from his strong desire to serve his sovereign rather than to challenge or disobey him. Melchiori and Gabrieli have argued that the play converts More into a type of Puritan hero; they suggest Munday would have wanted to please Puritans who increasingly emphasized the independence of the conscience against the claims of the state.[38] Protestants had no monopoly, however, on appeals to conscience. Harpsfield and Stapleton elevate More's conscience over unjust laws; recusant Catholic martyrologists writing in the 1580s and 1590s also privilege conscience in their arguments about other martyrs. Given the heavy emphasis on conscience in the Catholic recusant sources, it seems more likely that the play's authors capitalized upon the potential flexibility in common martyrological language, such as the claim that martyrs act on their consciences, to hide what the sources consistently reveal: the faith undergirding conscientious decisions.

In its early scenes, the play heightens expectations for a confession of conscience. More's first scene invokes the revelation expected from a convicted criminal. In this scene, an unwise judge entreats a cutpurse, "Wilt thou discharge thy conscience like an honest man?" (I.ii.98). At Lincoln's death such a discharging occurs, for Lincoln confesses clearly the lesson his death ought to teach: "learn it now by me, / Obedience is the best in each degree" (II.iv.58–9). The play, unlike the Holinshed source, details the confession a condemned man should make.[39] Lincoln capitulates to authorities after More convinces him that divine and political authorities dovetail: "to the king God hath his office lent" (II.iii.106). As the play progresses, however, in More's view those authorities begin to conflict; the play begins to question whether More is a traitor or engaged in conscientious nonobedience. Critics disagree over whether the play endorses More's nonobedience or depicts the need to obey the sovereign at all costs. The difficulty stems in part from More's refusal to confess, to follow the script either of the unjustly or rightfully condemned.[40] More cites a rather opaque "conscience" as his reason for not signing the unspecified articles presented to him: "Subscribe these articles? Stay, let us pause: / Our conscience first shall parley with our laws" (IV.i.73–4). Tilney seems to have objected to the play's portrayal of More's (and Rochester's) willingness to incur the king's displeasure; the lines following this declaration of conscience (81–105) are marked for alteration. Importantly, the line referring to "Our conscience" was itself unobjectionable. After More exits to reflect further, Surrey uses More's earlier argument against him: "'Tis strange that my lord chancellor should refuse / The duty that the law of God bequeaths / Unto the king" (IV.i.106–8). William Long argues that *More's* "theme . . . is . . . the unfortunate consequences of disobedience to the rule of the sovereign."[41] The difficulty is that More, unlike Lincoln, never gives us the lesson Long specifies. Despite the promptings and urgings of other characters,

More refuses to play the role of the traitor who dutifully confesses and repents for his transgressions.

The expectation for More's final confession is at least doubly charged, since martyrs were expected to make a clear confession as well. Numerous recusant Catholic texts, including those about More, recount martyrs' desires to confess what they believe is the true cause for which they die: religion, not treason. Munday's *A Discoverie of Edmund Campion, and his confederates* (London, 1582) shows his familiarity with Catholic martyrs' arguments. Instead of showing that More desires to reveal his beliefs, however, the play carefully intensifies his reticence, depicting his withdrawal even from his family. As More's family entreats him to capitulate (entreaties not found in the play's sources), More tantalizes them with the possibility of his acquiescence.[42] Towards the end of IV.iv, More's wife kneels before him, asking him to reconsider his position; he responds, "I have bethought me, / And I'll now satisfy the king's good pleasure" (146–7). Surrey praises this "fair conversion," and More clarifies his earlier position as a tease: "I will subscribe to go unto the Tower / With all submissive willingness" (151–2). Rather than interpreting More's sense of humor to reveal his inner state, as its source materials do, the play uses More's jokes to delay and even obscure such revelation.

In a similar incident, More's family visits him in the Tower and asks him to reconsider. More teases his son-in-law Roper, hinting that he will confess some wrongdoing: "I have deceived myself . . . And as you say, son Roper, to confess the same / It will be no disparagement at all" (V.iii.92–4). Seeing his wife's elation, More again offers a jest: "Nay, hear me, wife, first let me tell ye how. / I thought to have had a barber for my beard, / Now I remember that were labour lost, / The headsman now shall cut off head and all" (96–9). The joke reveals that More will not capitulate in order to be freed; it also resonates with an earlier episode in the play. In that episode, adapted from Foxe's *Actes and Monuments*, More confronts a ruffian, one Jack Falkner, who has taken what Falkner calls a "foolish vow" not to cut his beard. More's response, an addition to the Foxean source, counters Falkner's characterization of vows: "Vows are recorded in the court of heaven, / For they are holy acts" (III.i.113–14).[43] More sentences the man to prison till his vow expires. Shortly thereafter, Falkner changes his mind, cuts his hair and wishes to make "a new vow . . . to live civil" (III.i.222). More's later decision not to cut his beard symbolizes that he, unlike Falkner, will not break a vow to achieve his freedom. The later joke also invokes the Falkner scene's questions about whether vows are foolish or holy, and about whether one should break vows to "live civil." Those questions remain unanswered in the play's powerful conclusion.

In its closing act, the play shies away from the martyr's and the traitor's expected confessional scripts, retreating behind jests to render More's death both surprisingly generic and dramatically powerful. The play portrays the woe London's citizens felt at More's demise and recounts the two jests regarding an old woman's law case and More's upper garment. The play also adds a series of more bitter jests that encode More's withdrawal from public confession. Upon ascending the scaffold, for instance, More remarks: "In sooth, I am come about a headless errand, / For I have not much to say, now I am here. / Well, let's ascend a God's name" (V.iv.49–51). The source materials indicate that More wished to speak to the crowd and did in fact manage a brief confession of his faith. This jest, not found in the sources, indicates that it is not only More who has a faulty memory: the play's suppression of More's final confession encourages as well a temporary repression of cultural memory about the reasons for his death.

More's next jest compares the scaffold to his private rooms: "here's a most sweet gallery, I like the air of it better than my garden at Chelsea" (V.iv.63–4). McMillin has discussed this jest as an example of the play's sophisticated dramaturgy. The typical English Renaissance stage had a curtained pavilion or booth at its back that could be used for playing interior scenes (at stage level) and raised ones (on the roof of the booth or pavilion). McMillin speculates that the playwrights might have planned to use such a physical structure for both the private scenes at Chelsea and the public space of the scaffold.[44] If his conjecture is correct, the lines would highlight the fact that despite his movement from Chelsea to the scaffold, More does not move towards public disclosure; instead, he retreats from domestic privacy to an even more intense opacity achieved in one of the most public spaces in the play.

Indeed, Shrewsbury emphasizes the public function of the scaffold and of the condemned's last words: "My lord, 'twere good you'd publish to the world / Your great offence unto his majesty" (V.iv.68–9). More's response buries his supposed trespass beneath metatheatricality: "my offence to his highness makes me of a state pleader a stage player (though I am old, and have a bad voice) to act this last scene of my tragedy" (72–5). A martyr's last words were supposed to reveal the inward convictions beneath the joyful surface. Here More, a character in a dramatic performance, likens himself to a performer playing a tragedy; refusing the invitation to publish his supposed offence, he offers instead another layer of theatrical opacity. His remark frustrates the observers in the play. Surrey urges More, "My lord, my lord, hold conference with your soul: / You see, my lord, the time of life is short" (80–1). The drama of both the martyr's and the traitor's final moments is invoked but without the disclosures expected by the onlookers at Rigbie's execution and represented by More's hagiographers.

More does at last resign his jokes: "Here More forsakes all mirth, good reason why: / The fool of flesh must with her frail life die. / No eye salute my trunk with a sad tear; / Our birth to heaven should be thus: void of fear" (V.iv.115–18). The play substitutes this speech for the moment of confession and never explicitly interprets the remark as indicating an Erasmian understanding that God's wisdom seems foolish to the world. Instead, the play closes with Surrey's uneasy evaluation of the scene he has witnessed, an evaluation that evokes the conflicted rendering of More in the Holinshed source: "A very learned worthy gentleman / Seals error with his blood" (V.iv.119–20). The Revels editors suggest that these lines are unclear about whose "error" is meant. A common feature of martyrological rhetoric, however, was the martyr's assertion that he died to seal his testimony with blood.[45] The phrase hints at More's mistaken faith, while its juxtaposition with praise for More's learning points to the mixed feelings the Holinshed text voices about More. Because the play substitutes opaque jests and generic confessions for a specific revelation of what, exactly, More's blood is sealing – error, as Surrey suggests, or religious faith, as in the Catholic sources? – it separates the scene's pathos from what it might have confirmed.

Only one moment in the play implies the religious motivation behind More's fall. Shortly after More refuses to subscribe to the king's articles, his daughter reports a disturbing dream she had: while her father was praying at a church, a rood fell on him and killed him (IV.ii.37–41). The dream is doubly iconoclastic, collating the fall of a rood and the crushing of More. It further suggests the problem the playwrights faced as they attempted to resurrect More's image, damaged by Protestant propaganda, without resurrecting the convictions for which he died. The ultimate opacity of More's presentation should not be equated with the confusion Greg attributes to the play. Nor does it necessarily support the views of Fox, Candido, Forker, and Melchiori, who in finding evidence of careful dramaturgy and thoughtful composition attempt to unify the play into a single stance on a particular theme. Instead, the play's richness comes from its keen awareness of the interpretational problems in which its subject matter is implicated and the subtle negotiations it undertakes between the controversial stances outlined in its sources and the conflicted views of its

London audience. Balancing iconographic and iconoclastic traditions, the play exploits one of the discursive rifts opened by England's competing sets of martyrologies: the potential erosion of confidence in the common markers used to signal a martyr's authenticity. Its attempt to present a history capable of accommodating mixed feelings such as those outlined in Holinshed's account of More's death reveals, through what it conceals, the potential misalignments that Reformation controversy created between discursive conventions and inward convictions, between the performance of a martyr's joyful laughter and the beliefs of his heart.

### HENRY VIII AND CONFLICTS OF CONSCIENCE

*Sir Thomas More* has tantalized critics for over a century with the possibility that one of its revisers, the manuscript's famous Hand D, was William Shakespeare. While a definitive ruling on the authorship question may never be possible, there are intriguing thematic connections between Shakespeare's *Henry VIII* (1613), his last history play, and *Sir Thomas More*.[46] Specifically, *Henry VIII* extends the earlier play's interest in the ambiguities produced by Protestant and Catholic uses of similar testimonial conventions. *Henry VIII* most obviously invokes issues of martyrdom in that several of its characters, as the play obliquely and ominously reminds us, were considered martyrs for different causes, and *Henry VIII*, like *More*, draws on Foxe's *Actes and Monuments*. The play also engages with martyrological discourse more subtly in its characters' repeated appeals to conscience. While *More* does not give its lead character the opportunity to discharge his conscience, numerous figures in *Henry VIII* discharge theirs only to uncover conflicting testimony. Despite its debts to Foxe's martyrology, *Henry VIII* does not adopt Foxe's argument for the historical continuity of a Protestantism rooted in individual consciences and given official expression for the first time in the 1530s. Repeatedly undermining or qualifying the testimony of consciences, the play's ambivalent historiography refuses to reconcile the antagonistic histories that conflicting consciences dictate. The disparate testimonies offered under the authentication of "conscience" illuminate what More's opacity in *Sir Thomas More* elides: the fault-lines in the English religious histories martyrologists attempted to narrate.

The play's complex handling of appeals to conscience is all the more striking against the backdrop of martyrological writing on conscience. The language of conscience is not necessarily linked to martyrology, of course. Camille Wells Slights has read the play's references to conscience in the context of casuistical arguments about the primacy of the conscience in determining tough moral questions.[47] Yet the questions of conscience the play raises have to do not just with moral decisions *per se* but with larger testimonial concerns. The issue is not only whether the king makes the proper decision about his marital situation but, more fundamentally, whether he is being truthful when he claims to act only upon his conscience's promptings. As Gordon McMullan notes, "it is the question of 'testimony,' of pinpointing and recounting the truth, which is repeatedly at stake in the play's uncertainties."[48] Because Protestant and Catholic martyrologists are concerned with demonstrating how trustworthy consciences may be recognized, martyrological discourse forms a rich context for the play's examinations of conscience. In contrast to the play's probing of conflicting testimony, martyrological discourse values the consistency or constancy of a conscientious person and the mutual confirmation of the testimony of consciences, from which sound religio-historical narratives may be built.

Since the language of conscience is widely used in martyrological writing, it is best studied cross-confessionally. Arguing that *Henry VIII* celebrates the moral inviolability and potentially conflicting independence of individual consciences, Slights attributes this subjective understanding of conscience to Protestantism; she opposes that understanding to a Catholic reliance on external authorities to reconcile individual differences. Yet the individual conscience is not given such latitude in mainstream Protestant thought. Indeed, Foxe writes that Marian Catholic inquisitors frequently characterized Protestant consciences as independent and wholly subjective; the charge is one that Foxe's martyrs labor to disprove.[49] Further, recusant Catholic writers frequently privilege martyrs' consciences over obedience to the state's anti-Catholic legislation. While there are differences between Protestant and Catholic uses of conscience, it is significant that Protestant martyrologists who use the language of conscience to legitimate their martyrs seem compelled to link their martyrs' consciences to particular theological understandings. The term, then, does not necessarily signal Protestant associations, as writers like Foxe were well aware. Given Catholic claims on the language of conscience, Protestant controversialists must argue for associations between that rhetoric and their beliefs, as well as for the continuity of history which they hope to draw from the testimony of Protestant consciences.

Foxe negotiates the problem of conflicting consciences as he attempts to interpret the continuing history of English Protestantism through the difficult (from a propagandistic point of view) reign of Henry VIII. Next

to a sidenote that reads "Traitors made martyrs" Foxe discusses the simultaneous execution of three Catholics and three Protestants in 1540. As Foxe
indicates, his rendering of this episode was criticized by Nicholas
Harpsfield (alias Alan Cope) who argues that Catholics executed under
Henry suffered for conscience.[50] Foxe responds by insisting that the
Catholic "Martyrs" died not for religion but for treason. Specifying that
these Catholics died the traitor's death of "hangyng, drawyng, and quar-
teryng," Foxe hopes to settle the religious confusion that ensued among
spectators:

The which spectacle so happenyng upon one day, in two so contrary partes or
factions, brought the people into a marveilous admiration & doubt of their
religion . . . as might so well happen amongest ignoraunt and simple people, seeing
two contrarye partes so to suffer, the one for Popery, the other against Popery,
both at one time.

In order "to remove and take away all doubt hereafter from the posterity,"
Foxe admonishes readers that doctrine must distinguish true martyrs from
false: one group suffers for the "Gospell," another for "Popery."[51] Right
doctrine should corroborate conscientious testimony.

Yet even among Foxe's martyrs, right doctrine is not self-evident. Foxe
links the term "conscience" to understandings of the "gospel" in ways that
suggest a desire to reconcile Protestant consciences into a common body of
belief. For instance, John Philpot (to whose multiple examinations Foxe
devotes much space) repeatedly links his conscience's testimony to the
primacy of the Word and the absolute power of God. Against Catholic
claims that he stands only on the shifting sands of his own opinion, Philpot
insists that he relies not upon "any opinion of wylfulnnes, or singularity"
but "only upon my conscience, certainly informed by gods worde, from the
which I dare not go for fear of damnation." His "conscience," "grounded
on Gods worde," is thus connected to Protestant views of biblical primacy.[52] One of Philpot's Catholic inquisitors takes a rather unsympathetic
view of this insistence upon conscience: he charges Philpot not to
"stand . . . in [his] own conceit."[53] To such charges, Philpot responds
"I sit not in mine owne conscience: but I know it, & God there onely
ought to sit, and no man else."[54] Philpot's retort distinguishes his faith
from independent willfulness; even he does not control his own conscience
but rather God alone. Foxe attempts to reconcile conflicting Protestant
consciences because he values the consistency of martyrological testimony,
the reinforcement Protestant consciences were to give to each other.
Philpot, for example, argues that Catholics have never been able to answer

Germany's learned ministers and Calvin, implicitly linking closely Calvinist and Lutheran thinkers, and insists that " 'in the matter of pre-destination [Calvin] is in none other opinion then al the Doctors of the church be, agreeing to the scriptures.' "[55] Based upon the convergence of the testimony of consciences, Foxe builds his book's larger argument for Protestantism's historical and theological continuity.

Foxe's celebration of consistent Protestant consciences finds its antith-esis in his unfavorable (to put it mildly) portrait of Stephen Gardiner, one of his text's principal villains. In Foxe's view, Gardiner's theological waverings indicate that he was not truly learned because he was "variable" in matters of religion: "standing upon a singularity of his owne wit" he differed even from other "Papistes."[56] Because Foxe is so concerned with religious unity, this charge is one of the worst he can level. As Gardiner "inconstantly . . . varied from him selfe," Foxe attacks claims that his "con-science" was religiously sound.[57] Foxe's criticism mirrors, ironically, Gardiner's earlier attack on Protestants such as Luther and the martyr Anne Askew, celebrated by John Bale. In a 1547 letter to Somerset, Gardiner complains that "at one time Bale prayseth Luther, and setteth his death forth in English with commendation as of a saint, which Luther (whatsoever he was otherwise) stoutly affirmed the presence really of Christes natural body in the Sacrament of the Altar; and yet Bale, the noble clerke, would have Anne Askew, blasphemously denying the pre-sence of Christes natural body, to be taken for a saint also."[58] Gardiner argues that nobody can safely embrace Protestant beliefs since even Protestantism's own confessors and martyrs disagree about what those beliefs are. Robert Persons makes a similar argument about Thomas Cranmer, claiming that his acquiescence to Henry in all matters "sheweth no conscience to have byn in Cranmer at all."[59] Much as Foxe charges Gardiner with inconstancy, Persons accuses Cranmer of political oppor-tunism and religious waverings, noting his "so many turnings and wynd-ings, both in matter of Religion and manners," and sharply criticizes Foxe for calling Cranmer a constant man.[60] For Persons and Foxe, inconstant, willfully individualistic people cannot be people of conscience and thus cannot offer trustworthy testimony.

In addition to attacking Foxe's martyrs as inconstant waverers, recusant Catholic writers attempted to reclaim the rhetoric of conscience for their own cause. Writing in 1582 of the charismatic Edmund Campion, Thomas Alfield challenges the government's claim that Campion died not for religion but for treason; that claim, he insists, is "already generaly confutid in all mens consciences."[61] In his final note on the deaths of Campion and his priestly co-sufferers, Alfield asserts that the consciences of the men who died will provoke their countrymen's consciences to consider aright the reasons for their sacrifices. Those consciences will make supposed traitors into martyrs:

> as the cause, not the paine, or persecution . . . iustifieth all men: so Christ, and these good mens consciences formed in al pietie, mekenesse, and modesty, so their last protestation, washed, sealed, and confirmed with their blood, so their resolute death for religion, for our faith, for the church . . . may stirre up the minds of al men inwardly and in conscience to consider the cause of our sufferance, affliction, and imprisonments . . . that they may acknowledge our undeserved calamities.[62]

The martyrs' testimony that they die only for religion should correspond with others' internal promptings. Appealing to inward minds, Alfield hopes to establish a unified community of belief, interpretation, and historical understanding.

Writing in 1601 about the deaths of sixteen English Catholics, Thomas Worthington makes a similar appeal to conscience. He asserts that these Catholics died for religion and not for treason, as "in their consciences" those who level the treasonous charge "can not but knowe it to be farre oterwise."[63] The consciences of persecuted, persecutors, and martyrologist must agree; what sets the martyrs apart from persecutors who know but refuse to confess the truth is their willingness to let conscience inform all outward actions. Writing of John Rigbie's examination, Worthington stresses Rigbie's own inward impulses as motivating his Catholic conversion. In response to the inquisitor's question, "Who perswaded you to that course, to alter your Religion[?]," Rigbie replies, "No bodie my Lord, but myn owne conscience, for when I considered myn estate, I found that I was not in the right course to be saved. And therfore I resolved by Gods grace to professe that Religion wherby my soule might be saved."[64] At his martyrdom, Rigbie argues against charges of treason and echoes refrains found throughout Foxe's work: "I am a true Subiect, and obedient to her Maiestie and the Lawes, in anie thing which may not hurt my conscience . . . most readie I am, and willing to seale it with my bloode . . . knowing nothing wherin I have offended, but only uttered my conscience."[65] As Foxe's martyrs insist upon their obedience to monarchical authority, their adherence to their consciences, and their willingness to seal their consciences' testimony with their blood, so Rigbie's use of this common language argues for his own death as a martyrdom. Both Catholic and Protestant martyrologists, then, count on the persuasive force of appeals to conscience and work to reconcile consciences behind one faith. *Henry VIII*, in a less religiously integrated approach to the history of the English Reformation, examines the historical problems that arise when appeals to conscience do not result in believable testimony, when conflicting consciences produce ambiguous histories.

Given the play's less-than-straightforward approach to the Reformation, scholars have debated whether *Henry VIII* celebrates Protestantism's rise. Alan Young argues that the play praises Protestantism's emergence, while Lee Bliss, Frederick Waage, and Frank Cespedes argue that its darker elements are not outweighed by Cranmer's final prediction of Protestant England's glory.[66] Casting long shadows over Cranmer's hopeful prophecy is the play's undermining of the testimony of consciences, testimony that is crucially important in the play's Foxean source. Ivo Kamps has argued that the play is not "a disunified play about history but a play about disunified history."[67] As such, the play challenges the historiography of one of its own sources, as well as of other martyrologies dedicated to celebrating the bloody fates of several of its characters. Like *More*, *Henry VIII* is well aware of the interpretational problems engendered by the cross-confessional use of common martyrological rhetoric. Rather than repressing memories of religious conflict, however, *Henry VIII* actually alludes to conflicting controversial interpretations of Reformation history and in doing so doubts whether consciences may witness collectively to historical and religious continuity. These doubts are never fully resolved, suggesting not a staging of Protestant subjective consciences, nor a clear intention to celebrate Protestantism's rise, but rather a pervasive uneasiness about the supposedly conscientious origins of national Reformation.

This uneasiness may be perceived in the play's hints about the fates of Anne, Cromwell, Cranmer, and More – all claimed as either Protestant or Catholic martyr-heroes. The play does not avoid "the whole issue of persecution," as Julia Gasper claims, for these hints recall the conflicting sacrifices demanded by different consciences.[68] For instance, in III.ii the fates of More and Cromwell, highly controversial figures for Foxe and his Catholic opposition, are closely juxtaposed. After his fall, Wolsey is informed that More has been chosen Lord Chancellor in his place and offers a blessing upon him: "May he continue / Long in his highness' favor, and do justice / For truth's sake and his conscience; that his bones, / When he has run his course and sleeps in blessings, / May have a tomb of orphans' tears wept on him" (395–9).[69] Wolsey's blessing rather optimistically assumes that "truth," "conscience" and the king's "favor" all converge and that More need only continue in the king's favor in order to fulfill the demands of truth and conscience. Fifty lines later, Wolsey offers

Cromwell a similar injunction: "Be just, and fear not. / Let all the ends thou aim'st at be thy country's, / Thy God's and truth's: then if thou fall'st, O Cromwell, / Thou fall'st a blessed martyr" (446–9). Wolsey's injunction aligns truth with political "ends"; the trouble for Cromwell, of course, is that the "ends" he was to aim at in the near future, while ostensibly good for the Protestant cause, did not suit his king, so that in Foxe's view at least he fell a martyr.[70] Similarly, More obeys his conscience's demands to the death. The closely juxtaposed allusions to the fates of these two men suggest a fundamental misalignment between the king's wishes and the demands of truth and conscience.

Perhaps the most notorious ambiguity in the play concerns the character of the king himself. Young argues that we must take the king's scruples at face value; the play, however, makes that rather difficult. For example, one of only two references the play makes to a "reformation" of any sort occurs in a discussion criticizing French fashion at the court, so that there is a link between anti-French nationalism and this supposed "reformation."[71] Henry posts a "new proclamation" upon the court gate demanding the "reformation of our traveled gallants / That fill the court with quarrels, talk and tailors" (I.iii.17, 20–1); as Rolf Soellner suggests, this posting may allude to Luther's famous posting of the 95 Theses. The Englishmen to whom the proclamation pertains have become too enamored of French fashion and must, as Lovell remarks, "[renounce] clean / The faith they have in tennis and tall stockings" as "there's no converting of em" (29–30, 43). In the scene immediately following this religiously allusive banter about French fashion, Henry appears at Wolsey's banquet posing as a French-speaking shepherd and meets Anne.[72] Following on the heels of anti-French sentiment, the association of Henry's meeting Anne with the "French tongue" (I.iv.57) problematizes the notion that the play celebrates wholeheartedly the union that ushered in, officially at least, the English Reformation.

The play's rearrangements of Holinshed's chronology further undermine Henry's public declarations of the authenticity of his unquiet conscience. In Holinshed, no mention is made of Anne until after the trial scene (the Shakespearean parallel is II.iv); Wolsey's banquet is discussed in the context of proving how luxuriously the Cardinal lived but no mention is made of Anne's presence. In telling contrast, the play juxtaposes Henry's public explanation of his doubts' origins with Anne's entrance in II.iii. After Henry emphatically declares his reasons for separating from Katherine – "O my lord, / Would it not grieve an able man to leave / So sweet a bedfellow? But conscience, conscience! / O tis a tender place, and

I must leave her" (II.ii.139–42) – the next line the audience hears, spoken by Anne, is "Not for that neither" (II.iii.1). In contrast, Foxe's Henry VIII says that his doubts "daily & hourly trouble my conscience" and that if the marriage to Katherine were proved valid, he would gladly stay with her, for there would be nothing "more pleasant nor more acceptable to me in my life, both for the discharge & clearing of my conscience and also for the good qualities and conditions . . . in her."[73] In the play, as Judith Anderson remarks, "conscience" is juxtaposed with "bedfellow" and the potency implications of "able," so that the "tender place" seems not particularly spiritual.[74] Other characters' comments further undercut Henry's conscience. When the Lord Chamberlain remarks, for example, that "the marriage with his brother's wife / Has crept too near his conscience," Suffolk remarks: "No, his conscience / Has crept too near another lady" (II.ii.15–17). Because Suffolk's line is an aside, the audience is made privy to the undermining of Henry's conscience even as they witness the unfolding of the history launched by his supposed misgivings. At the moment of Anne's triumph, her coronation, the second gentleman's remarks remind the audience simultaneously of her beauty and the king's hypocrisy: "Sir, as I have a soul, she is an angel . . . I cannot blame his conscience" (IV.i.44, 47). Henry's conscience is associated not with inward, moralistic promptings but merely with sexual desires.

Further, the play refuses to associate his conscience with Protestant doctrines or causes, as Foxe and other Protestant Reformation writers attempted to do.[75] Although Slights finds that the play is unclear about the honesty of the king's revelations, she nevertheless argues that Henry's conscience is a Protestant one as he relies principally on it and not on external authorities to resolve his dilemma. Similarly, Bertram argues that as Henry increasingly relies on his conscience, he moves towards a Protestant endorsement of the conscience's freedom from papal jurisdiction.[76] Yet Henry's supposed reliance upon papal authority early in the play is not so clear. Cespedes notes that Wolsey is already "licking his political wounds" in I.ii.[77] Further, Henry's characterization of Wolsey as "the quiet of my wounded conscience" in II.ii is remarkably similar to his later comment about Cranmer: "My learned and well-beloved servant Cranmer, / Prithee return. With thy approach I know / My comfort comes along" (II.iv.236–8). Henry takes advantage of different church authorities to stamp his initiatives with ecclesiastical approval; he is willing to turn to whoever might give approbation to his desires. His conscience does not reveal a particularly Protestant bent, nor is the

opportunity for Protestantism's official incursion into England attributed to much more than Henry's sexual and political strategizing.

The play questions its king's conscience through its altered chronology
and its undercutting of Henry's public professions. It also extends this
questioning of the testimony of consciences to the historiographical process itself, as it repeatedly stages the difficulty of relying on individual
consciences for certain testimony. In Holinshed's version of events, for
example, only the king is associated with "conscience"; here, the term is
associated with Wolsey, More, Cromwell, Cranmer, and even the convicted traitor Buckingham. The problems of testimony in early modern
culture, exacerbated by martyrological battles, are made manifest as the
play repeatedly questions its major figures' consciences. Buckingham's
innocence or guilt, for example, becomes a pressing question for the
play's audience as well as for the gentlemen whose conversation reveals
his fate to us.[78] In the Holinshed passage which is this scene's source, the
details of the indictment against Buckingham are listed in full. While
Wolsey is blamed for instigating Buckingham's investigation out of envy,
Holinshed does not fully excuse the Duke, being careful not to question
too vigorously the king's justice.[79] In the play, the details of the testimony
against Buckingham are revealed to us secondhand, summarized in the
gentlemen's conversation ("examinations, proofs, confessions / Of divers
witnesses," II.i.16–17), while Buckingham is allowed to defend his innocence passionately.

Most marked are the contradictions staged in Buckingham's death
scene. In the Holinshed source, Buckingham dies "meekelie"; given this
meek and presumably silent death, only Buckingham could know whether
or not he was a traitor: "At the time of his death (no doubt) his conscience
(giving in greater evidence than 10,000 witnesses) told him whether he was
justlie condemned or no, for a mans dieng day is as a bill of information,
putting him in mind of his life well or ill spent."[80] Martyrologists make
manifest such bills of information, relying on martyrs' final words as
especially truthful since no believer would go to the grave with lies on
his/her lips. While *More* prevents its protagonist from discharging his
conscience, *Henry VIII* allows Buckingham to discharge his but also
makes it difficult for the audience to believe wholly in his testimony.
Buckingham invokes the tradition of truthful last words as he gives his
final advice, urging onlookers to heed it with the line "This from a dying
man receive as certain" (II.i.125). In this context, Buckingham's words are
all the more powerful: "And if I have a conscience, let it sink me / Even as
the axe falls, if I be not faithful!" (60–1). Like Philpot and recusant Catholic

martyrs, Buckingham envisions conscience as an internal moral arbiter which indicates with divine certainty his words' truthfulness. Similarly, his final self-vindication uses the standard martyrological trope of sealing one's testimony with blood, thus coupling martyrological bravado with the blood of a supposed traitor: "I am richer than my base accusers, / That never knew what truth meant: I now seal it; / And with that blood will make 'em one day groan for't" (104–6). He asserts his innocence powerfully and yet reminds auditors of the aristocratic imperiousness that prompted his ill-fated attack on Wolsey ("*base* accusers," emphasis added).[81] His claims of innocence contrast sharply with the gentlemen's earlier observations that though Buckingham would "fain . . . have flung from him" the evidence brought against him, "indeed he could not" (II.i.24–5). The conflicting testimony – traitor or victim, liar or martyr – is never clearly resolved.

Extending this concern with the believability of an individual's testimony, the play's treatment of its major villain, Cardinal Wolsey, considers whether the testimony of individual consciences may be used to construct historical narratives. Wolsey eventually undergoes a transformation in which he supposedly replaces his focus on the external, material world with an inward, more penitent perspective. In his final moments on stage, the Cardinal performs a change of heart. After renouncing worldly fame – "Vain pomp and glory of this world, I hate ye!" – Wolsey declares "I feel my heart new opened" and finds "within . . . A peace above all earthly dignities, / A still and quiet conscience" (III.ii.365–6, 378–9). As Anderson notes, however, the Cardinal's insistence on his inward peacefulness jars with his question to Cromwell that soon follows: "What news abroad?" (391).[82] His recurring concern with worldly issues raises a shadow of doubt about the inner transformation he professes. While Wolsey, unlike *More*'s lead character, does confess his conscience, that confession is rendered a potentially incomplete or inauthentic performance.

Holinshed's *Chronicles* draws upon Stow's selections from Cavendish's *Life of Wolsey* to produce its odd account of a man who lived a scheming villain and died a wholesome penitent.[83] Perhaps responding to the ambiguity in its source, the play presents an historiographical debate over the degree to which Wolsey's good end ought to inform history's assessment of him. Griffith asserts that Wolsey died "full of repentance, / Continual meditations, tears and sorrows" (IV.ii.27–8). Katherine counters with a diatribe on his faults, stressing that he was "ever double / Both in his words and meaning" (38–9). Griffith again praises his noble ending – "His overthrow heaped happiness upon him; / For then, and not till then, he felt

himself . . . he died fearing God" (64–8) – and Katherine is finally reconciled to this portrait of Wolsey thanks to the "honest chronicler" Griffith
(72). The exchange models how episodes of internal repentance and
quieting of consciences may be interpreted and indeed contested in the
course of producing histories.

Conflicting interpretations of history are again invoked in the play's
treatment of Katherine and Anne. The play repeatedly juxtaposes Anne's
virtues and beauty with highly sexualized accounts of and reactions to her
rise. This juxtaposition invokes historiographical controversies over the
degree to which she was the virtuous champion of Protestantism that
writers such as Foxe portrayed her to be.[84] For Foxe, Katherine's marriage
is a clear violation of godly law which the pope arrogantly sought to
manipulate: "This mariage seemed very straunge and hard . . . But what
can be . . . so harde or difficulte wherewyth the Pope, the omnipotent
Vicare of Christe can not . . . dispense, if it please him?"[85] For Foxe, Anne
is a Protestant heroine, renowned for her learning and devotion. Although
Holinshed's portrait of Anne is less partisan, Holinshed does reprint Hall's
prurient speculation over Katherine's virginity (or lack thereof) at the time
of her marriage to Henry.[86] In addition, both authors acknowledge some
disagreement over the validity of the king's divorce and the motives for his
remarriage. Mentioning these disagreements briefly, Holinshed's
*Chronicles* then attempts to show their resolution: "Of this divorce and of
the kings mariage with the ladie Anne Bullongne men spake diverselie;
some said the king had doone wiselie, and so as became him to do in
discharge of his conscience. Other otherwise judged, and spake their fansies
as they thought good: but when everie man had talked enough, then were
they quiet, and all rested in good peace."[87] Foxe claims that Katherine's
supporters were of low social status, either due to their class or their gender:
"the mouthes of the common people, and in especial of women, and such
other as favoured the Queene . . . were not stopped."[88] Discrediting
Katherine's supporters more than does Holinshed, Foxe argues for the
ungodliness of her marriage and the piety of the king's new wife. The play's
sources, then, both recognize the debates over the king's divorce. Foxe
attempts to resolve them into a coherent historical narrative of
Protestantism's rise, while Holinshed's text presents them but suggests
they eventually died down.

The play alludes to the debates over the two women through its sarcastic
commentary about the king's motives. It also explores more fully the
tensions embedded in the king's marital problems. Early in the play the
Old Lady's bawdy reading of Anne's situation counterpoints Anne's

insistence upon her own virtue; the Old Lady skeptically remarks on Anne's "soft cheveril conscience" which despite her protestations would quite willingly "stretch" for a queen's honors (II.iii.32). In Anne's insistence that she "would not be a queen" (24), the pun on "quean" is striking. Similarly, in the two major moments of Anne's triumph in the play, her crowning and Elizabeth's baptism, unruly, sexualized celebrations undercut official pageantry. The description of Anne's "saint-like" demeanor at her coronation is juxtaposed ironically with the turbulent, sexually charged crowd. In the third gentleman's remarks, the crowd's response to Anne's beauty virtually enacts the second gentleman's earlier declaration that he could not "blame" the king's "conscience" for being unsettled by that beauty:

> Believe me, sir, she is the goodliest woman
> That ever lay by man; which when the people
> Had the full view of, such a noise arose
> As the shrouds make at sea in a stiff tempest,
> As loud, and to as many tunes. Hats, cloaks
> (Doublets, I think) flew up; and had their faces
> Been loose, this day they had been lost. Such joy
> I never saw before. Great-bellied women
> That had not half a week to go, like rams
> In the old time of war, would shake the press
> And make 'em reel before 'em. No man living
> Could say 'This is my wife' there, all were woven
> So strangely in one piece.                     (IV.i.69–81)

The combination of jubilant tribute (the tossing of hats) and sexualized salute (the flying up of doublets) suggests that the strong sexual undercurrent in the play's depiction of Anne persists even into the moment of her triumph. Similarly, the inability of male celebrants to identify their wives comments ironically on the king's search to obtain what he would consider to be a true wife and a valid marriage. At Elizabeth's christening, a similar juxtaposition unsettles Anne's image as the virtuous mother of English Protestantism's champion. Just before the christening, the unruly crowd outside prompts the porter to exclaim, "Bless me, what a fry of fornication is at door! On my Christian conscience this one christening will beget a thousand; here will be father, godfather, and all together" (V.iv.33–5). The christening is connected to unlicensed, undifferentiated sexuality, a connection which problematizes the play's celebration of Anne and which contrasts markedly with Foxe's and Holinshed's defenses of Anne's rise to power.

The play's juxtaposition of Anne's goodness and beauty with intim-
ations of uncontrolled sexuality finds its counterpart in the play's celebration of the bold Queen Katherine. Katherine's speeches at the trial scene
proclaim her to be a good and a godly wife, casting doubt on Henry's
protestations that he leaves her bed due to his conscience's moral promptings. The play's treatment of Katherine as an upstanding (if somewhat
outspoken) wife is remarkable given her treatment by Protestant historians
like Foxe, for whom she was merely the pope's pawn, submitting to an
immoral marriage. Because of her consistently bold and honorable behavior (it is her intervention, for example, which leads to tax relief for the
commoners at the play's beginning) Katherine's vindication of her character later in the play seems trustworthy. Her concern with testifying about
her chastity implicitly responds to those such as Holinshed and Foxe who
hinted and supposed, respectively, that she was not a virgin at the time of
her marriage to Henry VIII: "Strew me over / With maiden flowers, that all
the world may know / I was a chaste wife to my grave" (IV.ii.168–70). At
her final exit, she again denies the king's claims against her, calling into
question the reliability of the king's conscience and of the historical
narratives regarding her marriage built upon that conscience. In its treatment of Anne, Katherine, and Wolsey, the play adduces controversies over
the proper interpretation of the English Reformation's origins by weighing
and never fully reconciling conflicting testimonies. That multi-faceted
approach persists, though in repressed form, into its final scenes.

The most emphatic weighing of conflicting consciences occurs when
Cranmer is called before the council. Francis Yates has argued that the play
"reflects the Foxeian apocalyptic view of English history."[89] Yet the play's
departures from Foxe's text reflect its skepticism about the martyrologist's
historiography and, more generally, about the ability to produce a unified
religious history built on the testimony of martyrs' consciences. The play
distorts historical time to allow Thomas More to preside over the council
meeting (it actually occurred in 1543; More was executed in 1535),[90] so that
Foxe's martyr-hero Cranmer is on stage next to More, a foundational
English Catholic martyr-hero. The play does not "dilute the political
problems of the Reformation";[91] it rather highlights the conflicts among
Henry's councilors by allowing More and Cranmer to face each other. The
scene prior to the council meeting reminds the audience of Cranmer's
future martyrdom. In an addition to the Foxean source, Cranmer claims
that he is "right glad . . . / Most throughly to be winnowed, where my
chaff / And corn shall fly asunder" (V.i.109–11). Shortly before Cranmer
makes this assertion, Gardiner threateningly predicts that "it will ne'er be

well ... Till Cranmer, Cromwell ... and [Anne] / Sleep in their graves"
(V.i.29–31). More's martyrdom is invoked more subtly. As Wegemer notes,
Cranmer stands accused of treasonous malice, the actual charge leveled
against More at his treason trial. The play allows space for both men to
defeat the charges against them, but that defeat comes only when the
religious conflict implied by the presence of these two martyr-heroes is
subsumed into the supremely conflicted character of the king.

At issue in the scene is the proper relationship between political and
religious authorities, just the issue on which Henry VIII and More found
themselves at odds. Earlier in the play, Katherine claimed ultimate, if not
earthly, victory over her troubles: "Heaven is above all yet; there sits a judge /
That no king can corrupt" (III.i.100–1). When the king sees how
Cranmer has been mistreated, he echoes his former wife's words while
substituting the king's authority for that of heaven. Angry at the councilors' behavior, the king grumbles "Tis well there's one above em yet."
Since at this moment, according to the stage directions, the king is
literally "at a window above," the line in performance would most clearly
refer to him, not to any divinity. Further, the play implies that Henry
VIII's displeasure with how Gardiner treats Cranmer stems mostly not
from religious sympathies but from the fact that Cranmer is "so near our
favor" (V.ii.30). In Foxe's text, it is Cranmer's virtue that primarily
motivates Henry to defend him; the play's shift of emphasis continues
its depiction of the Reformation as proceeding largely from the king's
own sexual and political initiatives.[92] Indeed, despite arguing that he is
not a heretical disturber of the public peace, Cranmer is able to save
himself only by producing the king's ring. In turn, More shields himself
and the other councilors from the king's wrath by voicing lines attributed
to anonymous councilors in Foxe: he insists that "What was purposed" to
Cranmer was "meant for his trial / And fair purgation to the world" rather
"than malice" (V.iii.151–2). The play allows More to vindicate himself
from the charge of treasonous malice, of which the historical More was
convicted. Accepting More's plea, the king urges reconciliation: "As I
have made ye one, lords, one remain; / So I grow stronger, you more
honor gain" (V.iii.180–1).[93] The problem, of course, is that the councilors
are not one at all. Though martyr-heroes for different causes have been
allowed to vindicate themselves, the implicit conflicts between their views
are not reconciled but merely suppressed at the king's insistence.

The play's ending emphasizes the forced historiographical processes that
mold the testimonies of different consciences into a united narrative. Its
final scenes both model this process and undercut it with subtle reminders

of darker ambiguities explored in the play. Critics who find a celebration of Protestantism in the play put considerable pressure on Cranmer's final prophecy of Protestant England's glory.[94] Yet that prophecy itself qualifies Cranmer's vision of a glorious, peaceful England. Interrupting his speech by remarking "(But few now living can behold that goodness)" (V.v.21), he unwittingly reminds the audience of his famous martyrdom under Mary, and his reference to Elizabeth's death – "(When heaven shall call her from this cloud of darkness)" (44) – pointedly contrasts England's future glory with the "cloud of darkness" beneath which earthly kingdoms necessarily languish. Finally, Henry's last lines are suggestive in what they omit. Rejoicing over Elizabeth's birth, he exclaims, "never before / This happy child did I get anything" (64–5), glossing ominously over his first daughter who would shortly make a martyr of Elizabeth's godfather.[95] The play celebrates Elizabeth's birth but simultaneously calls attention to the suppression of historical events that could disturb such a peaceful vision. Ultimately, subtle reminders of the suffering of those who adhere to their consciences qualify England's effervescent glory, in the future for the play's characters and in the past for its audience.

Probing the dubious reliability of appeals to conscience, the play is unwilling to reconcile conflicting testimonies into a single religio-historical narrative. Its insistence (as its subtitle proclaims) that "All is True" instead gives us a much more complex historiography. *Henry VIII* has more in common with earlier Shakespearean histories, which encompass (without reconciling) differing perspectives on historical events, than critics who argue for an integrative vision in the play have allowed. Inhabiting multiple, conflicting perspectives on controversial uses of consciences and historical interpretations of them, *Henry VIII*'s ambivalence argues for the impossibility of integrating conflicting sources and testimonies into a unified English Reformation history.

Both *More* and *Henry VIII* make room for potentially divided theatrical audiences. To do so, *More* presents a history stripped of confession, while *Henry VIII* gives us too many confessions. These adaptations of martyrological material produce a critique of martyrology's evidentiary assumptions and a comparatively unsettled, unorthodox historiography. By exploiting the potential ambiguities of common martyrological conventions, both plays interrupt martyrologies' somewhat circular argumentation, in which confessions of conscience confirm historical narratives and historical narratives confirm individual consciences. In *More*, the repression of confession turns martyrdom into an opaque performance, divorced from the silenced beliefs of the martyr, while in *Henry VIII* dubious

consciences and conflicting confessions generate irreconcilable performances. The historiographical approaches taken by *More* and *Henry VIII*, so
different from those of the plays' martyrological sources, suggest the
growing impossibility of staging a religiously unified historical vision for
England given the conflicting consciences whose testimonies martyrologists so insistently proclaimed. In this sense, the conflicting testimonies
martyrologies foregrounded contributed to the early seventeenth-century
shift in history plays towards less-integrated visions of the English past.

NOTES

1 Had the second part of *Sir John Oldcastle* survived, it presumably would depict a
  proto-Protestant martyr. On Jesuit martyr-plays, see Allison Shell, *Catholicism,
  Controversy, and the English Literary Imagination, 1558–1660* (Cambridge:
  Cambridge University Press, 1999).
2 During the late sixteenth and early seventeenth centuries, history plays on the
  Tudor period were in vogue, including *Sir Thomas Wyatt, When You See Me You
  Know Me, Thomas Lord Cromwell,* and *If You Know Not Me You Know Nobody*
  (parts I and II). *More* and *Henry VIII* are the earliest (1592–5; see note 4 below on
  dating problems) and latest (1613) contributions, respectively, to this trend. On
  Foxean historiography in these plays, see Marsha Robinson, *Writing the
  Reformation: Acts and Monuments and the Jacobean History Play* (Aldershot:
  Ashgate, 2002).
3 William Long, "The Occasion of *The Book of Sir Thomas More*" (*Shakespeare
  and Sir Thomas More: Essays on the Play and its Shakespearean Interest,* ed.
  T. H. Howard-Hill, Cambridge: Cambridge University Press, 1989, 45–56),
  asserts that *More* teaches the folly of disobeying one's king, while Alastair Fox
  argues that More's folly is akin to God's wisdom ("The Paradoxical Design of
  *The Book of Sir Thomas More*," *Renaissance and Reformation,* 5 [1981], 162–73).
  For *Henry VIII* as sympathetic to Protestant politics, see Donna B. Hamilton,
  *Shakespeare and the Politics of Protestant England* (Lexington, KY: University of
  Kentucky Press, 1992); Alan R. Young, "Shakespeare's *Henry VIII* and the
  Theme of Conscience," *English Studies in Canada* 7 (1981), 38–53; and Camille
  Wells Slights, "The Politics of Conscience in *All is True* (or *Henry VIII*),"
  *Shakespeare Survey* 43 (1991), 59–68. On the play as somewhat sympathetic to
  Catholicism, see Peter L. Rudnytsky, "*Henry VIII* and the Deconstruction of
  History," *Shakespeare Survey* 43 (1991), 43–57, and Gerard Wegemer, "Henry
  VIII On Trial: Confronting Malice and Conscience in Shakespeare's *All is
  True*," *Renascence* 52 (2000), 111–30.
4 G. Harold Metz, "The Scholars and *Sir Thomas More*," in *Shakespeare and Sir
  Thomas More,* 25–9. There is less agreement about the date of and reasons
  behind the revisions. The Revels editors propose 1593–4 for composition and
  revision (introduction, *Sir Thomas More,* ed. Vittorio Gabrieli and Giorgio

Melchiori, Manchester University Press, 1990). Scott McMillin (*The Elizabethan Theatre and The Book of Sir Thomas More*, Ithaca: Cornell University Press, 1987) and Gary Taylor ("The Date and Auspices of the Additions to *Sir Thomas More*," in *Shakespeare and Sir Thomas More*, 101–29) argue for a later date of revision (1602 and 1603–4, respectively). A final determination may never be made; still, Taylor and McMillin adduce persuasively the practices of theatrical companies and the Jacobean appetite for plays on Tudor subjects.

5 Anthony Munday, *The English Roman Life*, ed. Philip Ayres (Oxford: Clarendon Press, 1980), introduction.

6 Many (though not all) scholars find respectable the hypothesis that three pages of the manuscript – folios 8r–9r – are in Shakespeare's hand. For an overview of this contentious issue, see Metz, "The Scholars and *Sir Thomas More*," 13–25.

7 R. W. Chambers (*Thomas More*, Harcourt, Brace, & Co., 1935), and the Revels introduction.

8 The years 1593–4 saw a rise in xenophobia; Tilney may have feared the riot scenes would provoke violence. Greg indicates where Tilney marked the manuscript and concludes that the play was never performed, since to comply with Tilney's cuts and demands for revision would "[eviscerate] the play in a manner fatal to its success on the stage" (xv). Melchiori argues that the "overly realistic presentation" of the May Day riot was Munday's "only miscalculation ("*The Book of Sir Thomas More*: Dramatic Unity," *Shakespeare and Sir Thomas More, 80*).

9 Katharine Maus, *Inwardness and Theater in the English Renaissance* (Chicago: University of Chicago Press, 1995), 31–2.

10 Knott, "John Foxe and the Joy of Suffering," *Sixteenth Century Journal* 27 (1996), 721–34.

11 *Actes and Monuments* (London, 1583), 1984, 2002.

12 *A Briefe Historie of the Glorious Martyrdom of XII Reverend Priests* (Rheims, 1582), A6r; *Concertatio* (Trier, 1588), 138r–v.

13 *A Briefe Historie*, A7r.

14 John Mush, "The life and Death of Mistris Margarit Clitherow," Bar Convent (York) MS, 90.

15 *Ibid.*, 109.

16 *Ibid.*, 107.

17 *A Relation of Sixtene Martyrs: Glorified in England in Twelve Monethes* (Douai, 1601; facsimile reprint, Ilkley: Scolar Press, 1977), 28.

18 Melchiori and Gabrieli, introduction to *Sir Thomas More*, 6–7, and "A Table of Sources and Close Analogues for the Text of *The Book of Sir Thomas More*," *Shakespeare and Sir Thomas More*, 197–202.

19 *AM* (1583), 1069. Gabrieli and Melchiori ("A Table") note that the playwrights likely used this edition.

20 Like the playwrights, Harpsfield depicts More's political rise, then discusses his private life, wisdom, and learning, and finally relates his martyrdom. The shape of Harpsfield's narrative may have influenced the play's; the Revels editors suggest Munday may have come across a manuscript of Harpsfield's

work during his searches under Topcliffe, thus spurring his interest in writing this play (introduction to *Sir Thomas More*, 8).

21 Peter Ackroyd, *The Life of Sir Thomas More* (New York: Nan A. Talese, 1998), chapters 30–2.

22 Marius, *Thomas More: a Biography* (New York: Knopf, 1984), 509.

23 Chambers, *Thomas More*, 350.

24 *The Life and Death of Sir Thomas Moore, knight*, ed. Elsie Vaughan Hitchcock (London: Published for the Early English Text Society by Oxford University Press, 1932), 193.

25 *Ibid.*, 204.

26 *The Life and Illustrious Martyrdom of Sir Thomas More*, trans. Philip E. Hallett, ed. E. E. Reynolds (New York: Fordham University Press, 1966), 124.

27 *Ibid.*, 128. Alastair Fox cites Hall's remark to argue that the play celebrates More's embracing the wisdom of God that seems like foolishness to the world ("The Paradoxical Design"). As Stapleton implies, however, Protestant writers use Hall's remark to disparage More while recusant Catholic writers vindicated More's mirth by reading it in Erasmian ways. James McConica discusses changing depictions of Erasmus and More's relationship in sixteenth-century recusant writing ("The Recusant Reputation of Thomas More," in *Essential Articles for the Study of Sir Thomas More*, ed. R. S. Sylvester and G. P. Marc'hadour, Hamden, CT: Archon Books, 1977, 136–49).

28 *Life and Illustrious Martyrdom*, 187.

29 *Ibid.*, 196–8. Stapleton's editor asserts that the letter was probably not Erasmus's.

30 *Ibid.*, 188–9.

31 On the authors and perspectives contributing to "Holinshed's" *Chronicles*, see Annabel Patterson, *Reading Holinshed's Chronicles* (Chicago: University of Chicago Press, 1994). I use "Holinshed" for convenience, not to indicate sole authorship.

32 *Chronicles* (London, 1587), 938.

33 *Ibid.*, 938.

34 *Ibid.*, 939. The sermon is by Bishop Elmer of London; a sidenote indicates that Abraham Fleming extracted the sermon for the 1587 edition of the *Chronicles*.

35 Candido and Forker, "Wit, Wisdom, and Theatricality in *The Book of Sir Thomas More*," *Shakespeare Studies* 13 (1980), 85–104.

36 Harpsfield, *Life and Death of Sir Thomas More*, 23–4.

37 *Ibid.*, 57.

38 See the introduction to their edition.

39 Patterson argues for a pro-citizen bias in Holinshed's version of the Lincoln episode (*Reading*, 195–8). Holinshed does not record that Lincoln upheld obedience to the state, as the play represents, but that he reasserts his right to complain of injustice to authorities (*Chronicles*, 843).

40 Melchiori, "Dramatic Unity"; Long, "The Occasion of *The Book of Sir Thomas More*."

41 Long, "The Occasion of *The Book of Sir Thomas More*," 50.

42 More's relationship with his family was, according to modern historians, vexed. Ackroyd (*Life of Sir Thomas More*) and McConica ("Recusant Reputation") suggest it took family members some time to understand why More was willing to die. On early More biography and its increasing characterization of More as a martyr, see Michael A. Anderegg, "The Tradition of Early More Biography," in *Essential Articles for the Study of Thomas More*, 3–25.

43 Foxe tells this anecdote about Cromwell, Foxe's hero and More's arch-enemy. Ackroyd's biography outlines Cromwell's attacks on More (*Life of Sir Thomas More*, chapter 29). Melchiori claims that Munday used this anecdote because Cromwell represents an ideal statesman who, like More, was "above all factions" ("*The Book of Sir Thomas More*: Dramatic Unity," 79). This is certainly how Foxe wished to represent Cromwell; its accuracy is, however, questionable, and there were numerous anecdotes about More in recusant Catholic sources which could have served as well. The transfer of the anecdote seems typical of the playwrights' willingness to use their sources flexibly.

44 McMillin, *The Elizabethan Theatre*, 104.

45 The phrase recurs in Foxe, Allen, Worthington, Alfield, and in Harpsfield's *Life and Death of Sir Thomas More*: "God provided that . . . in this Realme . . . should be those that should first . . . confirme and seale the unitie of the . . . Churche with their innocent blood" (212). Surrey's remark is steeped in irony: as the audience would know, he was executed at the end of Henry's reign, ostensibly for Catholic sympathies.

46 If Shakespeare collaborated on *More*, he could have been influenced by its entirety. Masten argues that attempts to delineate different hands in *More*'s manuscript ignore the fact that collaborators could influence each other in ways that preclude individual attributions ("More or Less: Editing the Collaborative," *Shakespeare Studies* 29 [2001], 109–31). There is also a notorious authorship question about *Henry VIII*. My research does not bear directly on whether Shakespeare collaborated with John Fletcher on this play. Linda Micheli discusses the controversy (*Henry VIII: An Annotated Bibliography*, New York: Garland Press, 1988, introduction). Peter Rudnytsky argues that the collaborative hypothesis "is unsupported by any external evidence"; because Heminges and Condell were present at the 1613 performance of *Henry VIII* which resulted in the burning of the first Globe, "their inclusion of the play in the First Folio . . . must have taken place with full knowledge of the circumstances of its composition and . . . provides a measure of tangible evidence that it is *not* a collaboration" ("*Henry VIII* and the Deconstruction of History," *Shakespeare Survey* 43 [1991], 43).

47 "The Politics of Conscience in *All is True* (or *Henry VIII*)," *Shakespeare Survey* 43 (1991), 59–68. Elsewhere Slights acknowledges that when Henry VIII questioned his marriage "he was posing a case of conscience . . . The literature justifying Henry's divorce took polemical rather than casuistical form" (*The Casuistical Tradition in Shakespeare, Donne, Herbert, and Milton*, Princeton: Princeton University Press, 1981, 4).

48 McMullan, "Shakespeare and the End of History," *Essays and Studies* 48 (1995), 17.

49 Claire McEachern notes the distrust of individual interpretive acts among many Protestant leaders (*The Poetics of English Nationhood, 1590–1612*, Cambridge: Cambridge University Press, 1996).

50 *AM* (1583), 1201.

51 *Ibid.*

52 *Ibid.*, 1800, 1805.

53 *Ibid.*, 1809.

54 *Ibid.*, 1822.

55 *Ibid.*, 1804–5.

56 *Ibid.*, 1785, 1788.

57 *Ibid.*, 1785–6.

58 *The Letters of Stephen Gardiner*, ed. James Arthur Muller (Cambridge: Cambridge University Press, 1933), 277.

59 Persons, *A Treatise of Three Conversions* (1603–4), 372. On Cranmer's life, see Diarmaid MacCullough, *Thomas Cranmer: a Life* (New Haven, Yale University Press, 1996).

60 *A Treatise of Three Conversions*, 378, 383.

61 *A True Report of the Death and Martyrdome of M. Campion Jesuit and prieste* (London, 1582), B1.

62 *Ibid.*, C4v–D1.

63 *A Relation of Sixtene Martyrs* (1601), 4.

64 *Ibid.*, 14.

65 *Ibid.*, 17–18.

66 Young, "Shakespeare's *Henry VIII* and the Theme of Conscience"; Bliss, "The Wheel of Fortune and the Maiden Phoenix of Shakespeare's *Henry VIII*," *English Literary History* 42 (1975), 1–25; Waage, "*Henry VIII* and the Crisis of the English History Play," *Shakespeare Studies* 8 (1976), 297–309; Cespedes, "'We are one in fortunes': the Sense of History in *Henry VIII*," *English Literary Review* 10 (1980), 413–38.

67 Kamps discusses historiographical strategies in the period, though not those underpinning martyrologies ("Possible Pasts: Historiography and Legitimation in *Henry VIII*," *College English* 58 [1996], 195).

68 Gasper, "The Reformation Plays on the Public Stage," in *Theatre and Government Under the Early Stuarts*, ed. J. R. Mulryne and Margaret Shewring (Cambridge: Cambridge University Press, 1993), 212–13.

69 I cite the Viking Penguin edition (New York, 1977).

70 *AM* (1583), 1184.

71 The second is the Lord Chancellor's announcement that Cranmer's "new opinions" ought to be "reformed" (V.iii.17,19). Soellner suggests that these allusions to the Reformation imply religious conservatism ("Reformation and Deformation in Shakespeare's *Heinrich VIII*," *Shakespeare Jahrbuch* 120), [1984], 68–76). They at least suggest keen historical irony. As Gordon McMullan argues, "conscience, conversion, faith, Reformation itself: each of these words is detached from its ostensibly higher meaning and degraded to the level of the material" ("'Swimming on bladders': the Dialogics of Reformation

in Shakespeare & Fletcher's *Henry VIII*," in *Shakespeare and Carnival: After Bakhtin*, New York: St. Martin's, 1998, 219).

72 Allusions to France and French fashion possibly invoke Anne's girlhood, spent in France, and her association with French fashion; on Anne's life, see Retha Warnicke, *The Rise and Fall of Anne Boleyn* (New York: Cambridge University Press, 1989).

73 *AM* (1583), 1050.

74 Anderson, *Biographical Truth: the Representation of Historical Persons in Tudor-Stuart Writing* (New Haven: Yale University Press, 1984), 129. Bliss notes that Henry's "must" implies the verdict he wishes others to reach ("The Wheel of Fortune," 8).

75 One qualification is needed: Foxe insists on the continuity of a suffering church throughout time but acknowledges the instability of many Henrician leaders, including the king himself; he blames Catholic leaders and bad councilors for Henry's waverings.

76 "*Henry VIII*: The Conscience of the King," in *In Defense of Reading*, ed. Reuben A. Brower and Richard Poirer (New York: E. P. Dutton & Co., 1962), 153–73.

77 Cespedes, "'We are one in fortunes,'" 422.

78 Cf. Rudnytsky: "the downfall of Buckingham turns on a series of antithetical perspectives, between which it is both necessary and impossible to choose" ("*Henry VIII* and the Deconstruction of History," 48).

79 *Chronicles*, 865. Kamps argues that Holinshed "was clearly not convinced of Henry's justice in this matter" ("Possible Pasts," 200).

80 *Chronicles*, 865.

81 Rudnytsky, "*Henry VIII* and the Deconstruction of History," 48.

82 Anderson, *Biographical Truth*, 139.

83 See Anderson on the play's engagement with Cavendish's *Wolsey* (through Holinshed, drawing on the 1580 edition of Stow's *Chronicles* and, possibly, more directly through the 1592 edition of Stow's *Chronicles*; *Biographical Truth*, 135–42).

84 On the accuracy of Foxe's depiction of Anne, see Thomas Freeman, "Research, Rumour, and Propaganda: Anne Boleyn in Foxe's 'Book of Martyrs,'" *The Historical Journal* 38 (1995), 797–819. Freeman argues that Foxe's portrait is biased but faithful to his sources.

85 *AM* (1583), 1049.

86 *Chronicles*, 912–13.

87 *Ibid.*, 930.

88 *AM* (1583), 1049–50.

89 Yates, *Shakespeare's Last Plays: a New Approach* (London: Routledge, 1975), 72.

90 Wegemer, "Henry VIII On Trial."

91 Gasper, "Reformation Plays," 212–13.

92 Cespedes notes that Henry's rescue of Cranmer is temporally and politically motivated ("'We are one in fortunes,'" 434).

93 Hugh Richmond compares this enforced reconciliation to the similarly flawed reconciliation at Edward IV's bedside in *Richard III* ("The Resurrection of an Expired Form: *Henry VIII* as Sequel to *Richard III*," *Shakespeare's English Histories: a Quest for Form and Genre*, ed. John W. Velz, Tempe, AZ: Medieval and Renaissance Texts and Studies, 1997, 205–28).

94 Judith Doolin Spikes argues for the myth of the elect nation as the play's unifying theme ("The Jacobean History Play and the Myth of the Elect Nation," *Renaissance Drama* 8 [1977], 117–49). Yet Cespedes notes that Cranmer's prophecy of a golden age would be unavailable to stage characters or audience in 1613, due to the recent death of the Prince of Wales (" 'We are one in fortunes'"). Bliss finds Cranmer's prophecy disjunctive at best, an image not of what the English kingdom is but what it ought to be ("The Wheel of Fortune"). See also Rudnytsky's reading of topical nuances regarding Princess Elizabeth's nuptials: her wedding did not, of course, cement James I's alliance to continental Protestantism, as militant Protestants had hoped ("*Henry VIII* and the Deconstruction of History," 55–6). Gasper notes that Cranmer's biblical allusions are to Old Testament prophets, not to Revelation which was so central to Protestant apocalypticism ("Reformation Plays").

95 The Viking editors gloss "get" as "achieve" with an obvious quibble on "beget."

# CHAPTER 7

# Martyrdom, nostalgia, and political engagement

Martyrologists' insistence on interpreting the world as sharply divided between true and false churches, wonders, and martyrs persisted into the mid-seventeenth century. In particular, martyrological habits of reading the world continued to shape the ways that the religiously implicated conflicts of the seventeenth century were understood. Dekker and Massinger's play *The Virgin Martyr* and mid-seventeenth-century Catholic martyrologies simplify contemporary conflicts, somewhat nostalgically, into stark confrontations between right religion and idolatry or heresy, in keeping with earlier martyrologists' attempts to differentiate true from false religions. Dekker and Massinger's play and these later Catholic martyrologies use martyrs typically portrayed relatively passively – namely female martyrs and Catholic martyr-priests – to articulate political resistance through the marvel of martyrs' endurance. In this combination of resistance with nostalgia for a martyrological worldview, the latter seems to enable the former, yielding an aggressive passivity legitimated by the stark oppositions these texts formulate.

*The Virgin Martyr* (1620) is the last saint's play staged in early modern England. Although based on Catholic legends of two female virgin martyrs, it serves, perhaps surprisingly, as militant Protestant propaganda.[1] Specifically, the play exploits the paradoxes of the bold yet persecuted female martyr in order to articulate, legitimate, and somewhat soften broader forms of religiously motivated resistance. This resistance includes, most importantly, allegorically veiled criticism of James I's foreign policy in the early years of the Thirty Years' War, which seemed to some militant Protestants to be accommodating Catholic aggression on the continent. The play's conclusion blurs the lines between passive martyr and active, religiously motivated soldier even as it hearkens back to traditional legends and a traditional dramatic form. Catholic martyrologies documenting the execution of English priests during the 1640s undertake a similar project, as they incorporate more articulate, outspoken forms of political resistance into their portrayals of priests wrongly executed. These texts formulate the English civil wars as purely religious conflicts and portray Catholic martyr-priests as religious soldiers who voice much more straightforward political commentaries than did earlier, Elizabethan martyr-priests. These martyrologies both long for a clearly articulated showdown between right religion and heresy and recognize that in the midst of a civil war Catholic martyrdom is inevitably caught up in very worldly power struggles.

The play and these later martyrologies demonstrate the flexibility of martyrological conventions, as a Protestant play celebrates a virgin martyr and Catholic martyrologists puncture the myth of martyrs' political disinterestedness. These texts' willingness to play with conventions and polemical arguments scholarship usually associates with the other side, so to speak, indicates the dependence of martyrological conventions upon particular religio-political circumstances as much as on seemingly neater theological or polemical distinctions. These texts long nostalgically for a searingly clear conflict between right religion and damnable falsehood, using the somewhat simplified martyrological vision of history to read a complicated present. At the same time, these texts are only too aware of the epistemological, interpretational, and representational problems competing testimonies provoked; they invoke, so as to dispel, competing formulations of religious heroism even as they insist upon and redeploy martyrology's stark oppositions between godly passive resistance and devilish, persecutory machinations.

GENDER, MARTYRDOM, AND RESISTANCE IN DEKKER AND
MASSINGER'S *THE VIRGIN MARTYR*

*The Virgin Martyr* is largely unknown today. Yet this play, first performed in 1620, was quite popular in its own time. The title page of its first quarto printing proclaims "The Virgin martir, A Tragedie. As It Hath Bin Divers times publickely Acted with great Applause." Title pages are of course primarily advertisements, but the record shows that the play was acted "Divers times" to "great Applause." A new scene was licensed in 1624, probably because the play was being performed again by a new company, and the play enjoyed four quarto printings, in 1622, 1631, 1651, and 1661. It was revived for the Restoration stage (we have evidence of performances from 1661 to 1668), and Benjamin Griffin adapted it in 1715 under the title *Injur'd Virtue, or, The Virgin Martyr.*[2] Despite its long-lived success, it has seemed to many critics an anomalous, simple-minded throwback to England's dramatic and religious past.[3] Performed nearly 100 years after almost every English saint's play was destroyed in the monastic dissolutions,[4] the play conflates St. Dorothy's and St. Agnes's legends into the story of a virgin martyr named Dorothea who suffers at the hands of the Roman emperors Diocletian and Maximinus. Yet the play is not just an anachronistic recycling of a defunct dramatic genre, for it is closely implicated in contemporary martyrological controversies.

Specifically, the play uses its lead character's virginity to polarize conflict between true and false religion against the backdrop of a much murkier religio-political situation, including England's tepid response to continental Protestants' calls for help at the outbreak of the Thirty Years War. The play portrays a world in which the true Christian martyr may be clearly distinguished from her pagan persecutor. This is not the world of *Henry VIII*, in which conflicting testimonies are explored but never firmly resolved and consolidated behind a single reading. Here the political ruler is Diocletian, the arch-villain of Christian martyrdom, not the conflicted figure of England's first nominally Protestant monarch; the title of the play – *The Virgin Martyr* – advertises what the audience is to see (as opposed to the subtitle of *Henry VIII*, "All is True," which epitomizes the play's irresolution of its conflicting testimonies). Still, the play is not naïve: it acknowledges the interpretational problems fostered by competing martyrdoms, using its stark oppositions of Christian to pagan to attempt to resolve them more definitively than does *Henry VIII*.[5] In particular, *The Virgin Martyr* takes advantage of martyrological ambiguities about the testimony of female martyrs. The play alters its martyrological sources to highlight religious competition; to resolve that competition it intensifies the resistance of the female martyr so that her purity may facilitate the separation of true from false religion. Further, it exploits tensions inherent in contemporary portrayals of defiant female martyrs to suggest how easily the desire for martyrdom may inspire larger forms of political and even military resistance, implicitly asking its audience to move beyond pity and horror towards taking retributive action against persecutors.

The play challenges many of our assumptions about ways to distinguish Catholic from Protestant female martyrdom and about the sorts of resistance female martyrdom could inspire. With the important exception of Julia Gasper, scholars usually either dismiss the play's portrayal of religion as diffuse and generic or categorize the play as Catholic-leaning.[6] Of course, people of every religious predilection thought their beliefs constituted generic Christianity: their opponents did not represent a competing creed but a departure from true religion. Readings of the play as Catholic propaganda are equally problematic, for they presume that Dekker could write both the rabidly anti-Catholic *The Whore of Babylon* and Catholic propaganda, and that Jacobean censors were broad-minded enough to allow it.[7] With the possible exception of Foxe's *Actes and Monuments*, the play's sources are Catholic martyrologies: *De Probatiis* (Surius), Edward Kinesman's translation of Alfonso Villegas's *Flos Sanctorum* (a Counter-Reformation compendium of saints' lives), and Caxton's translation of *The Golden Legend*.[8] But the readerships of Catholic martyrologies included Protestants of all persuasions, and as Spenser's *Faerie Queene* shows, Protestants often tried to recuperate Catholic legends for their causes.[9] If source material cannot determine the play's religious leanings, its attitude towards virginity has seemed a firmer indication of Catholic perspective. Theodora Jankowski argues that because the play celebrates Dorothea's determination to remain a virgin, it contains "strong hints of Roman Catholicism."[10] Yet her virginity cannot clearly demarcate the play's confessional allegiances if that virginity is read more allegorically, as the play's generalities seem to invite. Furthermore, Foxe himself praises the physical purity of early church martyrs as coextensive with the purity of their consciences, and both Protestant and Catholic martyrologists celebrated married and single women for their refusal to be sullied by contrary religious teachings.

This purity of conscience combined with the female martyr's supposedly weaker nature produced powerful martyrological propaganda. The play seems determined to adapt and exploit this power. For early modern martyrologists a martyr's religion, not his/her gender, was the foundational analytical category. Still, the gender of female martyrs could prove extraordinarily useful to their (usually) male martyrologists. Discourses of femininity could be employed to highlight persecutors' cruelty and to endorse a particular faith by pointing to its extraordinary female witnesses. For Foxe, martyrs of lower social status (lower-class or uneducated men as well as women) are valuable precisely because their violations of common expectations for their behavior make their testimony powerful. In his account of Agnes Potten and Joan Trunchfield, Foxe rejoices that these two, "beyng so simple women," nevertheless "manfully stoode to the confession and testimony of Gods worde and veritie."[11] The adverb "manfully" genders martyrdom as masculine while simultaneously the fact that "simple" women behaved "manfully" evinces their sanctity; only God could inspire such constancy and zeal in otherwise unremarkable people. Similarly, in his preface to his translation of *Flos Sanctorum* Kinesman writes that "to every age and sexe, though weake, and frayle by nature, hath [God] given strength, and courage to overcome all the temptations, & enticementes of the world . . . and in the end resolution, and constancy to dye for him, making their bloud...the seed of his Church."[12] Witnesses "frayle by nature" testify all the more to the strength God has given them. Most scholarship on female martyrs has asked whether their resistance to government, church, and domestic authorities could have larger political repercussions outside martyrdom's dire circumstances.[13] Generally, the answer has been cautiously pessimistic. Yet *The Virgin Martyr* imagines female martyrdom primarily as resistance to domestic hierarchies, imperial authority, militant masculinity, and even, implicitly, the absolutist politics of James I himself. Female martyrdom's ambiguities are exploited both to articulate resistance and to blunt somewhat the force of that resistance.

The play is staged at a moment when England, in the militant Protestant view, seemed to be shirking its duty to support continental Protestants, embroiled in the beginnings of the Thirty Years War. In 1617 Ferdinand of Styria, a Catholic and a Habsburg, was named King of Bohemia and attempted to recatholicize Bohemia and to roll back the religious freedoms granted to Bohemian Protestants since 1609. In 1618 the Bohemian nobility rebelled, and in August of 1619 they chose a new king, Frederick of the Palatinate, married to James I's daughter Elizabeth. Unfortunately for the Bohemians, Ferdinand was elected Emperor of the Holy Roman Empire two days later. A Habsburg-Catholic coalition quickly developed to threaten Frederick, and the Bohemians soon found they could not count on their supposed allies.[14] James I did not act immediately to rescue his son-in-law Frederick and his daughter for several reasons: he was intent on pursuing a Spanish match for his heir Charles, he saw himself as a diplomatic peace-maker in European affairs rather than a militant combatant, and he resisted supporting the Elector Palatine's unorthodox method of attaining the Bohemian crown, for Frederick had acted against a crowned prince.[15]

His seeming reluctance to aid the Protestant Elector Palatine's cause abroad did not sit well with militant Protestants at home. Julia Gasper has proposed that *The Virgin Martyr*'s somewhat generalized allegory of suffering and passive resistance is meant to rouse Londoners to support the Bohemian cause.[16] Indeed, for many early modern Protestants contemporary persecutions were seen as revived forms of early church persecutions; the use of an early church martyr to evoke the suffering of contemporary continental Protestants fits that perspective. Further, as Gasper notes, the Holy Roman Empire portrayed itself as a renewed Roman Empire; contemporary English propaganda pamphlets on the Bohemian situation repeatedly characterize Ferdinand as "Caesar," "Roman Emperor," or "King of Romans," and Catholicism as "Romish

Religion."[17] The play could have easily suggested connections between its late classical Rome and the newly revived Roman (and, in Ferdinand's hands, threateningly Catholic) Empire on the continent. The play was first performed at the Red Bull, a theatre used to stage militant Protestant plays.[18] It also likely encountered trouble with the censor. Bentley notes that the censor charged 40s. for reading the play, twice the usual amount, and there are indications of rewriting; it is the "reformed" play that was entered in the Stationers' Register.[19] Though we cannot know what was changed, Gasper's guess that the play contained politically sensitive material seems reasonable.[20] Yet the play's significance is greater than its immediate political import. Its attention to the female martyr's double nature – her defiance and her supposedly natural weakness, her impenetrable conscience and her sensationally threatened body – suggests that the playwrights extend martyrological tensions inherent in depictions of female martyrs to inspire defiant, even militant forms of resistance to persecution and, most importantly, to religio-political compromises.

Given the play's relative obscurity, a plot summary is in order. During the reigns of the notorious persecutors Diocletian and Maximinus (a fictive conflation), a Christian named Dorothea is singled out because a governor's son, Antoninus, has fallen in love with her instead of with Diocletian's daughter, to whom he is betrothed. Dorothea is arrested when her Christianity is discovered in the course of Antoninus's overtures. Throughout her ensuing trials, a servant boy, transparently named Angelo, comforts her and is revealed to the audience to be a guardian angel. Diocletian's loyal underling Theophilus, a furious persecutor of Christians, offers to have his daughters Caliste and Christeta, formerly Christians themselves, persuade Dorothea to reconvert to paganism as they did.[21] Not only do they fail, but Dorothea reconverts the two to the Christianity they once embraced. Enraged by their reconversion and encouraged by a servant named Harpax – a devil, Angelo's counterpart – Theophilus promptly martyrs his own daughters. In the meantime Antoninus has fallen gravely ill for lack of Dorothea's love. Impatient with his son's infirmity, the governor drags Dorothea into his bedchamber and orders his son to rape her, in the hope that he will then be cured. After a brief struggle with his conscience, Antoninus refuses, and so does every other man the governor attempts to recruit. At last the governor collapses as if dead and is only revived in response to Dorothea's prayers. Meanwhile, Spungius and Hircius provide a grim comic relief; their names are appropriate to their vices (drunkenness and lechery). Dorothea has taken these two into her household. While she has attempted to convert them and to use them to further her good works, they are markedly unreformed; they aid in the discovery of Antoninus as he tries to woo Dorothea and are later persuaded by Harpax to participate in their mistress's torture. Despite the fact that she proves impervious to her former servants' blows, she is soon martyred; at her martyrdom, Antoninus converts and promptly dies as well. The play's final act performs St. Dorothy's traditional iconography. Just before her death, Dorothea brags to Theophilus of the rich heavenly gardens to which she goes. Theophilus taunts her, challenging her to send him fruit and flowers from that garden. In the last act, Angelo delivers fruit and flowers to him, and Theophilus undergoes his own conversion and martyrdom.

Several changes from the play's martyrological sources suggest how the playwrights adapted them for the religious situation as they saw it. The playwrights added Spungius, Hircius, and Harpax, and expanded the Catholic sources' anonymous angel into the character Angelo. Drawn from morality plays' stock figures, these four characters function to distinguish firmly between true and false religion. The addition of Spungius and Hircius attacks the hypocrisy of supposed Christians. In his first scene, Spungius complains: "when I was a Pagan and kneeld to this Bachhus, I durst out-drinke a Lord, but your Christian Lords out-boule me: I was in hope to leade a sober life, when I was converted, but now amongst the Christians, I can no sooner stagger out of one Alehouse but I reel into another" (II.i.25–9). Hircius is the virginal Dorothea's radical opposite; he makes sexual jokes even as, betrayed by Harpax, he is led to his eventual execution. The fates of these two characters warn against deserting one's Christian alliances. Other morality figures also serve as an attack on hypocrisy. Angelo appears much sooner than in the Catholic sources and Harpax, his devilish counterpart, has the play's second line. While Harpax is able to uncover hidden Christians, Angelo exposes hypocrisy. Spungius proclaims, "I am resolved to have an Infidels heart, though in shew I carry a Christians face" (II.i.47–8). But Angelo sees easily through such pretences: "Your hearts to me lie open like blacke bookes, / And there I reade your doings" ( II.i.111–12). The development of the Catholic sources' angel into four morality-play characters coerces interpretation and emphasizes that there is no room for negotiation or compromise with a Christian-hating Roman Empire.

Although these characters are adapted from morality plays, *The Virgin Martyr* has no Everyman figure. The morality play characters instead compete over several others, notably Antoninus and Theophilus, to determine which side, heavenly or devilish, they will join.[22] To clarify the corporate nature of the battle and to make the play resonate with contemporary religious conflicts, the play greatly expands its sources' allusions to Roman religion into a fully realized competing religious system. Theophilus persecutes out of misguided religious zeal:

> Weare all scepters
> That grace the hands of kings made into one,
> And offerd me, all crownes layd at my feete,
> I would contemne them all, thus spit at them,
> So I to all posterities might be cald
> The strongest champion of the Pagan gods
> And rooter out of Christians.           (I.i.66–72)

Christeta uses familiar martyrological rhetoric in support of Roman religion; she says that she and her sister will "seale" their beliefs "with our bloods"(53). Significantly, Christianity's newness is represented in the terms Catholic controversialists used to represent Protestantism. In I.i Theophilus praises his daughters for returning "to the faith that they were borne in"(193), echoing the common controversial charge that Protestants departed from the faith of their forefathers. Importantly, in the opening Diocletian is shown being merciful to conquered kings. Collusion with Rome is clearly an option but would mean endorsing the persecution of Christians.[23] The play explicitly invokes competing versions of martyr-like suffering – perhaps, given the complexities of early modern martyrdom this book has traced, it must – in order to resolve the problems such competition provokes, for the play makes clear that the supposedly newer religion, which rejects Rome's iconic perversions and errors, is the true one. This fully realized sense of competing religions updates the Dorothea and Agnes legends and contrasts true Christianity with the Roman errors Dorothea opposes.

   Also at stake in the play's insistence on starkly opposed religions is the gendering of the heroic resistance to authority that helps Christianity articulate itself amid persecution. Forms of heroism too are imagined competitively. The play considerably expands its sources to depict a Roman culture that idealizes and masculinizes stoicism, constancy, and military conquest. When Harpax first describes Antoninus, his masculinized, sexualized military prowess wins praise: "So well hath [he] fleshd his maiden sword, and died / His snowy plumes so deepe in enemies blood, / That besides publicke grace, beyond his hopes, / There are rewards propounded" (I.i.95–8). The play expands the executioner's viewpoint, so to speak, developing his version of heroism so that it may be controverted. By the play's end, Roman heroic masculinity is converted by the eloquence of a defiant virgin into a new form of heroism figured as an androgynous conquest-through-suffering. Competing religions are troped as competing heroisms: a martial, militaristic, Roman stoicism is eventually transfigured into a passive endurance that is nonetheless frequently characterized in militaristic terms. As the play's martyrs endure passively yet claim militaristic bravado while they do so, the play articulates a Protestant call-to-arms, without renouncing the powerful cultural position (and political safeguard) of the persecuted but enduring martyr. Each of the major conversions Dorothea helps bring about – of Christeta, Calista, Antoninus, and Theophilus – reworks major flashpoints in Protestant and Catholic female martyr accounts: the benefits and potential risks of celebrating female martyrs' verbal testimony, the legitimacy of rebelling against patriarchal domestic authority, and the simultaneous strength and vulnerability of martyrs' bodies. Taking female resistance further than do contemporary martyr accounts, the play pits right religion against the impiety of violent Roman rites, with the result that even passive resistance may be converted into more militant action.

OPEN MOUTHS, CLOSED BODIES: FEMALE ELOQUENCE AND
BODILY INTEGRITY

In early modern anti-feminist writing, the openness of a woman's mouth signified her supposed unchaste openness in other ways.[24] The play's first conversions turn on the question of whether the female martyr's eloquence may co-exist with bodily integrity. Dorothea confronts Calista and Christeta to determine whose eloquence, hers or theirs, will emerge victorious. The play's emphasis on the special force of female eloquence both echoes and overgoes contemporary martyrologies, in which female martyrs' words are valuable precisely because their powerful speech violates expectations for female behavior. For instance, Foxe claims that Alice Driver, a 30-year-old woman from Suffolk, was "better learned than the popish doctors." For Foxe Driver's gender and class heighten the force of her anti-transubstantiation arguments; one of his sidenotes reads "The papists [are] put to silence by a simple woman."[25] Her gender and social station make her defense of her beliefs all the more powerful.

For Catholic writers, too, female martyrs' transgressions of patriarchal expectations of and for women serve as valuable testimonial evidence. Margaret Clitherow's martyrologist, the priest John Mush, registers with pride the challenge that a woman of her "constant virtue" might pose:

She, a woman, with invincible courage, entred combate against you all, to defend the most ancient faith, where in both she & you were baptized, and gave your promis to God to keepe the same untill death: where you, men, cowardish in the quarrell & faithlesse in your promise, laboured, all at once, against her to make her partaker of your turpitude & dishonestie . . . hath not the fortitude of one woman showed the injustice of [your tyrannie and Impious lawes]?

In militaristic language, Mush subjects non-Catholic masculinity to Catholic femininity: heretics and church-papists cowardly forsake the true faith while Clitherow, a supposedly weak woman, has the strength to defy "Impious lawes."[26]

Yet in comparison with Foxe's female martyrs sixteenth-century Catholic female martyrs often look more docile.[27] Catholic authors must defend their martyrs against charges of treason; they usually emphasize that their martyrs are otherwise compliant.[28] Accounts of the Catholic martyr Anne Line struggle to balance the martyr's requisite verbal challenges with the meekness and modesty expected of virtuous and nontreasonous women. Two versions of her last words and actions demonstrate martyrologies' uneven treatment of bold female speech. In John Gerard's *Autobiography*, a sharp-tongued martyr appears, as Line chides religious antagonists: "'When she reached the place of execution she found the ministers there ready to pester her with exhortations to abandon her errors. But she would have none of it. 'Away, I have nothing in common with any of you,' she said shortly."[29] Yet a note in another source suggests a slightly different scene: "She behaved herself most meekely, patiently and vertuously to her last breath. She kissed the gallowes and before and after her private prayers blessinge herself, the carte was drawne awaye, and she made the signe of the crosse upon her, and after that never moved."[30] The propagandistic uses for female martyr accounts and the controversial atmosphere in which they were circulated mean that there was little consensus about how female martyrs' speech should be portrayed, though the value of that speech, emanating from the supposedly weaker sex, was consistently emphasized.

Of course, female martyrs' outspokenness could also be read as transgressive, disruptive, and distinctly unsaintly. The Catholic controversialist Robert Persons called the Protestant martyr Anne Askew "a coy dame, and of very evill fame for wantonnesse: in that she left the company of her husband *Maister Kyme*, to gad up & downe the countrey a ghospelling & ghossipinge where she might, & ought not."[31] Speaking publicly – "ghospelling & ghossipinge" – prompts the charge of "wantonnesse." Defending against such easily anticipated charges, martyrologists sever the connection between outspokenness and sexual misconduct, sometimes by softening a woman's words but more often by defending her purity of conscience *and* body, her virginity of spirit. Thus Foxe recovers virgin martyrs like Agnes: God protected her virginity so as not to allow "his giftes of holy integritie or chastitie to be polluted."[32] Foxe celebrates her resistance to sexual affronts through conflating physical chastity with integrity, a goal to which all outspoken female martyrs may aspire.

The play counts on the power of female eloquence, as do both Protestant and Catholic martyrologists. Yet it surpasses contemporary martyrologies by allowing Dorothea to voice more fundamental forms of resistance to the patriarchal discourses of Roman society as the play portrays it. Act III contains the play's first conversions to Christianity, conversions centered on a concern with gender and appropriate speech. Theophilus's daughters Caliste and Christeta attempt to persuade Dorothea to forsake Christianity for Roman religion. Instead, they are converted back to Christianity, a conversion that also redeems feminine eloquence. The play registers the special power of female speech; as a priest in its opening scene notes, the sisters "teach their teachers with their depth of judgment, / And are with arguments able to convert / The enemies of our gods, and answer all / They can object against us" (I.i.46–9). Priding herself on their verbal prowess, Caliste boasts that "We dare dispute against this new sprung sect / In private or in publicke" (I.i.50–1).

Dorothea's conversion of Calista and Christeta turns on making women's religious speech and practices independent of sexual transactions. The play also suggests that silence in the face of heretical beliefs is worse than loose sexual behavior, an assertion contemporary martyrologists are not willing to make. The two sisters characterize their previous, temporary conversion to Christianity as a sexual and material fall. They were "Ruin'd" by Dorothea's "perswasion" and link the rise in their material fortunes to Roman religion. Dorothea's religion is "a toyle / Slaves would shrink under" and unfit for noblewomen: "Learn to be happy, the Christian yokes too heavy / For such a dainty necke" (III.i.78–9, 99–100, 94–5). They attempt to separate suffering from virtue, a link Dorothea firmly reinforces. Dorothea justifies female speech in godly causes:

> Have you not cloven feete? are you not divels?
> Dare any say so much, or dare I heare it
> Without a vertuous and religious anger?
> Now to put on a Virgin modesty,
> Or maiden silence, when his power is question'd
> That is omnipotent, were a greater crime,
> Then in a bad cause to be impudent. (III.i.101–7)

Dorothea invokes the common association between chastity and silence only to reject it. Importantly, this speech does not incorporate its source's anti-feminist statements. Kinesman's Dorothea exclaims that the two sisters "seem to be women" because they embrace paganism out of fear of dying.[33] Kinesman thus genders martyrdom and the bravery it requires as exclusively masculine. The play instead seeks to capitalize on the female martyr's combination of bold, persuasive speech with what Foxe calls "holy integritie and chastitie." Dorothea sheds "Virgin modesty" and "maiden silence" to argue that Roman religion is linked to sexual impurity; the suggestion of Rome as a Whore of Babylon haunts the scene. In a lengthy anti-hagiography, Dorothea attacks the Roman gods "canoniz'd" (III.i.144) by the sisters' culture, linking those gods to impudence, incest and whoredom, pointing out their "unchast loves, anger, bondages, wounds" (III.i.149). She suggests that any woman who follows Venus, no matter how chaste she might be, is tainted by Venus's sexual immorality. The sisters' reconversion to Christianity represents a reclaiming of their chastity and a rededication of their eloquence in true religion's service.

Their quick reconversion is characterized in the militaristic terms used to celebrate masculine Roman heroism in the play's opening. In Act I, Antoninus's military prowess justifies his elevation as the betrothed of the emperor's daughter; here, Calista and Christeta convert military conquest into spiritual conquering: "We are caught our selves / That came to take you, and assur'd of conquest / We are your Captives" (III.i.199–201). In response, Dorothea casts Christian paradoxes of victory-through-loss in the discourse of militarism: "in that you triumph: / Your victory had beene eternall losse, / And this your losse immortall gaine, fixe heere, / And you shall feele your selves inwardly arm'd / Gainst tortures, death, and hell" (201–5). Dorothea's characterization of Roman religion and of the sisters' reconquest for Christianity links the shedding of virgin modesty with military triumph. The sisters agree to surprise those waiting for the three of them to sacrifice to Roman gods. Roman religion evokes Catholic liturgical practices as the Roman priest in III.ii enters "with the Image of Jupiter, Incense and Censors." The sisters' iconoclastic response wins them martyrdom at the hands of their own father. Altering its sources to emphasize a feminine blend of outspoken sharpness and bodily integrity, the play shows female martyrs resisting the pressures of Rome's religious and military establishment by adopting the language of conquest and by being willing to suffer. The controversial environment in which early modern martyrologies were articulated pits forms of feminine eloquence against each other. The play does the same, and suggests that the sharper form of female speech is the more virginal and virtuous. Its militarizing of female martyrdom and defiant speech suggests the thinning of the line between passive though defiant resistance and defiant action.

### LIKE A VIRGIN: MARRIAGE, INTEGRITY, AND THE FEMALE MARTYR

The play's second conversion is Antoninus's, Dorothea's suitor. Her insistence on maintaining her virginity despite his ardent attentions is the aspect of the play that has seemed most Catholic to many scholars. Catholic writers like Kinesman and Persons (*Three Conversions*) do often single out virgin martyrs for praise. Yet writers like Foxe were willing to celebrate the virginity of early church martyrs provided that their spiritual integrity wins just as much praise: "Agnes for her unspotted & undefiled virginitie, deserved no greater praise and commendation, then for her willing death and martirdome."[34] There is evidence Dekker felt similarly. In the same year in which *The Virgin Martyr* was first performed, Dekker published an apocalyptic poem, *Dekker His Dreame*, in which his vision of heaven includes martyrs alongside "Virgins, whose soules in life from Lust liv'd cleare, / Had Silver robes, and on their heads did weare / Coronets of Diamonds."[35] Gasper also notes that Dekker used images of persecuted virgins to represent the Netherlands in *The Whore of Babylon* and *The Magnificent Entertainment*.[36] Further, Catholic writers sometimes celebrate married women. Kinesman praises the martyr Marta as "equall to her husband, in nobilitie, and nothing inferiour to him in vertue and Holiness";[37] Mush praised Clitherow's domestic virtues; and Southwell's *Short Rule* adapts the Rule of St. Benedict to the situation of married Catholic women. Both Protestant and Catholic martyrologists wrestle with cases in which a woman must decide whether to defy her husband for conscience's sake. Because the play is concerned with a particular suitor who is a pagan when he woos Dorothea, martyrologies' portrayals of the dilemmas women in religiously mixed marriages faced are especially relevant.

At issue are the precise circumstances under which a woman may assume a virginal imperviousness to domestic authority. In editing Anne Askew's account, John Bale portrays her departure from her husband's home as unwilling; he then argues that her departure confers virginal righteousness. Bale claims that Askew was compelled to marry Thomas Kyme, but

"Notwithstandynge . . . [she] demeaned her selfe lyke a Christen wife, and had by hym (as I am infourmed) ii chyldren." She left her husband because he disobeyed a higher authority: "She coulde not thynke hym worthye of her marriage which so spyghtfullye hated God the chefe autor of marriage."[38] For Bale, Askew's departure earns her a renewed bodily wholeness: in her steadfastness to the truth, she is "a vyrgyne . . . redeemed from the earthe and folowynge the lambe, and havynge in her forehead the fathers name written. Apocalypsys 14." The biblical passage which Bale invokes (Revelation 14:4) alludes to virgin *men*, men "not defiled by women"; in the Geneva gloss this masculine virginity is interpreted as an imperviousness to idolatry. Bale confers on Askew a pure, masculinized virtue. Still, her martyrologists seem to worry that her leaving her husband would (as indeed it did) prompt criticism. Editing Askew's story for his *Actes and Monuments*, Foxe does not directly discuss the details of her marriage, instead adding a sidenote in the 1570 and subsequent editions that carefully refers readers to Bale's discussion.[39]

Generally, the *Actes and Monuments* praises women who leave their marriages for reasons of conscience but tends to contain such behavior within a rhetoric of exception. One female martyr resolves conflicts between domestic and religious duties by an inward motion she interprets as divinely inspired. When Catholic interrogators insist that the devil deludes her, she counters: "it is the spirite of God whiche leadeth me, and which called me in my bed, & at midnight opened his truth to me. Than was there a great shout and laughing among the priestes and other." Foxe's sidenotes legitimate her explanation: "How God reveled his truth unto her."[40] Yet Foxe stresses how unusual this "weake vessell" is; her uniqueness validates her testimony but also mutes her account's more radical implications. Despite her insistence that she must be dutiful first to God rather than to her family, Foxe closes the account by returning her, textually at least, to her husband. After narrating her martyrdom, Foxe writes, "Touching the name of this woman (as I have nowe learned) she was the wife of one called Prest."[41] Even in the 1570, 1576, and 1583 editions Foxe begins this account by stating that he has not yet learned the woman's name and ends by noting that she is "the wife of one called Prest"; the woman who spent much of her interrogation defending her right to leave her husband for conscience's sake is finally identifiable only by his name.[42]

For recusant Catholics, the question of whether a wife should obey a Protestant husband was especially important, since Catholic wives played key roles in the English mission.[43] Since Catholic liturgies were often conducted in private homes, women helped shelter priests and stockpile materials necessary for Mass. In his 1593 treatise *Christian Renunciation*

Henry Garnet supports the freedom of a woman's conscience more emphatically than do contemporary Protestant ministers: wives, servants and children are "subjecte to their masters, husbandes, Parents" "in those things onely . . . which are not contrary unto Gods commaundements."[44] In practice, however, this rationale was difficult to invoke. Clitherow's martyrology reveals that Catholics and Protestants alike were unsure how to react to this apparently dutiful housewife who defied domestic and political authorities; Mush implies that even York Catholics were divided over whether Clitherow's behavior was justifiable. He depicts Clitherow as both patiently submissive to her husband and disobedient to him in matters of religion; her husband claims that "hee could wish noe better a wife than she was, except onely for two faults, as hee thoght; that was because she fasted much & would not goe with him to Church."[45] The account's ending attempts, not entirely successfully, to resolve tensions between religious and domestic allegiances. Mush claims that when John Clitherow heard of his wife's condemnation, "he fared lyke a madman out of his witts, and wept . . . vehemently . . . and said, Alas, will they kill my wife? Let them take all I have, & save her, for she is the best wife in all England, and the best Catholick also."[46] Yet in reporting Clitherow's final words about her husband, Mush indicates that she still reserved her conscience from his control: "if ever I have offended him, but for my conscience, I ask him forgivenes."[47] Her martyrologist emphasizes her consistently dutiful behavior even as she dies for the one thing in which she would not submit to her husband.[48]

The play intensifies the danger that a Christian wife might be dominated by a differently believing husband. It draws on St. Agnes's legend to give Dorothea a suitor whose advances she rejects in favor of a heavenly kingdom.[49] Her rejection, however, has as much to do with her unwillingness to be dominated by a pagan husband as with her desire to maintain her virginity *per se*.[50] Dorothea's insistence on remaining a virgin may be read allegorically: in resisting Antoninus's overtures she resists Rome's pagan, idolatrous religion and hypermasculine militarism. Most obviously, Dorothea's virginity resists a rather clichéd conception of love. The playwrights update their sources' hints of a young man's love-sickness by turning Antoninus into a hyperbolic Petrarchan suitor: in the opening act Antoninus compares himself to a ship without an anchor and claims to be "scorchd / With fire" (I.i.411, 423–4). In Shakespearean fashion Antoninus urges procreation, associating virginity with vanity: "glaze not thus your eyes / With selfe-love of a vowed Virginity" (II.iii.74–5). While Antoninus accuses Dorothea of cruelly wielding power over him, the play makes it clear that Antoninus's wooing has her domination as its goal. In the first act, Antoninus explains why he prefers Dorothea to Artemia, the emperor's daughter: "with Artemia / I still must live a servant, but enjoying / Divinest Dorothea, I shall rule, / Rule as becomes a husband" (I.i.451–4). The play's upholding of Dorothea's "vowed Virginity" does not necessarily endorse Roman Catholicism but rather preserves her from the difficult position of Askew and "Prest's wife," true-believing women married to idolaters. Antoninus does claim that he would not wrest her "conscience" and would allow her to practice her religion. But the play insists on an even starker form of purity for its heroine than that found in many contemporary martyr accounts, for sexual submission to a differently believing man too closely implies religious impurity.

This is made clearer as the challenge to Dorothea's virginity intensifies. In the fourth act, Antoninus's wish to rule over Dorothea threatens to turn violent. When she is forced to his bedside, the threat that Antoninus will "play the Ravisher" (IV.i.100) represents more than a physical attack; however horrifying that may be, the play insists that ravishment has spiritual meaning as well. Earlier in the play, Dorothea describes how her servant Angelo has ravished her: "Thy voice sends forth such musicke, that I never / Was ravisht with a more celestiall sound . . . when I tooke thee home, my most chast bosome / Me thought was fil'd with no hot wanton fire, / But with a holy flame, mounting since higher" (II.i.175–6, 198–200). Linked to spiritual ecstasy, ravishment is also associated with conversion. Hircius claims that he is "ravished" by Harpax, while Theophilus is "ravisht" by his daughters' eloquent ability to reconvert Christians to paganism (III.iii.203, III.ii.36). The threat that Antoninus might ravish Dorothea literalizes and sensationalizes a threat not against her body only but her "holy integrity" read more broadly. Despite his father's taunts ("A souldier, and stand fumbling so," IV.i.98), Antoninus chooses not to rape Dorothea; neither will any other man the governor attempts to force on her. In one pointed exchange a captured British soldier is offered his freedom if he will "ravish" Dorothea but refuses and decrees rape unmanly: "ravish her! is this your manly service, / A Divell scornes to doo't, tis for a beast, / A villiane, not a man" (IV.i.151–3). The soldier, beaten for his troubles, challenges the governor's definition of masculine soldiery, much as Dorothea does in various responses to her impending martyrdom. The not-very-subtle point is that the British ought to be willing to suffer rather than aid attacks upon victimized true-believers.

Eventually Antoninus is ravished by Dorothea, converted to her versions of love and heroism. In Act IV's opening, Antoninus vows "constant love" and anticipates that he will have "seald it with my death" (IV.iii.27, 30). Yet he soon transfers to Dorothea the supreme virtue of constancy and conflates it with defiance of military threats: "She smiles, / Unmov'd by Mars, as if she were assur'd / Death looking on her constancy would forget / The use of his inevitable hand" (IV.iii.66–9). Dorothea herself likens Theophilus to a foolish rapist who glories "in having power to ravish / A trifle from me I am weary of" (IV.iii.71–2). As Dorothea's language and bearing imply the victory of Christian over Roman ideals, her explicit prayer for the conversion of Antoninus's love to religious passion requests a parallel sort of victory: "Grant that the love of this young man to me, / In which he languisheth to death, may be / Chang'd to the love of heaven" (IV.iii.150–2). His passion is converted to the "holy fire" (IV.iii.160) Dorothea felt at seeing Angelo; he now feels, rather than illness, a "comfortable heate" (IV.iii.161). Dorothea receives from him a "religious kisse" on the hand now that his "fire" is "holy." As a result of Dorothea's prayer, his soul is released when her head is stricken off and in the final act Dorothea and Antoninus return to greet Theophilus and welcome him into heavenly bliss. In this drama of morality play abstractions and broad religious conflicts, Dorothea's resistance to married domestication is not just a resistance to marriage *per se* but an unwillingness to be linked to a non-Christian. Her imperviousness to an idolater's wooing intensifies the forms of domestic resistance Protestant and Catholic female martyrs undertook and stresses all the more firmly that Protestants can have no dealings with the Catholic enemy.

## PLAYING THE MAN: THE GENDERING OF MARTYRDOM

The play's final conversion is of Theophilus, persecutor of Christians and father of Christeta and Calista. This conversion explicitly masculinizes and militarizes martyrdom while also emphasizing the piteousness of martyrs' suffering. Stressing sensationally and graphically Roman torture of Christian bodies, the play as a whole draws on martyrological depictions of suffering bodies as both remarkably resilient and pitifully victimized. More broadly, the issue of the gendering of the martyr's body – its combination of passive strength and vulnerability to execution – speaks to the gendering of martyrdom itself. Mary Beth Rose identifies a seventeenth-century shift from a "heroics of action," gendered masculine, to a "heroics of endurance," predominantly gendered feminine.[51] In martyrological literature, the gendering of a "heroics of endurance" is always problematic, for despite the martyr's typically passive resistance the gendering of martyrdom as a form of masculinized heroism has a long history. According to the first extra-biblical Christian martyrology, the *Martyrium Polycarpi*, on the way to his martyrdom Polycarp hears a heavenly voice saying "Be strong, Polycarp, and play the man."[52] Thomas Worthington's *A Relation of Sixtene Martyrs* (Douai, 1601) also genders a martyr's passive courage as male, reporting that the Catholic martyr John Rigbie behaved "manfully."[53] Foxe uses the phrase Polycarp hears – "play the man" – in his 1576 account of the deaths of Nicholas Ridley and Hugh Latimer. Polycarp's phrase is a later addition to the account; either Foxe received additional information or he felt the need to remasculinize the martyrdoms of an old man (Latimer) and a man who suffered piteously for lack of sufficient fire (Ridley). In Foxe's 1576 edition, Latimer's final words to Ridley urge him to assume a masculine stoicism: "Bee of good comfort, M. Ridley, and plaie the manne: we shall this daie light suche a candle by Gods grace in Englande, as (I trust) shall never be put out."[54] The candle, of course, is both their own bodies and the Protestant faith they hope to ignite; their bodies are sites of pity recuperated as sites of defiant strength.

When the suffering bodies are female, "playing the man" becomes especially vexed. The female martyr's body, with its presumably greater vulnerability, may be exploited to show the amazing strength of God made visible through weakness and also the horrific cruelty of persecutors who attack women viciously. The suffering female body was extremely useful for propaganda.[55] In Richard Verstegan's *Theatrum Crudelitatem Haereticorum Nostri Temporis* (Antwerp, 1588), an illustration of a mute Margaret Clitherow being pressed to death serves to arouse pity and sympathy for Catholics in England. Foxe claimed that Askew was so weakened by torture that she had to be carried to her execution in a chair. Robert Persons recognized the value of such propaganda, complaining that Foxe related Askew's story "so pittifully...as he would moove compassion on her side."[56]

Yet martyrologists balance the female body's supposed weakness with the martyr's spiritual imperviousness to suffering, highlighting the spiritual strength contained within the weak vessel of the female body and at least potentially rehabilitating the female body as a site of passive resistance. Foxe reprints the early church martyr Julitta's final words praising the strength of suffering women: "Not flesh only God used in the creation of the woman, in signe and token of her infirmitie, & weaknes, but bone of bones is she, in token that shee must be strong in the true and living God, all false Gods forsaken."[57] Catholic authors too stressed the female body as a site of impervious resistance. Margaret Ward (*d.* 30 August 1588), sentenced to death for helping a priest escape from prison, insisted that her daring act sprang directly from her true femininity: "as to what she had done in favouring the priest's escape, she believed the Queen herself, if she had the bowels of a woman, would have done as much, if she had known the ill-treatment he underwent."[58] Breaking a priest out of prison is, remarkably, just an outpouring of feminine sympathy from the center of the female body; the Queen's own femininity is figured only in a conditional ("if she had the bowels of a woman"), for it is the Queen's government's lack of sympathy for Catholic priests that causes them to suffer.

Equally frequently, however, an emphasis on the female martyr's vulnerability to torture could undermine her other defiant attributes, such as her sharp tongue or quick mind. Perhaps the most infamous suffering female body in the English Protestant imagination is Anne Askew's. Askew was subjected to torture at the rack, a punishment almost unheard of for women and especially women of her social standing. Askew tersely renders her racking: "Then they ded put me on the racke, bycause I confessed no ladyes nor gentyllwomen to be of my opynyon, and theron they kepte me a longe tyme. And bycause I laye styll and ded not crye, my lorde Chauncellour and mastre Ryche, toke peynes to racke me their owne handes, tyll I was nygh dead."[59] Bale's commentary stresses her frailty: "lyke a lambe she laye styll without noyse of cryenge, and suffered your uttermost vyolence, tyll the synnowes of her armes were broken, and the strynges of her eys perysshed in her heade."[60] Repeatedly asking the reader to envision her suffering, broken body, Bale does not elaborate on Askew's remarkable assertion that after her torture, she "sate ii. longe houres reasonynge with my lorde Chauncellour upon the bare floore" about matters of faith.[61] He focuses instead on how her "weakenesse" reveals Christ's suffering with her. Although Foxe draws on a version of Askew's text printed without Bale's commentary, he follows Bale's emphasis on her physical fragility, changing the preface to her account to stress her physical suffering.[62] In the 1563 preface, readers are encouraged to study her text carefully: "Here next foloweth . . . the true examinations of Anne Askew . . . by the which (if thou marke dilligently) the communications bothe of her, and of her examiners thou maist easely perceive the tre by the frute and the man by his worke."[63] The much shorter 1570 preface simply states that the reader will "heare" her "tragicall story & cruel handlyng."[64] Her infamous torture is now the primary hook. In the 1570 version (the basis for the subsequent English editions published during Foxe's lifetime), Askew needs to be a weak, physically broken woman in order to serve as an example for readers.

In gendering its martyrs' suffering, the play gradually moves from the kind of piteousness invoked by Verstegan's mute depiction of Clitherow's pain, to the more mixed form of a woman who is able to speak somewhat (as in Askew's account) and whose body wondrously resists tortures, to a defiant, resistant "playing the man" in the martyrdom of Theophilus. The play can only imagine this last, most defiant martyrdom as a man's (though inspired by the marvels associated with a woman's martyrdom). The marvel of martyrs' perseverance is amplified by increasingly defiant speech. The play greatly expands Theophilus's role, making the doubter at the execution (in Caxton, Villegas, and Surius) the chief persecutor. Theophilus's conversion engenders a parallel conversion of his hyper-masculinized attacks on vulnerable Christians into a militarized martyr-dom. In developing its three on-stage martyrdoms from silent, piteous spectacle to defiant, articulate suffering, the play moves martyrdom from a position of passive endurance to one of at least potential action and engages with the broader problems of characterizing the martyr's body in contem-porary martyr accounts.

In the play's opening, the mute piteousness of Christians is stressed. In a lengthy expostulation to Harpax, Theophilus surveys his victims. They include all sorts of people *except* virile men: "Babes torne by violence from their mothers brests / To feed the fire, and with them make one flame: / Old men as beasts, in beasts skins torne by dogs: / Virgins and Matrons tire the executioners, / Yet I unsatisfied thinke their torments easie" (I.i.61–5). This list of horrors resembles atrocity propaganda circulated in support of the Bohemian cause, in which Ferdinand's minions were accused of "continuall Rapines, Murders, Combustions, Devastations, plentifull effusion of Innocent blood, violation and ravishing, both of Wives and honest Virgins, dismembring of little sucking Children, with many other inhumane, most Cruell, and Barbarous insolences."[65] The martyrs in Theophilus's catalogue are silent, suffering victims, like those in the propaganda pamphlet. Similarly, Calista and Christeta's eloquence is stifled at their martyrdoms. They are killed in a way that likens their execution to a perverse Mass: Theophilus asks the "incensed power, / Which from my infancy I have ador'd," to "Looke downe with favourable beames upon / The Sacrifice (though not allow'd thy Priest) / Which I will offer to thee, and be pleasde / (My fierie zeale inciting me to act it) / To call that justice, others may stile murther" (III.ii.104–10). The lines clearly indicate that Theophilus kills them on stage, before a "holy altar" (112). The two speak only briefly before their martyrdoms, to insist on their constancy to Christianity, and do not respond verbally to Theophilus's long speech prefacing his double murder.

Unlike Calista and Christeta, Dorothea has long been preparing for martyrdom. That preparation is couched in the conventional terms of donning God's armor. Just before her verbal confrontation with Calista and Christeta, Angelo urges her to "claspe thine armour on, / Fight well, and thou shalt see, after these warres, / Thy head weare Sun-beames, and thy feet touch starres" (II.iii.192–4). Later, as she is beaten for her convictions Dorothea marvels that torture (as in many virgin martyr legends) has little effect on her: "Joy above joys, are my tormentors wearie / In torturing me, and in my sufferings / I fainting in no limbe: tyrants strike home / And feast your fury full"( IV.ii.90–3). Dorothea's martyrdom allows her more powers of speech than were granted to Calista and Christeta. Still, her martyrdom is presented graphically; in IV.iii a stage direction, "Her head strucke off," indicates that her beheading is to be shown. Her last words balance the female martyr's piteousness with impervious resolve: "Say this of Dorothea with wet eyes, / She liv'd a virgin, and a virgin dies" (IV.iii.178–9).

Theophilus's conversion also inspires "wet eyes." But even as his martyrdom turns him into an on-stage spectacle, his rhetoric configures a new sort of militarism from the martyr's impenetrable resolve. Acts I and V contrast two forms of militarism. In the first, Roman military conquests are celebrated; in the fifth Theophilus, steadfast persecutor of Christians, undergoes a conversion that rewrites militarism as conquest-through-suffering. At the beginning of Act V, Dorothea's martyrdom has taken place, at which Theophilus issues the legendary taunt that she send him fruit and flowers from a heavenly garden. Retiring to his study, Theophilus works on an anti-martyrological catalogue, recording the gruesome persecutions he has overseen (the fact that many of the atrocities listed take place in the British Isles would not have been lost on the play's spectators). As in the play's sources, Angelo brings Theophilus a gift of fruit and flowers culled from a heavenly garden. The implication of this marvel is that the fruit or profit of reading martyrologies is a self-sacrificing response, when one is called by God; the legendary marvel is used to resolve the problem of conflicting interpretations of Christian deaths (just execution or religious martyrdom?), suggesting both that such resolution sometimes requires extraordinary means and that the play is anxious to provide them. The Angel responds to Theophilus's request to see the garden in generally Calvinist terms: "Yes, if the Master / Will give you entrance" (V.i.55–6). Clearly this is the case, as Theophilus takes the gifts from Angelo, that "ravishing Boy" (V.i.166) and determines for martyrdom: "That my last act, the best may Parallel" (V.i.172).

The opening of V.ii echoes the play's beginning. Artemia is about to be betrothed again, to Diocletian's co-emperor Maximinus. This may allegorize loosely the Catholic division of Frederick's lands between the Spaniards and Maximilian, Duke of Bavaria, after Frederick's 1620 defeat at the Battle of White Mountain;[66] Dekker and Massinger could have known about this from contemporary pamphlets. In any case, the consolidation of Rome's forces is clearly ominous. Artemia and her father expect Theophilus to glory anew in the Christians he has slain. Instead, Theophilus reinterprets his life's work: he presents a Christian martyrology (V.ii.101–2), praises Dorothea, and argues for her superiority to "canoniz'd" Spartan and Roman women who endured death stoically (V.ii.110ff.). His words invoke the specter of competing martyrologies; the proper resolution to such religious competition is the definitive, defiant action he has undertaken. We know that before he speaks to Diocletian he has sent Macrinus, Antoninus's friend, to release all Christians in his prisons and put them on boats to escape. He has, in other words, taken action. Tortured on stage at the end of V.ii, Theophilus talks throughout his ordeal and characterizes his conversion in military terms. His last words are: "witnesse for me, all these wounds and scarres, / I die a souldier in the Christian warres"; Angelo, reappearing to welcome him into heaven, hails him as "this souldier" (V.ii.232–3, 237). The stage directions indicate the iconography Foxe's title page tried to claim for English Protestantism: Antoninus, Caliste, and Christeta enter wearing the martyr's white robes; Dorothea appears yet more glorious with crowns on her robe and one on her head; and Angelo brings Theophilus his own martyr's crown.

The play shows a gradual shift of the gendering of the martyr's body from a piteous, feminized spectacle, to a more verbally resistant martyr, to a martyr who suffers but "plays the man" both in his militaristic rhetoric and in his preemptively defiant actions. The play cannot imagine that a woman might take this final step. Still, Theophilus's martyrdom broadens the possibilities for resistance by blurring the lines between a victimized martyr and a militant insurgent. The play as a whole uses a female martyr's defiant resistance to stir up anger and action against Roman/Catholic persecutors. In its final blending of martyrdom with militant resistance it echoes the rhetorical strategies of contemporary pamphlets on the Bohemian situation. A ballad printed in 1619 entitled "Gallants, to Bohemia, Or, let us to the warres againe" characterizes soldiering as righteous self-sacrifice; it celebrates those who "for true Religions right . . . spend their lives in bloudy fight / For God and for his Gospel" and views this self-sacrifice as truly manly: "To armes and fight it out like men."[67] Other pamphlets justify the

Bohemians' rebellion against Ferdinand and the crowning of Frederick on the grounds of cruel persecutions. In the pamphlets, the suffering of piteous but steadfast victims bleeds easily into the decisive action of sympathetic co-religionists. In *The Virgin Martyr*, the rehabilitation of an early virgin martyr's legendary purity invokes the problems of competing martyrologies and competing interpretations of martyrdom in order to resolve them by drawing a firm line between right religion and frighteningly violent Roman impiety. Through intensifying motifs in contemporary female martyr accounts, the virgin martyr's traditional endurance and imperviousness is converted into a Protestant mythology inspiring militant resolve.

## PLAYING THE POLITICIAN: ENGLISH CATHOLIC MARTYRDOM ON THE INTERNATIONAL STAGE, 1641–1649

If Catholic female martyrs tended to be portrayed as more docile than their Protestant counterparts, such docility was usually even more marked in the case of Catholic martyr-priests. In the mid-seventeenth century, however, Catholic martyrologies exhibit a blend of nostalgic simplification and also depict priest-martyrs as increasingly outspoken. Until recently, much literature by or about English Catholic martyrs has been relegated to the margins of the early modern canon. The scholarship that does exist focuses primarily on the late sixteenth and early seventeenth centuries.[68] But as William Ward would have been quick to point out, Catholic martyrdom did not end with Elizabeth I's death. Ward was the first of nineteen priests executed under treason legislation during the 1640s.[69] The lives of Ward and his co-sufferers were documented in Latin martyrologies published on the Continent. These texts are at the intersection of several scholarly blindspots: they were not written in English, they were not published in England, and they concern Catholicism. Yet they were an important way in which passionate, religiously motivated readings of the English civil wars were disseminated internationally; they are also an important barometer of the changes Catholic martyrology underwent in the mid-seventeenth century.[70]

In the 1640s four texts were published about the suffering of seventeen English Catholic priests.[71] All were printed in the Spanish Netherlands or in Douai, France, where readers presumably had an intense interest in English Catholicism's fate. Published in Brussels in 1645, Jean Chifflet's *Palmae Cleri Anglicani* documents the ordeals of nine priests executed between 1641 and 1644. Ambrose Corbie published a narrative about the Jesuit priest Henry Morse, *Narratio Gloriosae Mortis... Henricus Mors* in Graet in 1645. In the same year he published *Certamen Triplex*, which includes Morse with two other martyrs, Thomas Holland and Ralph Corbie, the author's brother. This work, first published in Antwerp, went through two editions in 1645 and 1646. Richard Mason published *Certamen Seraphicum Provinciae Angliae Pro Sancta Dei Ecclesia* at Douai in 1649; his work celebrates four martyrs and one confessor of the Franciscan order. These texts were quickly incorporated into the libraries of Catholic colleges on the continent. Of course, one did not have to be Catholic to read them; Mason's book, for instance, made its way into John Selden's library.[72] All three authors were fairly prominent churchmen. Jean Chifflet was a priest and the son of Jean-Jacques Chifflet, physician to Phillip IV of Spain.[73] Richard Mason was a prominent Franciscan and doctor of divinity.[74] Ambrose Corbie, a Jesuit, taught at the English Catholic college at St. Omer and was appointed confessor at the English college in Rome in 1645, a position he held till his death in 1649.[75]

By writing in Latin, these authors follow the precedent of writers who memorialized earlier Catholic martyrs in the language. Like those writers, Chifflet, Corbie, and Mason conclude that despite charges of treason, their subjects died as Catholic martyrs. Yet Chifflet, Corbie, and Mason depart significantly from earlier writers' attempts to separate Catholic martyrs from political concerns. It is a scholarly commonplace to note the political activity of English Catholics until the Gunpowder Plot in 1605 and their relative political quietism thereafter.[76] In martyrologies, however, the reverse seems true: Elizabethan martyrologists are at pains to deny that English Catholic martyrs have any political goals, while later martyrologists are willing to portray their priests as quite outspoken on political matters. Chifflet, Corbie, and Mason see the relationships between Reformation, revolution, and religious persecution through the lens of Catholic arguments about political loyalty, heroic self-sacrifice, and the national consequences of heresy. Theirs is a dual vision: they portray these martyrs as religiously motivated and politically engaged. Broadcasting to an international audience, their texts filter the struggles of the English civil war through the agendas, convictions, and dying words of Catholic priests.

The martyrs of the 1640s found themselves embroiled in the struggles between Charles I and Parliament. Earlier, in the 1630s, Charles's reluctance to prosecute priests on charges of treason and his pro-Spanish foreign policy deepened suspicions that he was not fully committed to the Reformation and angered those who felt England should aid continental Protestants in their struggles against Catholic powers.[77] The fear that Charles was betraying the Protestant cause at home and abroad directly affected the fate of Catholic priests. As conflict between king and Parliament flared, Parliament demanded that Elizabethan treason legislation be put into effect and proclaimed that all priests were to leave the country by 7 April 1641 on pain of death. The Irish Catholic rebellion further invigorated prosecution of the Elizabethan statutes.

Of course, those who perceived in Charles's foreign policies a "popish plot" to bring England back into the Roman fold simplified the international situation.[78] The Thirty Years War was no longer being fought along strictly religious lines; instead, dynastic concerns were now at the forefront. Sharon Achinstein has recently pointed out that Milton and other English Protestant writers still saw the war through the simplifying lens of confessional differences.[79] Catholic martyrologies show that this type of thinking was not limited to Puritan-leaning Protestants. These martyrologies exhibit nostalgia for the days when Catholics and heretics squared off across sharply demarcated religious lines – though those days only really existed in martyrologies' pages. These later martyrologies implicitly respond to the confusion of the late stages of the Thirty Years' War and of the Dutch Revolt, arguing that although on the Continent religious lines were no longer drawn as clearly as they might or should be, in England Catholic priests drew those lines clearly in blood.

This nostalgia is evident in Chifflet's dedication. Chifflet argues that English priests wish to protect

ancestral religion, and they do not suffer it to be snatched away by any fever of pestilential opinions. Their struggles presented to us the certain likeness or image, as it were, of those times in which the Christian religion was born, and we seemed to see in this extreme age of the church something just like its first infancy, and its same cradle sprinkled with blood, which [things], although most bitter and painful to the mind, are most useful and just for the health of the church, for the glory of Christ, and for an example of constancy and fortitude.[80]

The notion that contemporary religious struggles echoed the early church's struggles was widespread cross-confessionally, foundational for the historiography of Bale, Foxe, Persons, and William Cardinal Allen. In Chifflet's volume, this historiography somewhat nostalgically simplifies contemporary complexities into starkly, irreconcilably opposed ideologies.

Despite this nostalgia, these martyrologies are also intensely involved in the conflicts of civil war England. Together with Elizabethan martyrologists, Chifflet, Mason, and Corbie insist that those who suffer die for religion, not treason. John Gibbons's *Concertatio Ecclesiae Catholicae in Anglia* (Trier, 1588) follows the lead of English-language martyrologies by recording that many priests prayed devoutly for Elizabeth I before dying and proclaimed their loyalty to her in everything but religion. Yet Chifflet, Mason, and Corbie must also negotiate the pressures civil strife exerted on Catholic martyrdom. Most importantly, priests could no longer simply protest that they are loyal English subjects when the nation to which they are presumably loyal is so deeply divided.

To what or whom should the loyal Englishman pledge fealty in the 1640s? Catholic priests were not the only ones who wrestled with this question, of course, though the problem of negotiating conflicting loyalties was a long-standing one for English Catholics. Elizabethan Catholics who wished to formulate a discourse of Catholic loyalism faced almost insurmountable difficulties. As Alison Shell and Arnold Pritchard have shown, many Catholic attempts at formulating loyalist positions produced deep rifts within the Catholic community and were not terribly persuasive to authorities.[81] In the 1640s, Catholic priests promulgate new forms of loyalism made possible, ironically, by the fragmenting of their nation. Many of the priests executed by order of Parliament defend themselves at length, more so than did priests in earlier martyrologies which often stress how forcefully Catholics were silenced.[82] In their self-defenses, Catholic priests take advantage of the conflicts between Parliament and king to proclaim their loyalty to the monarch and to the nation torn apart by civil war.[83] Chifflet records that the martyr Hugh Green (*d.* 29 August 1642) gave a final speech defending the Catholic Church's antiquity and integrity and bewailing English civil strife. In his view, this strife proceeds directly from Protestantism's interminable quarrels: "above all I certainly feel sorry for my most miserable country, lacerated with the struggles of such contentious opinions."[84] Green prays earnestly for "the King and for the establishing of peace" and asserts "that there would never be a cessation from discordant war, until there would be an end of such divisions of sects and religions."[85] Explicitly linking king, peace, and Catholicism, Green proclaims that he has always prayed for Charles while saying Mass, the very activity for which he is condemned: "I testify truly to God, that never did I wish evil to the King or to the country; always I was most mindful of the health of the King, to such an extent that I never fail to remember [him] in the most holy sacrifice of the Mass."[86] Green does not say that he has honored Parliament in the same way.

As Green's final words indicate, the martyr-priests both insisted on their loyalty to their divided nation and maintained that the civil wars were God's punishment for the nation's heresy. The priests proclaim their loyalty to the *idea* of the nation while criticizing the nation's religious policies and practices. Such forceful criticism intensifies earlier Catholic thinking about the Elizabethan persecutions. In his martyrology about twelve priests executed between 1577 and 1580, William Cardinal Allen argues that priests suffer because of heretics' cruelty and warns his nation of God's pending vengeance.[87] Other Elizabethan Catholics saw their sufferings as an appeasement for late medieval corruptions in the church. Southwell's "St. Peter's Complaint" has often been read as expressing the need for the Catholic Church to do penance for its missteps and return, like the repentant Peter, to Christ's embrace. Catholic martyrologies published in the 1640s still see England as a hotbed of Protestant persecution but argue explicitly that England now suffers for its Protestant excesses; the civil wars are read as a large-scale instance of the providential retributions pervasive in earlier martyrologies. Barbara Donagan has recently shown that Protestant ministers of royalist and Parliamentary persuasions also read the civil wars as punishment for sinfulness.[88] Yet the tone of righteous vindication the Catholic martyrologies assume distinguishes them both from Protestant criticisms of national immorality and from Elizabethan Catholic martyrs' claims that they would never meddle in political affairs (a dubious claim in some cases but one that almost all the Elizabethan martyrs made). The 1640s martyrologies instead invoke Catholic theology to argue that only Catholicism with its expiatory sacrifices is able to atone for the sins under which the nation groans.

Earlier Catholic martyrologies sometimes claimed that martyrs were offered as sacrifices. In one late sixteenth-century poem probably written by Henry Walpole, the speaker claims that he dies in part as a sacrifice for his country: "Let all Distresse to me befale: to doe my Countrie good / and let the thirst of Tyrantes all: be quenched in my blood."[89] In the 1640s, this notion of sacrifice is insistently and specifically politicized. Perfectly loyal Catholic priests claim that they die as sacrifices *for* their country, rather than as willing martyrs at their country's hands; they become the ultimate patriots, giving their very lives for the peace of their *patria*. In his final words, the Jesuit Henry Morse prays that my death may to some extent make satisfaction for the sins of this kingdom. Certainly, if there were for me as many lives as there are grains of sand washed up by the sea, I would most gladly lay them all down to this end, and as a testimony to the faith of Catholicism . . . Truly I hold one thing to be most certain: that the cause of all these disturbances and calamities in England is heresy and the filth of so many sects. As long as these, as bad as poison, slither through the bowels of this kingdom, you will in vain hope for quiet, peace, or any remedy for your evils.[90]

In Corbie's representation, Morse deftly weaves together political sacrifice with religious ends: he takes his nation's sins upon him as a scapegoat and identifies those sins as the heresies against which his faith is starkly opposed. Corbie records that Father Thomas Holland makes a similar claim. After forgiving his persecutors,

with a fervency of spirit he added prayers by name for the king, for the queen, for the royal family, for the parliament, and for the whole nation; for whose general good, restoration to the faith, and eternal welfare, he said, 'If there were for me as many lives as there are hairs on my head, drops in the ocean, stars in heaven, perfections in the Lord of the heavens, I would most willingly lay them all down for this purpose.' The people's great applause showed their approval of these his last words.[91]

A French manuscript account of Holland's death includes this final wish in slightly altered form but does not record the crowd's applause; Corbie stresses the English crowd's endorsement of Holland's reading of the English situation and of his sacrifice.[92]

Two forms of Catholic loyalism surface repeatedly in these texts: loyalty to the monarch and self-sacrificing fealty to a suffering nation. For the 1640s martyrs, religious error clearly leads to political confusion, and political confusion may only be cured by a return to a right religious state. In this way, the 1640s texts complicate their own nostalgia for a simpler time when religious lines and conflicts were stark and clear, for even martyrology itself becomes explicitly bound up with political struggles. In Elizabethan martyrologies, martyrs commonly defend themselves by separating strictly (if somewhat dubiously) their political duties from their religious beliefs and practices. In the later material this denial is occasionally present as well. But more commonly the later martyrologies argue that political activities and political entities are directly affected by religious choices and practices (a connection perhaps obvious to modern observers but one which earlier martyrs strive to deny).[93]

Several martyrs volunteer extensive political commentary at the moments of their deaths. Two sources survive for Thomas Reynolds's martyrdom (21 January 1642): Chifflet's account and a Latin manuscript dated 1 February 1642 (new style), which made its way to Nymphenburg (the central Bavarian site of the Institute of the Blessed Virgin Mary). In the manuscript, Reynolds asserts that he suffers for religion, forgives his executioners, and dies meekly and peacefully.[94] In Chifflet's book, Reynolds speaks at length about one of the most vexed historiographical questions – the causes of the English Civil Wars – and comes up with an answer not to be found in Conrad Russell's volume on the subject. Reynolds prays fervently that Parliament may return to the truth:

'O if between king and Parliament there were good agreement! If all things everywhere in this our nation were made to the greater glory of God! At last, [my] prayers having been granted . . . England would return to the beauty of piety; there is nothing that may be requested that is any more beautiful or blessed' . . . That man said these things, to which he added, that he most firmly believed that it was not possible to have security without Catholic observance of the law.[95]

The cause of the civil war is simply England's apostasy. In Mason's *Certamen Seraphicum*, the martyr Arthur Bell offers a lengthy explanation of what his countrymen must do if they desire peace:

Listen to me, most dear countrymen, because if you wish to be freed from your miseries you first must necessarily put an end to your sins . . . the causes of these calamities & miseries. Truly, most importantly, rise again from heresy, by which now and for so many years you lie so miserably downcast: because of this, truly (for I say it again sadly), from the true body of Christ you have been cut off like putrid limbs, like dead branches cut from the tree of the Church. If you continue to love great darkness more than light, long afflictions will attend you: & certainly, many calamities and hardships threaten this city of London and the whole kingdom of England, unless they should immediately stop pursuing and persecuting priests and the Catholic people. Consider, I ask you, & see the afflictions with which God has now begun visibly to punish you . . . All these chastisements, wars, calamities, are inflicted on you by God to this end, that you may hereafter be recalled from shipwreck into the port of the Catholic Church.[96]

Bell's words show the forcefulness of the religio-political arguments advanced by these martyrologies. England's conflict is a religiously motivated battle in which priests may metaphorically engage because it will end only when England returns to Rome's embrace. With similar fervor, Chifflet says that Catholics have "spurned" Elizabeth I's laws. One priest, Edward Morgan, responds to these unjust laws by militarizing his own martyrdom: Morgan wishes to "prove myself an unconquered soldier with God as [my] General."[97] Earlier Catholic martyrologies attacked the stereotype of militaristic, seditious Jesuits waiting to destroy the English state; those who celebrated famous martyrs like Edmund Campion distinguished the martyr's passivity from militaristic aggression.[98] Compared to a contemporary Latin manuscript about Morgan's martyrdom, Chifflet's Morgan is meeker; yet Chifflet also relishes the image of Morgan discharging his religio-military duty amid the first blows of the civil wars.[99]

Mason's portrait of Thomas Bullaker, executed in 1642, epitomizes the changes Catholic martyrology went through in this period, as it blends political challenge with royalist loyalty and religious devotion. Mason claims that his source for Bullaker's examinations is a manuscript written by Bullaker himself. An independent manuscript of Bullaker's life contains none of the detail in Mason's book, which is much more inflammatory.[100] For instance, while answering questions the Sheriff of London puts to him, Bullaker inserts a pro-monarchical attack on iconoclastic excesses by linking rebellion to the notorious January 1642 attack on the Cheapside cross:

Certainly I have been persuaded that you proceed in this [my case] with the utmost hate, when you were in no way able to endure to look with temperate eyes at the statue & image of Christ (to whose sacred passion, and to our redemption equally the [Cheapside cross] stands as a memorial) . . . 'Where,' they said, 'does Christ in holy scripture order his image or statue to be made?' To whom I answered . . . should not he who would . . . bespatter, trample, and tear the image of the King be punished as a traitor, betrayer, and culprit of the terrible crime of high treason? If therefore such deeds should be punished in this way, I ask that you consider how much of a crime it is to abuse, to injure the image of the King of Kings, Jesus Christ our Saviour, in the way that you did recently.[101]

These words were spoken on 11 September 1642, one month after the king's banner was raised at Nottingham. Arguing for the value of religious images, Bullaker attaints with high treason those who do not honor the king or respect his image; he charges his interrogators with the very crime laid at his feet.

Bullaker proceeds to even more inflammatory statements, predicting the downfall of Parliament and its religious reforms. During Bullaker's second examination his interrogators try to argue that he dishonors the king. Bullaker insists that Parliament and the religion it tries to establish are in the wrong:

One of my interrogators said, Mr. Bullaker, don't you well know that it has been written in scripture, Fear God, and honour the King? [I replied] I know it truly, nor am I unaware that it is that Parliament [the Elizabethan Parliaments] which has decreed and ordained that priesthood is a crime of high treason: that same Parliament decreed and affirmed by law episcopacy, the liturgy, ecclesiastical offices, and ceremonies, all of which you rescind in this present Parliament. [My interrogator responded:] Because such things were ordained badly, it is permitted that we amend them. I understand well, I answered: you have attempted and have plotted this, but a Parliament will come, it will come I say, and the very next one too, which will follow this one, by which the religion you attempt to establish and institute will be obstructed and undone.[102]

Bullaker predicts the hostility of Restoration parliaments to the religious changes of the 1640s and lays the outlawing of priesthood firmly at parliament's feet, not the monarch's. He likens the instability of parliamentary rule to the instability of the Protestant Reformation, to its wavering on the question of how far to go. His prediction of the downfall of this parliament's innovations directly challenges parliament's attempt to usurp power. Religiously motivated attacks on Protestant instability are seamlessly woven into attacks on parliamentary rule.

Bullaker's account closes by attacking the simplistic anti-Catholicism that saw popish plots lurking in every corner:

Traitor! they exclaimed, and clamored that these tumults of the kingdom had been stirred up by me and by those like me. To whom I replied, would that in this kingdom there were not another kind of traitors, from which they should fear truer and worse dangers. Since many (supposed) treasonous acts have been attributed to and cast at the Catholics by invented lies, declare, show, announce to me, if you can (do) this, even one (which has been) proved.[103]

Bullaker's argument is that the current ways many English Protestants understood the English civil struggle are insufficient; popish plots are nothing but phantasms. The Latin martyrologies give a broad audience a counter-view of the English situation which simplifies things in its own way: Catholics are loyal to the monarch; they die willingly as scapegoats for their country's sins; heresy is responsible for the nation's suffering. These texts do not assume, as did earlier Catholic martyrologies, that political and religious selves may or indeed *can* be separated. Blending martyrological paradigms with political commentary, these texts pick up where *The Virgin Martyr*'s allegory left off. Interweaving political commentary with religious sacrifice, Mason, Corbie, and Chifflet show how civil strife changed the shape of English Catholic martyrdom, compromising its nostalgia for straightforward religious conflict but expanding the power of its political reach.

These martyrologies and Dekker and Massinger's play engage with the question of how to reconcile the nation and its goals with the relatively simple martyrological framework of conflicts between devilish persecutors and holy martyrs. Drawing on martyrology to argue for sharper religious demarcations at moments when religiously motivated identities, policies, and actions are becoming considerably complicated, these works show the persistent appeal of earlier martyrological habits of representation and interpretation. They show as well an awareness that earlier ways of depicting martyrs – in particular, earlier habits of down-playing martyrdom's political implications – are no longer completely sufficient. In this sense they anticipate the blend of political self-justification and regal apotheosis in *Eikon Basilike*. Finally, they suggest, through hearkening back to earlier paradigms, a nostalgic longing for a simpler way of reading the world: through the starkly unforgiving oppositions of martyrology.

NOTES

1 I develop a line established by Julia Gasper (*The Dragon and the Dove: the Plays of Thomas Dekker*, Oxford: Clarendon Press, 1990).

2 G. E. Bentley, *The Jacobean and Caroline Stage* (Oxford: Clarendon Press, 1956), vol. 3, 263–6. See Larry Champion for the play's printing history ("'Disaster with my so many joys': Structure and Perspective in Massinger and Dekker's *The Virgin Martyr*," *Medieval and Renaissance Drama in England*, New York: AMS Press, 1984, vol. 1, 199–209).

3 Peter Mullaney sees the play as merely "entertaining," not "artistically" or "aesthetically" interesting (*Religion and the Artifice of Jacobean and Caroline Drama*, Salzburg: Institut für Englische Sprache und Literatur, 1977); George Price calls its religious conception "sincere but shallow" (*Thomas Dekker*, New York: Twayne Publishers, 1969, 95).

4 Peter Happé, "The Protestant Adaptation of the Saint Play," and John Wasson, "The Secular Saint Plays of the Elizabethan Era," in *The Saint Play in Medieval Europe* (Kalamazoo: Medieval Institute Publications, 1986), 241–60.

5 On the play's sophisticated awareness that the meaning of spectacles like martyrdom depends on viewers' assumptions, see Nova Myhill, "Making Death a Miracle: Audience and the Genres of Martyrdom in Dekker and Massinger's *The Virgin Martyr*," forthcoming in *Early Theatre* 7 (2004). I thank the author for sending me a copy of her essay.

6 Ruano de la Haza writes that "Dorothea could just as well have been a Roman matron or a Greek priestess dying for her beliefs" ("Unparalleled Lives: Hagiographical Drama in Seventeenth-Century England and Spain," in *Parallel Lives: Spanish and English National Drama, 1580–1688*, ed. Louise and Peter Fothergill-Payne, London: Associated University. Presses, 1991, 257). Price (*Thomas Dekker*) arrives at a similar conclusion.

7 Cf. Champion's challenge ("'Disaster with my so many joys,'" 200) to Louise Clubb's reading of the play as Catholic propaganda ("*The Virgin Martyr* and the *Tragedia Sacra*," *Renaissance Drama* 7), [1964], 103–26).

8 Gasper, "The Sources of *The Virgin Martyr*," *Review of English Studies* 42 (1991), 17–31.

9 Gasper cites evidence that Kinesman was read by an anti-Catholic Puritan ("The Sources").

10 Jankowski, *Pure Resistance: Queer Virginity in Early Modern English Drama* (Philadelphia: University of Pennsylvania Press, 2000), 124.

11 *AM* (1583), 1893.

12 *Flos Sanctorum*, trans. Edward Kinesman (Douai, 1623), 2v. The dedication to this, the fifth edition, ties the work to the Dutch-Spanish conflict: "To the right honourable and most religious knight, Syr William Stanely, Coronell, one of the Maiesters of his Cath. Majesties Army, and of his Counsell of warre in the Low-Countries & c" (2r).

13 On female martyrdom, see Marsha S. Robinson, "Doctors, Silly Poor Women, and Rebel Whores: the Gendering of Conscience in Foxe's *Acts and Monuments*," in *John Foxe and His World*, ed. Christopher Highley and John N. King (Aldershot: Ashgate, 2002), 235–48; Steven Mullaney, "Reforming Resistance: Class, Gender, and Legitimacy in Foxe's *Book of Martyrs*," in *Print, Manuscript, and Performance: the Changing Relations of the Media in Early Modern England*, ed. Arthur F. Marotti and Michael D. Bristol (Columbus: Ohio State University Press, 2000), 235–51; Thomas Freeman, "'The Good Ministrye of Godlye and Vertuouse Women': the Elizabethan Martyrologists and the Female Supporters of the Marian Martyrs," *Journal of British Studies* 39 (2000), 8–33; D. Andrew Penny, "Family Matters and Foxe's *Acts and Monuments*," *The Historical Journal* 39 (1996), 599–618; Carole Levin, "Women in the *Book of Martyrs* as Models of Behavior in Tudor England," *International Journal of Women's Studies* 4 (1981), 196–207; and my "The Inheritance of Anne Askew, English Protestant Martyr," *Archive for Reformation History* 94 (2003), 134–60, and "Foxe's Female Martyrs and the Sanctity of Transgression," *Renaissance and Reformation* 25 (2001), 3–22.

14 J. V. Polišenský, *War and Society in Europe, 1618–1648* (Cambridge: Cambridge University Press, 1978), 55–65.

15 The anti-absolutist implications of the Bohemians' actions are clear in a pamphlet entitled *The Reasons Which Compelled the States of Bohemia to Reject the Archduke Ferdinand &c. & Inforced Them to Elect a New King*, trans. John Harrison (London, 1619), which defends the nobility's power to choose a monarch.

16 Gasper, *The Dragon and the Dove*, 136–65.

17 See *The Declaration and Information of the High and Puissant King of Bohemia* (London, 1620); *A Declaration of the Causes, for the which, Wee Frederick . . . Have Acccepted of the Crowne of Bohemia*, trans. John Harrison (London, 1620); *Prosopopoeia. Or, a Conference . . . Between the pope, the Emperor, and the King of Spaine* (London, 1619?); *The popes Complaint to His Minion Cardinals, Against the Good Successe of the Bohemians* (London, 1620?); *News from Bohemia. An Apologie Made by the State of the Kingdome of Bohemia* (London, 1619); and *The True Copies of Sundrie Letters Concerning the Affaires of Bohemia* (London, 1620).

18  Gasper, *The Dragon and the Dove*, 140.
19  *The Jacobean and Caroline Stage*, vol. 3, 263.
20  *The Dragon and the Dove*, 142–3. Massinger was not afraid of anti-absolutist plays: he had recently gotten into trouble for his part in *Sir John van Olden Barnavelt*, a play about the situation in the Low Countries which, while taking the part of the Calvinist Maurice of Orange against the Arminian Barnavelt, nevertheless harbors republican sympathies. See Ivo Kamps, *Historiography and Ideology in Stuart Drama* (Cambridge: Cambridge University Press, 1996).
21  Whereas in the source materials they are unrelated to Theophilus (*Flos Sanctorum*) or are Dorothea's sisters (*The Golden Legend*), the play turns Christeta and Calista into Theophilus's daughters.
22  See Champion ("'Disaster with my so many joys'") on how the play adapts morality formulas.
23  Shepard remarks that the play's initially more merciful Diocletian makes Rome look "temptingly familiar" (*Amazons and Warrior Women: Varieties of Feminism in Seventeenth-Century Drama*, New York: St. Martin's Press, 1981, 194).
24  Anthony Fletcher, *Gender, Sex, and Subordination in England, 1500–1800* (New Haven: Yale University Press, 1995).
25  *AM* (1583), 2048. In the 1563 edition, this martyr is known as Elizabeth Driver; in subsequent editions, her first name is corrected to Alice.
26  *The life and Death of Mistris Margarit Clitherow*, Bar Convent (York) MS, 121–2. Matchinske argues that Clitherow's account reveals the intensely private character of recusant Catholicism (*Writing, Gender, and State in Early Modern England: Identity Formation and the Female Subject*, Cambridge: Cambridge University Press, 1998). Yet Mush uses Clitherow's domestic virtue to justify this dutifully submissive woman's challenges to public, legal authorities.
27  Of course, sharp speech is not the only measure of verbal challenge. Clitherow's silences were as unsettling to authorities as what she said: faced with charges of treason, she refused to plead. The 1594 edition of *Concertatio Ecclesiae Catholicae in Anglia* explains this refusal: "She would not be the cause of any death, nor would she drag any into such miseries of torture, or give occasion to any of ruin in faith" (41ov, translation mine). Her silence inspired imitators: see the account of Jane Wiseman, a would-be martyr, in John Gerard, *John Gerard: Autobiography of an Elizabethan*, trans. Philip Caraman (London: Longmans, 1951), 53.
28  In addition to Clitherow, these include Margaret Ward, martyred in 1589 for helping a priest escape from prison (see Diego de Yepez, *Historia Particular de la Persecucion de Inglaterra*, Madrid, 1599, 614–18), and Anne Line, martyred 27, February 1601 for sheltering a priest in her home (Gerard, *Autobiography*, 85).The playwrights were unlikely to know Clitherow's story but I adduce it here because works like the *Actes and Monuments* and *Flos Sanctorum* (which they knew) are best studied in comparison with a range of martyrological materials.
29  Gerard, *Autobiography*, 85.

30  Hist. MSS commission, Rutland MSS, i, 370; cited by Caraman in Gerard, *Autobiography*, 86.
31  *A Treatise of Three Conversions* (Saint Omer, 1603–4), 495.
32  *AM* (1583), 94.
33  *Flos Sanctorum* (Douai, 1609), 124.
34  *AM* (1583), 94.
35  *Dekker His Dreame* (London, 1620), 7.
36  Gasper, *The Dragon and the Dove*, 147.
37  *Flos Sanctorum* (1609), 54.
38  *The Examinations of Anne Askew*, ed. Elaine Beilin (Oxford: Oxford University Press, 1996), 92–3.
39  *AM* (1570), 1470; *AM* (1576), 1208; *AM* (1583), 1237.
40  *AM* (1583), 2051.
41  *Ibid.*, 2052.
42  Many of Foxe's female martyrs are referred to as someone's wife. Still, there is an unresolved tension between Foxe's identification of this martyr only through her marital status and her rejection of her ungodly family.
43  John Bossy, *The English Catholic Community, 1570–1850* (London: Darton, Longman, and Todd, 1975). Married women were initially under less pressure from recusancy laws. Still, Catholic wives provoked high levels of anxiety; see Frances Dolan, *Whores of Babylon: Catholicism, Gender, and Seventeenth-Century Print Culture* (Ithaca: Cornell University Press, 1999), and Arthur Marotti, "Alienating Catholics in Early Modern England: Recusant Women, Jesuits, and Ideological Fantasies," in *Catholicism and Anti-Catholicism in Early Modern English Texts*, ed. Marotti (New York: St. Martin's, 1999), 1–34.
44  *Christian Renunciation* (London, 1593), 83. The question of whether a wife may disobey her husband in matters of conscience figures prominently in Protestant marriage discourse; see Heather Dubrow, *A Happier Eden: the Politics of Marriage in the Stuart Epithalamium* (Ithaca: Cornell University Press, 1990) and Susannah Brietz Monta, "Marital Discourse and Political Discord: Reconsidering *Perkin Warbeck*," *Studies in English Literature* 37 (1997), 391–413.
45  *The life and Death of Mistris Margarit Clitherow*, 73–4.
46  *Ibid.*, 91.
47  *Ibid.*, 111.
48  On Clitherow's children's staunch Catholicism, see Mary Claridge, *Margaret Clitherow, 1556?–1586* (London: Burns & Oates, 1966), 116–17.
49  The play follows *The Golden Legend* which conflates the Dorothea and Agnes legends; see Gasper, "The Sources."
50  By 1715, when the elevation of marriage was firmly established and the need to portray continental Protestantism as a virgin struggling to remain intact had faded, Benjamin Griffin could alter this aspect of the play. In Griffin's *Injur'd Virtue, or, The Virgin Martyr* (London, 1715) Dorothea states that she has not returned Antoninus's love only because they were of different religions; at her

execution Antoninus and Dorothea vow to love each other after death with a pure, angelic love, and at the play's end they reenter together.

51 *Gender and Heroism in Early Modern English Literature* (Chicago: University of Chicago Press, 2002).

52 Reprinted in *Documents of the Christian Church*, ed. Henry Bettenson (Oxford: Oxford University Press, 1963).

53 *A Relation of Sixtene Marytrs* (1601), 45.

54 *AM* (1576), 1662. On the problem of the source for Latimer's words, see John King, "Fiction and Fact in John Foxe's *Book of Martyrs*," in *John Foxe and the English Reformation*, ed. David Loades (Menston: Scolar Press, 1997), 12–35, and Thomas Freeman, "Text, Lies, and Microfilm: Reading and Misreading Foxe's 'Book of Martyrs,'" *Sixteenth Century Journal* 30 (1999), 23–46.

55 See Anne Dillon, *The Construction of Martyrdom in the English Catholic Community, 1535–1603* (Aldershot: Ashgate, 2002), on the propaganda value of stories of Catholic suffering.

56 *A Treatise of Three Conversions*, 492.

57 *AM* (1583), 95.

58 Richard Challoner, *Memoirs of Missionary Priests*, ed. John Hungerford Pollen (London: Burns, Oates, and Washbourne, 1924), 145; see also Yepez, *Historia* book V, ch. 2.

59 *Examinations*, 127.

60 *Ibid.*, 129. In Foxe's papers, a note survives about this incident; see British Library Harley MS 419, 2r.

61 *Examinations*, 130.

62 Sarah Wall and Thomas Freeman demonstrate the editorial shaping of Askew's account in Foxe's text ("Racking the Body, Shaping the Text: the Account of Anne Askew in Foxe's 'Book of Martyrs,'" *Renaissance Quarterly* 54 [2001], 1165–96). On the ways Foxe and his abridgers dealt with Askew's torture, see Monta, "The Inheritance of Anne Askew."

63 *AM* (1563), 669. The preface recurs in STC 853. On STC 852.5 and its relevance to Foxe's work, see Freeman, "Text, Lies, and Microfilm." This preface is borrowed, with slight changes, from William Hill's 1548 reprinting of Askew's story (STC 852), and is derived from Bale (19).

64 *AM* (1570), 1413.

65 *A Declaration of the Causes*, 1.

66 Mark Kishlansky, *A Monarchy Transformed: Britain, 1603–1714* (London: Penguin, 1997), 92. There were a number of pamphlets printed on these events. See for instance *A Most True Relation of the Late Proceedings in Bohemia, Germany, and Hungaria* (London, 1620). The articles stipulated that no country could be invaded on the basis of religion but pointedly excluded Bohemia, which soon fell to the Habsburg-Catholic League alliance.

67 "Gallants, to Bohemia" (London, 1619).

68 Ceri Sullivan, *Dismembered Rhetoric: English Recusant Writing, 1580 to 1603* (London: Associated University Presses, 1995), and Anne Dillon, *The*

*Construction of Catholic Martyrdom*, have published important work on Elizabethan Catholic writing; Arthur Marotti considers several mid-seventeenth-century texts in "Manuscript Transmission and the Catholic Martyrdom Account in Early Modern England," in *Print, Manuscript, and Performance: the Changing Relations of the Media in Early Modern England*, ed. Arthur Marotti and Michael D. Bristol (Columbus: Ohio State University Press, 2000), 172–99.

69 I take the numbers from Richard Challoner's *Memoirs of Missionary Priests*. The life of Peter Wright was published at Antwerp in 1651, the same year he suffered (*R. P. Petri Writi . . . mors, quam ob fidem passus est Londini XXIX maii M. DC. LI*); he and John Southworth (*d.* 28 June 1654) were the only priests to suffer during the Interregnum.

70 Important texts in other languages include *Relation de Martyre du R. P. Philippe Powel autrement dict le Pere Morgan, Religieux Benedictin de la Congregation d'Angleterre.* (Paris, 1647) and Sieur de Marsys, *Histoire de la Persecution presente des Catholiques en Angleterre* (Paris, 1646). Sieur de Marsys would later make a controversial Catholicizing French translation of *Eikon Basilike*. See Philip A. Knachel, ed., *Eikon Basilike* (Ithaca: Cornell University Press, 1966), xviii–xix.

71 Other sources on these martyrs include manuscripts that circulated on the Continent and records in continental seminaries, such as the Douai diary. I concentrate on published Latin texts because they seem designed to disseminate widely religious explanations of the civil wars.

72 One of the Bodleian's copies of *Certamen Seraphicum* was part of Selden's library; another copy has an inscription on its engraved title page that reads "Bibliothecae Collegii S. Antonii de Padua Louanii." The Bodleian's copies of Chifflet's work indicate prior ownership by the Catholic college in Brussels. I thank Geoff Groom, Assistant Librarian of Rare Books and Printed Ephemera at the Bodleian Library, for this information (personal communication).

73 *Biographie Universelle Ancienne et Moderne* (Paris, 1854), 138–9, 141.

74 Mason published under the pseudonym Angelus Sancto Francisco. For Mason's biography, see the on-line *Catholic Encyclopedia* (http:// www.newadvent.org/ cathen/ 09770a.htm).

75 On Corbie see the *Catholic Encyclopedia* (http: // www.newadvent.org/cathen/ 04355b.htm).

76 A. G. R. Smith, *The Emergence of a Nation-State: the Commonwealth of England, 1529–1660* (New York: Longman, 1997), 263.

77 William Prynne attacked Charles I's leniency towards the priest John Goodman in *Hidden Workes of Darkenes Brought to Publike Light* (London, 1645). On Goodman's fate see Challoner, *Memoirs*, 378–82. The seventeenth of the Nineteen Propositions of 1 June 1642 ask Charles to align himself with the Dutch Provinces in their nearly 80-year struggle against Spain; see Simon Adams, "Spain or the Netherlands? The Dilemmas of Early Stuart Foreign Policy," in *Before the English Civil War: Essays on Early Stuart Politics and Government*, ed. Howard Tomlinson (New York: St. Martin's, 1984), 79.

78  On the importance of "popish plot" thinking, see Caroline Hibbard, *Charles I and the Popish Plot* (Chapel Hill: University of North Carolina Press, 1983).

79  Achinstein, "Milton and King Charles," in *The Royal Image: Representations of Charles I* (Cambridge: Cambridge University Press, 1999), 141–61.

80  *Palmae Cleri Anglicani*, 4–5. Translations from Chifflet are my own.

81  *Catholicism, Controversy, and the English Literary Imagination, 1558–1660* (Cambridge: Cambridge University Press, 1999); *Catholic Loyalism in Elizabethan England: the Development of Loyalism* (Chapel Hill: University of North Carolina Press, 1979).

82  See chapter 1.

83  The pro-royalist leaning of many English Catholics must have been well known in the Low Countries, where English mercenaries, many of them Catholic or Catholic sympathizers, had been fighting for Spain but left their posts in the early 1640s to return home and fight for their king. See Philip Caraman, *Henry Morse: Priest of the Plague* (New York: Farrar, Straus and Cudahy, 1957); on the recruiting of these mercenaries see Adams, "Spain or the Netherlands?, " 85.

84  Chifflet, *Palmae Cleri Anglicani*, 54–5.

85  *Ibid.*, 55.

86  *Ibid.*, 51.

87  *A Briefe Historie of the Glorious Martyrdom of XII Reverend Priests* (Rheims, 1582), aiiir.

88  "Casuistry and Allegiance in the English Civil War," in *Writing and Political Engagement in Seventeenth-Century England*, ed. Derek Hirst and Richard Strier (Cambridge: Cambridge University Press, 1999), 89–111.

89  Cited in Karen Batley, "Martyrdom in Sixteenth-Century English Jesuit Verse," *Unisa English Studies* 26 (1988), 5.

90  *Certamen Triplex*, 137–8. This text is available in English translation (*The Threefold Conflict*, trans. W. R. T., London: Catholic Publishing and Bookselling Company Limited, 1858). I consulted this translation in writing my own.

91  *Certamen Triplex*, 36–7.

92  J. H. Pollen, ed., *Acts of English Martyrs* (London: Burns and Oates, 1891), 367. A Latin manuscript on Edward Morgan's life and death (printed and translated in Pollen, *Acts*, 344–52) attributes a similar statement to him, though Chifflet does not include it in his text. Given the differences between this manuscript and Chifflet's account, I question Pollen's conclusion that the manuscript he reprints was the English text from which Chifflet worked.

93  On the implications of this denial for subjectivity, see Roland Corthell, " 'The Secrecy of Man': Recusant Discourse and the Elizabethan Subject," *English Literary Review* 19 (1989), 272–90.

94  *Acts*, 338–41.

95  Chifflet, *Palmae Cleri Anglicani*, 26–8, *passim*. "Sine Catholica legis observatione" could refer to canon law or the implication could be that Catholics observe law and order while Protestants do not, a common polemical charge.

96  *Certamen Seraphicum*, 154. Translations from Mason are my own.
97  Chifflet, *Palmae Cleri Anglicani*, 35–6, 40. Compare Mason, *Certamen Seraphicum*, 48, for Thomas Bullaker's similar criticism of Elizabethan laws.
98  See my discussion of Walpole's "Why do I use my paper, ink, and pen," chapter 1.
99  *Acts*, 344–52.
100  *Ibid.*, 352–7.
101  *Certamen Seraphicum*, 48–9. In a passage I omit, Bullaker refers explicitly to the Cheapside Cross ("Crucis monumentum in Platea Cheapside...."). In January 1642, the Cheapside monument was attacked. Despite the setting of armed bands to guard it, on 2 May 1643 the entire monument was pulled down and the Book of Sports burned on the site (Margaret Aston, *Faith and Fire: Popular and Unpopular Religion 1350–1600*, London: Hambledon Press, 1993, 287–8).
102  Mason, *Certamen Seraphicum*, 51.
103  *Ibid.*

# Conclusion:
## admiration and fear

I looked straight at the condemned man's face, which at times was hidden by the crowd ahead of me. And I saw the face of a man looking at something that is not of this earth, as I had sometimes seen on statues of saints in ecstatic vision. And I understood that, madman or seer as he might be, he knowingly wanted to die because he believed that in dying he would defeat his enemy, whoever it was. And I understood that his example would lead others to death. And I remain amazed by the possessors of such steadfastness only because I do not know, even today, whether what prevails in them is a proud love of the truth they believe, which leads them to death, or a proud desire for death, which leads them to proclaim their truth, whatever it may be. And I am overwhelmed with admiration and fear.[1]

In the epigraph above, Adso of Melk responds to an impending execution with a dazzled perplexity. He juxtaposes the condemned man's claim to truth with the subjectivity of that truth, qualifying "truth" as "their truth," the truth which "they believe." The links Eco both forges and undermines between the condemned man's would-be martyrdom and this subjective truth is a skeptical twentieth-century descendant of early modern concerns about the interpretation of competing martyrological literatures. Representations of martyrs' unshakeable convictions that they speak godly truths to worldly powers are considerably complicated when the fact of competing martyrologies is acknowledged, when the reading of martyrs' sacrifices is troubled by the sacrifices of their religious opponents. This complication is not, however, merely visible to a modern academic perspective: it was a real and persistent problem in early modern martyrologies and in the texts they influenced.

The variety and persistence of literary engagements with conflicting martyrologies demonstrate that martyrology was a key discourse through which writers attempted to come to grips with the major religious upheavals of the period. Martyrology deserves sustained scholarly attention for its complexities, its concern with hermeneutics, its literary influence, and its importance to early modern culture. Martyrology focused

Reformation-era questions about authority and resistance in excruciatingly human terms; it provided powerful frameworks for the imagining of spiritual struggles; it revolutionized the writing of religious history. At the same time, religious upheaval challenged the epistemologies of martyrdom as centuries of Christian tradition became fragmented, slowly and painfully, into various religious and martyrological traditions. Careful reading of competing martyrologies and the texts they influenced is thus a powerful way to uncover the central concerns and anxieties of the Reformation period.

Early modern martyrologists both insisted on using martyrdom to distinguish between conflicting religions and used overlapping assumptions and representational strategies to make those distinctions. It is clear that martyrologies, arguably the most partisan of religious genres, were read cross-confessionally. Because martyrologists themselves are well aware of the difficulties posed by competing sets of similar martyr-stories, cross-confessional reading of martyrologies is crucially important. Only through such a comparative methodology does the sophistication of early modern martyrologies become clear; only through comparative study may we read martyrologies as many early modern authors read them. Cross-confessional reading reveals that the process of generic separation in the case of martyrologies was slow and complex. The stark oppositions polemicists tried to establish between particular religions should not be allowed to obscure this fact. Writers drawing on martyrologies for source material or for more general forms of inspiration did not work in a religiously isolated vacuum but read widely, discovered overlaps in assumptions and conventions, and either tried to resolve those overlaps (by pushing beyond them to formulate particular distinctions) or chose to dwell on them at length, thus troubling the conclusions martyrologists hoped to foster. The fact that early modern writers read martyrologies cross-confessionally holds important implications for how we understand contemporary habits of religious reading. Literary efforts were not and could not have been religiously segregated; the complexity and fluidity of early modern religious culture did not allow for it.

As I have shown, the interpretive difficulties presented by competing martyrologies are troped in literary works. Sometimes these difficulties are represented as problems ultimately to be resolved through various fictive, allegorical, or poetic strategies, as in Spenser, Dekker and Massinger, Copley, or Southwell. Sometimes these interpretive difficulties demand a rethinking of martyrdom, as in Shakespeare, Munday, or Donne. As the work of martyrologists and those influenced by them reveals, religious aesthetics in the period are not neatly divisible by religious tradition. Even in the case of martyrology, a genre devoted to dividing true from false religion, absolute formal distinctions are difficult to draw. Martyrologies thus demonstrate that religious beliefs and representational practices were not neatly aligned in the period but were in flux. Virginity was not an ideal which only Catholic writers deployed; miracles were not eliminated in Protestant martyrological writing; Catholic writers reworked and relied upon the language of inwardness and conscience. There is no direct line between particular religious beliefs and the conventions used to represent those who held them. Rather, the connections between theology and aesthetics were precisely those which martyrologies contested and attempted to resolve. The implications of this finding are broad: we should see the development of religiously inspired literary genres and theories (as in so-called Reformation poetics, or Counter-Reformation aesthetics, or Protestant hagiography, etc.) as agonistic, not as organic developments from stable sets of doctrinally inspired representational habits through which one faith is readily distinguishable from the next. Representational and rhetorical habits do not emerge from a space of religious or literary purity but are embroiled in the turmoil, unrest, and shifting polarities of controversial polemics. The boundaries between polemics and aesthetics are thin and permeable; the Reformation era's religious upheavals and massive cultural changes produced not neatly distinct representational systems but ongoing struggles over how to adapt literary conventions, forms, and representational habits to a newly complicated religious landscape.

Questions about the literary aspects of martyrologies are rich ones for further study. More research is needed into the debt both Protestant and Catholic martyrologies owe to early church and medieval hagiographic traditions, a debt implicit in the shared or overlapping conventions I have traced. Much more work remains to be done on Latin-language Catholic martyrologies and on the ways Catholic writers on the continent responded to English controversies. Further, it is patently clear to those who study John Foxe that the richness of his work has only begun to be tapped. More scholarship is also needed on sermons about martyrdom from a range of writers and on links between martyrdom, performance, and the early modern theatre.

While martyrological ways of thinking certainly persist past the period I discuss (particularly in nonconformist and Catholic writings), I would hypothesize that ongoing contestations over martyrological rhetoric ultimately contributed to the growing privatization of religion in England. For instance, the shrinking of the conscience from the indicator of divine will and the core of true belief to something more like personal judgment[2] may have been hastened by intensified competition over martyrological tropes and constructs during and in the aftermath of the long English Reformation. The force of the argument Milton attempts in *Eikonoklastes* – that the cause, not the death, makes the martyr – is more blunted than it was 86 years prior as Foxe first published his *Actes and Monuments* and as Catholic writers began to defend their own cause with the truths of their martyrs. Writers like the Catholic J. A. who recorded Thomas Cranmer's dramatic martyrdom make it clear that martyrs could win admiration even from those who were not their co-religionists. Returning to the second half of Eco's phrase, competing martyrs seem also to have inspired a form of fear: the fear that, to adapt Milton's powerful image, Truth now might appear fragmented, herself martyred by religious controversies, and that this early modern Osiris could not be easily reassembled from persecution's textual remainders.

NOTES

1 Umberto Eco, *The Name of the Rose*, trans. William Weaver (New York: Harcourt Brace Jovanovich, 1983), 282.
2 Compare Kevin Sharpe, "Private Conscience and Public Duty in the Writings of Charles I," *The Historical Journal* 40 (1997), 665.

# Index